Organisations, Anxie

Organisations, Anxieties and Defences

Towards a Psychoanalytic Social Psychology

Edited by

R.D. HINSHELWOOD FRCPsych
Centre for Psychoanalytic Studies,
University of Essex

and

MARCO CHIESA MD MRCPsych
The Cassel Hospital, Richmond and
University College London

Routledge
Taylor & Francis Group
New York   London

Published in the USA by
Routledge
Taylor & Francis Group
711 Third Avenue
New York, NY 10017

Simultaneously published in Great Britain by
Routledge
Taylor & Francis Group
2 Park Square, Milton Park
Abingdon, Oxon OX14 4RN

Routledge is an imprint of the Taylor & Francis Group, an informa business

ORGANISATIONS, ANXIETIES AND DEFENCES

A CIP catalog record for this book is available from the British Library.

Library of Congress Cataloging-in-Publication Data

Available from the publisher

ISBN: 1-158391-336-X

Contents

Series foreword

After the first hundred years of its history, psychoanalysis has matured into a serious, independent intellectual tradition, which has notably retained its capacity to challenge established truths in most areas of our culture. The biological psychiatrist of today is called to task by psychoanalysis, as much as was the specialist in nervous diseases of Freud's time, in turn of the century Vienna. Today's cultural commentators, whether for or against psychoanalytic ideas, are forced to pay attention to considerations of unconscious motivation, defences, early childhood experience and the myriad other discoveries which psychoanalysts brought to 20th century culture. Above all, psychoanalytic ideas have spawned an approach to the treatment of mental disorders, psychodynamic psychotherapy, which has become the dominant tradition in most countries, at least in the Western world.

Little wonder that psychoanalytic thinking continues to face detractors, individuals who dispute its epistemology and its conceptual and clinical claims. While disappointing in one way, this is a sign that psychoanalysis may be unique in its capacity to challenge and provoke. Why should this be? Psychoanalysis is unrivalled in the depth of its questioning of human motivation, and whether its answers are right or wrong, the epistemology of psychoanalysis allows it to confront the most difficult problems of human experience. Paradoxically, our new understanding concerning the physical basis of our existence – our genes, nervous systems and endocrine functioning – rather than finally displacing psychoanalysis, has created a pressing need for a complementary discipline which considers the memories, desires and meanings which are beginning to be recognised as influencing human adaptation even at the biological level. How else, other than through the study of subjective experience, will we understand the expression of the individual's biological destiny, within the social environment?

It is not surprising, then, that psychoanalysis continues to attract some of the liveliest intellects in our culture. These individuals are by no means all psychoanalytic clinicians, or psychotherapists. They are distinguished scholars in an almost bewildering range of disciplines, from the study of mental disorders with their biological determinants to the disciplines of literature, art, philosophy and history. There will always be a need to explicate the meaning of experience. Psychoanalysis, with its commitment to understanding subjectivity, is in a premier position to fulfil this intellectual and human task. We are not surprised at the upsurge of interest in psychoanalytic studies in universities in many countries. The books in this series are aimed at addressing the same intellectual curiosity that has made these educational projects so successful.

We are proud that the Whurr Series in Psychoanalysis has been able to attract some of the most interesting and creative minds in the field. Our commitment is to no specific orientation, to no particular professional group, but to the intellectual challenge to explore the questions of meaning and interpretation systematically, and in a scholarly way. Nevertheless, we would be glad if this series particularly spoke to the psychotherapeutic community, to those individuals who use their own minds and humanity to help others in distress.

Our focus in this series is to communicate the intellectual excitement which we feel about the past, present and future of psychoanalytic ideas. We hope that our work with the authors and editors in the series will help to make these ideas accessible to an ever-increasing and worldwide group of students, scholars and practitioners.

Peter Fonagy
Mary Target
University College London

Foreword

This is an absorbing and important book, important both to students of society and its institutions but important also to psychoanalysts, not only to those who work in healthcare institutions but also to those other psychoanalysts who confine themselves to work with individual patients in consulting rooms. The interest of this last group in institutions and society is usually confined to puzzlement over the strange antics of their professional societies, but perhaps Hinshelwood and Chiesa will persuade them into other pastures.

The authors present a scholarly and wide-ranging examination of the development of psychoanalytic interest in society from Freud's early attempt to treat the whole of human history as a recapitulation of the Oedipus complex to recent detailed and careful analyses of unconscious anxieties and defences in particular institutions and social processes. They note Freud's progression from his 'tribal fantasy' in which he equated the individual and society in *Totem and Taboo* (1913) to his much more sophisticated analysis of the relation btween the individual and the group in *Group Psychology and the Analysis of the Ego* (1921) and in *Civilization and its Discontents* (1930).

From there the authors branch out to describe the development of psychoanalytic social psychology in Continental Europe, South America, the United States and Britain, emphasising in each case the effect of the cultural background and the local political and social context as well as the effect of the thinking of particular psychoanalysts. For each region they have asked a particularly well-informed author to contribute his (or her) view of relevant developments.

In Europe psychoanalysis has always had a radical tinge, greatly heightened by the rise of fascism and Nazism, the persecution of Jews and of psychoanalysts and the effects of the Second World War. Continental and South American analysts, especially those South American analysts who were émigrés from Europe, had to grapple not only with the dispersal of analysts and the effects of the war but also, in the case of Argentinian analysts, with the effect of violent political oppression. The theories of this group of analysts show, in particular, the way groups and institutions express and integrate both psychotic and non-psychotic levels of functioning and how this integration breaks down in situations of catastrophic change. Not surprisingly, the contributions of these analysts convey a sense of political and emotional urgency, and they are also concerned to link the 'groupiness' of individuals into the general theory of psychoanalysis.

Things have been rather different in the United States and Britain – much less political urgency, more interest in the 'efficiency' of institutions and their effect on the individual. Most of the use of psychoanalytic ideas in the United States has been carried out by people trained primarily in other disciplines, and their research has often been on industrial consultancy and has used the ideas of ego-psychology with its emphasis on adaptation. This has led to a view that institutions are, or should be, supportive of individual maturity – a view very different from that of Freud and Continental and South American analysts. There is another strand of thought in the United States, however, which is shown in Otto Kernberg's thoughtful review and psychoanalytic critique of the work of various British contributors on groups, work that developed at the Tavistock Institute in Britain.

The second part of the book concerns British contributions, originating especially in the very fruitful coming together during the 1939–45 war of psychiatrists from the Tavistock Clinic, psychoanalysts from the British Society of Psycho-Analysis and social psychologists such as Eric Trist. This led to Bion's original study of 'basic assumption groups' in relation to the 'work group'. His work, combined with the thinking of Eric Trist, led to studies of social systems as systems of defence against anxiety, followed by many other projects, some carried out by psychoanalysts, some by anthropologists and social psychologists; some projects were funded by special research grants, some were paid for by the institutions studied. Gradually this rapid development crystallised into three main types of work: training in group relations; the study of 'socio-technical systems'; and the application of 'systems theory' to the understanding of institutions. In spite of the fact that some of this work was carried out by psychoanalysts, it has not had much effect on psychoanalytic theory as used in the consulting room, except, perhaps in the sense that Bion's first understanding of the effect of projective identification on the analyst was based on his experiences in therapy groups.

Hinshelwood and Chiesa describe a further development based especially on the study of healthcare institutions. This work goes back to the earlier Tavistock ideas of the institution as encouraging a system of defences against the anxieties aroused by the work, and it makes much use of 'culture' which was such an important bridging concept when used by Trist and his early colleagues. Sometimes these healthcare studies have been carried out by an outside consultant, sometimes by members within the organisations as in some of the studies reported in detail in Hinshelwood's and Skogstad's recent book *Observing Organisations*. This study of one's own institution is an important departure from customary research procedure in which it is assumed that one cannot study one's own situation even though this is exactly what clinical psychoanalysts constantly have to do.

So what, Hinshelwood asks finally, has become of Freud's baby, his remarkable psychoanalysis? 'It has grown up', is his reply. 'There is now a wide respect', he says in the last sentence of this unusual book, 'that psychoanalysis can speak to most other disciplines in the human sciences, whilst according them a respect for their own method and object of study.'

And, though Hinshelwood does not express such a desire, I hope that clinical psychoanalysts too may be led by reading this thoughtful book to consider its relevance to their own clinical work and to the general body of psychoanalytic theory.

Elizabeth Spillius
June 2001

Acknowledgements

We would like to thank the contributors for taking part and for the patience to stay with us through the long process of bringing this particular project to fruition. We must also thank Elizabeth Spillius for repeated encouragement over the period of this book's genesis and completion. She has been extremely thoughtful about the project, and has conveyed her own enthusiasm to us as an inspiration. Sue Budd saw the whole manuscript in an earlier form, and from her expertise in social science made comments that were very helpful for us in polishing the work and bringing it to a conclusion. Finally there are the innumerable colleagues in the National Health Service, at Essex University and elsewhere who have contributed to our book with suggestions and encouragement.

It seems appropriate to dedicate this book to the memory of Barry Palmer, who died during the preparation of the manuscript.

The use of personal pronouns is not consistent throughout the book and varies with the individual authors. No particular inferences should be made regarding the usage each author employs.

Contributors

Marco Chiesa is Consultant Psychiatrist in Psychotherapy at the Cassel Hospital, Richmond, and Honorary Senior Lecturer at University College London. Formerly he was Senior Clinical Tutor in Psychotherapy at the Institute of Psychiatry (London) and Honorary Consultant Psychotherapist at the Maudsley and Bethlem NHS Mental Health Trust (London). He is a member of the British Psychoanalytical Society and engaged in private psychoanalytical practice. In recent years he has been involved in psychotherapy research and has published several scientific papers on the outcome of psychosocial interventions for personality-disordered patients.

Antonello Correale is a specialist in psychiatry, consultant psychiatrist and head of the Department of Mental Health, ASL Roma B Area II, Rome, Italy. He is a member of the Italian Psychoanalytical Society and one of the original founders of the Roman group for the psychoanalytic studies of groups and institutions. His approach is described in *Il Campo istituzionale* (Rome: Borla, 1991). He has edited several books, including *Quali psicoanalisi per le psicosi* (with Luigi Rinaldi) and *Psicoanalisi e psichiatria* (with Giuseppe Berti Ceroni).

Giuseppe Di Leone is head psychologist and co-ordinator of the Department of Mental Health, ASL Roma B Area II, Rome, Italy. He has a special interest in group psychotherapy within institutional settings.

Karl Figlio is Director of the Centre for Psychoanalytic Studies at the University of Essex, an Associate Member of the London Centre for Psychotherapy and a psychoanalytic psychotherapist in private practice. He has published on various aspects of psychoanalysis and psychotherapy in relation to science, culture and professionalisation, including *Psychoanalysis, Science and Masculinity* (London: Whurr, 2000). He was a founder member of the editorial board of *Free Associations: Psychoanalysis, Groups, Politics, Culture.*

R.D. Hinshelwood is Professor in the Centre for Psychoanalytic Studies, University of Essex; and previously Clinical Director of the Cassel Hospital, Richmond. He has written extensively on organisations from psychodynamic and psychoanalytic points of view, and on the 'therapeutic community'. He is a Member of the British Psychoanalytical Society. He wrote *What Happens in Groups* (1987), *A Dictionary of Kleinian Thought* (1987), *Clinical Klein* (1995), *Therapy or Coercion: Does Psychoanalysis Differ from Brainwashing?* (1997) and recently *Observing Organisations* (2000).

Larry Hirschhorn is a principal with the Center for Applied Research, a management consulting firm in Philadelphia. He is also an Adjunct Associate Professor of Management in the Wharton School, University of Pennsylvania, and a founding member and past president of the International Society for the Psychoanalytic Study of Organizations. He is the author of *The Workplace Within: Psychodynamics of Organizational Life*, and most recently, *Reworking Authority: Leading and Following in the Post-Modern Organization.*

René Kaës is Emeritus Professor at L'Université Lumière in Lyon, France. He is a psychologist and a psychoanalyst, a member of the psychoanalytic organisation known as the Quatrième Groupe. He is president of a study circle, CEFFRAP; a member of the International Association of Group Psychotherapy; and a member of the French Society for Group Psychoanalytic Psychotherapy. He is a founder member of the European Association of Transcultural Group Analysis, and of a number of other French and foreign scientific societies. He is scientific director of the book series 'Inconscient et Culture' for Dunod, Paris.

Otto F. Kernberg is a training and supervising analyst at the Columbia University Center for Psychoanalytic Training and Research, Professor of Psychiatry at Cornell University Medical College, and Associate Chairman and Medical Director of the New York Hospital-Cornell Medical Center, West Chester Division. He was president of the International Psychoanalytical Association between 1997 and 2001. He is the author of over 250 papers and has published numerous books in the field of psychoanalysis.

Barry Palmer unfortunately died during the preparation of this book. He was a member of the Tavistock Association, a staff member of many Leicester-type group relations conferences and a fieldworker on a Tavistock Institute research study. He was a Professional Associate of the Grubb Institute and was a member of its professional staff from 1962 to 1982. He was also a member of OPUS (Organisation for Promoting Understanding of Society), and of the Working Group on Groups and Organisations, which is affiliated to the Centre for Freudian Analysis Research.

Janine Puget is a full member of Associacion Psychanalyse de Buenos Aires, a full member of Associacion Argentina de Psicologie y Psicotherapie de Grupo (AAPPdeG), and teaches at both institutions. In 1995 she chaired the International Group Congress (Buenos Aires) with more than 100 papers on transference and countertransference, the epistemological status of psychoanalytical interpretation, psychic reality, couple psychoanalysis, group psychoanalysis, state violence, etc. She has written several books: *Psychoanalysis and State Violence*, *El grupo y sus configuraciones*, *Psicoanálisis de la Pareja Matrimonial*, *Lo vincular*, and contributed to several books in Argentina, France and Italy. She has participated in many national and international congresses.

Barry Richards is head of the Department of Human Relations at the University of East London. He has written *Images of Freud: Cultural Responses to Psychoanalysis* (Dent, 1989), *Disciplines of Delight: the Psychoanalysis of Popular Culture* (Free Association Books, 1994), *The Dynamics of Advertising* (with I. MacRury and J. Botterill, Harwood Academic Press, 2000), and numerous articles on psychoanalysis and society. He was a founder member of the editorial group of *Free Associations*, and convenor of the 'Psychoanalysis and the Public Sphere' conference committee. He is now chair of the editorial committee of the journal *Psychoanalytic Studies*. He is currently working on a book provisionally entitled *Repairing Leadership*.

1 General Introduction

R.D. HINSHELWOOD AND MARCO CHIESA

Psychoanalytic interest in social science is prevalent, not least an interest of Freud's. Indeed, across the world of psychoanalysis there has been a growing interest in the links between social processes and psychoanalysis. In this introductory chapter we outline and discuss from a historical prospective the most significant developments and contributions in a psychoanalytic social science or a social psychology.

This chapter covers the main founding ideas, notably Freud's, that have contributed to this interdisciplinary bridge. We have been tempted to employ the term 'social psychology' not to privilege psychology over sociology, but because the term does itself indicate the connection that we are seeking. The book then takes an overview of the later developments, by surveying a global perspective. It does this in two ways; firstly by introductory chapters by the editors on general trends, and secondly by chapters written by prominent contemporary thinkers and practitioners. These are set out in a geographical order. Part One looks at developments internationally, and Part Two at developments in Britain. No doubt some readers will find it contentious to privilege Britain in this way. However, in the view of the editors, this is justified by the tradition starting in the late 1940s in Britain, at the Tavistock Clinic (later the Tavistock Institute) which has had a specially powerful impact on the development of the field of work in Britain, and has developed a wider influence across the world as well (Trist and Murray, 1990a).

Psychoanalysis has contributed basic tenets, which must be sustained in the transition from one discipline to another. That psychoanalytic framework which we take as minimal will encompass the notions of 'the unconscious', 'psychological defences', 'transference/counter-transference' and the particular intrapsychic process which has interpersonal aspects – notably 'introjection', 'projection' and 'identification'. We will not pause to define these terms, as they are available in the psychoanalytic literature (Laplanche and Pontalis, 1973; Sandler, Dare and Holder, 1973; Hinshelwood, 1989).

However, as powerful influences have come from outside the psycho-analytic world, we also include in our outline contributions from the emerging new experimental science of social psychology. The work of Mayo (1933), Sherif (1936) and Asch (1952) established that the individual was highly influenced and determined, by his social context, not only in his behaviour but also in his relations with others, in his morale at work, in his perceptions, and in his moral conduct (Milgram, 1964).

Certain reductionist problems

We can address one fundamental query at the outset with the example of mythical stories (a social phenomenon), which are sometimes simply treated as the dreams of individuals. It has been common since Freud for psychoanalysts and others to apply thinking from individual psychology to the group and to society (e.g. Badcock, 1980). There is a considerable attraction to this point of view since crossing from the individual to the collective considerably simplifies the problems. However, this method bypasses the complex differences of conceptual levels present in the human sciences. Initially psychoanalysis was a method of interpreting symbols, and thus potentially amenable to explore any cultural manifes-tation – dreams, myths and culture itself (Freud, 1913). The rationale of this method, whereby a process encountered within an individual (i.e. Oedipal phantasies of an individual) can be elevated to a social phenomenon, has been called into question (Devereux, 1967). On the whole it would seem to be best to try not to conflate these two levels, assuming for instance that a symbol at one level is equivalent in function (and meaning) with one at another. Equally it should not be assumed that the structure of an individual personality would be recreated in the structure of social entities. For one thing, the therapeutic test by which individual interpretation is steadied cannot be applied to the interpre-tation of cultural myths. In the past several psychoanalytic discoveries about the individual have been applied to social entities; at first the Oedipus complex, and then repression (in place of social oppression), the superego, and so on. To move from the individual to the group requires greater sophistication of understanding of how the collectivity of individuals constitutes the group; and likewise how the individual is in considerable measure influenced in his own being by being a part of a collective, to which he also contributes. Freud himself was not consistent. His initial reductionism – of society to individual psychology (Freud, 1913) – was later modified when he wanted to understand group behaviour (Freud, 1921).

This is an emphasis on the group of individuals *as if* they were similar to an individual; as if the group entity operates similar psychic mechanisms, suffers its own anxieties, and uses symbols in the ways of individuals, rather than as semiotic systems in their own right. Originating as an individual psychology, any putative psychoanalytic social psychology has to address why it is, in the first place, that individuals do cohere into institutions. And it is worth briefly listing the possible candidates that exist, psychoanalytically, as this 'glue' that sticks individuals together to form a social entity. Trotter (1916) described the collectivisation of individuals as the product simply of an instinct, a view taken originally by Bion (1961) with his initial view of inherent 'valencies'. LeBon (1895), whom Freud took seriously, and McDougall (1920) regarded the key element as a suggestibility, a potential to relate to other's affects with similar affects. Freud (1921) elaborated this in terms of the process of identification, which he first found in the Oedipus complex, and the emerging child's adoption of a gender identity through linking specifically to one or other parent, a link composed of the 'being-like' quality. And this bonding was particularly potent through the phenomenon of leadership – the leader being a common identification for a whole group. Prior to that Freud had tended to think of the commonality that brought individuals together as an innate similarity of their phantasy life – the Oedipal phantasies are common to all mankind and therefore link us closely to each other with common phantasies. Later Freud (1930) discussed how civilisation is a massive project of self-interest held together by social sanctions against inevitable aggression. It is important to recognise that psychoanalytically this question is not yet settled. Frequently not addressed by psychoanalytic writers on social science, the nature of the social glue has nevertheless to be implicit in what they say.

Freud and social psychology

Freud eagerly extended the domain of psychoanalysis towards an understanding of the individual in his relations with society. He had already postulated in his theory of hysteria that certain phantasies were common in the whole human race, and that the Oedipus myth reflected the core of a ubiquitous childhood unconscious trauma. To establish this universality Freud had extended its application from dreams to the psychopathology of everyday life, and jokes. In *Totem and Taboo* (Freud, 1913), he entered the realm of anthropology to explain the occurrence of the Oedipus complex in savage societies. In this work Freud attempted to show that psychoanalytic discoveries, in particular the Oedipus complex, were universally relevant to the whole of human science. And linked to this was his idea that, should this be shown as a human universal, this would bolster the whole of psychoanalysis itself. Therefore his purpose was to prove psychoanalysis, which seemed to demonstrate his fear at the time that psychoanalysis would have to be justified from outside psychoanalytic practice.

He created a sort of genesis myth about the origin of society, based on the Oedipus complex. A tribal chief was killed and eaten by the younger males (the chief's sons), who were ambitious to take over from their father. Their patricidal act then drove them through guilt and fear to institute a collective system for guilty co-operation and the suppression of rivalry. Freud hovered on the brink of assigning this phantasy to an actual historical event, the founding moment that ushered in civilisation itself.

Anthropologists were respectful but critical of Freud's imagined hypothesis. First was Kroeber (1920), soon followed by Malinowski (1922), Elliott Smith (1923) and Rivers (1923). There is little doubt that Freud's views have been a greater or lesser stimulus to anthropological fieldwork ever since. Malinowski was quite laudatory in some ways, respecting Freud as providing the first bridge social scientists needed for understanding how individual instincts can take part in social formations. Malinowski accepted the unconscious, and the idea of a social taboo within a culture, and the intimate link between the taboo and the structure of the family in that culture. On the other hand Malinowski was quite scornful of Freud's armchair speculations and reported different conclusions from his own fieldwork with the Trobriand Island tribes. In those tribes, the individuals did not have a classical Oedipus complex. Instead the taboo was against brother–sister incest (rather than mother–son), and the figure enforcing the taboo was not the biological father but the maternal uncle. Malinowski therefore claimed to disprove Freud's contention that the Oedipus complex was rooted biologically in the human race; instead it was a culturally determined phenomenon.

Malinowski's partial endorsement of Freud's work, coupled with his criticism that psychoanalysts had not been there in the field, was not enough, as it did not satisfy the psychoanalysts' need to prove the discovery of a human universal. In 1926 Ernest Jones published a long and detailed response to Malinowski's conclusions. Like Freud, he mastered a great deal of anthropological literature in order to show that the manifest structure of taboo and prohibition, resting on a shallow denial that parental intercourse produced babies, was an example of repression of the classical Oedipus complex, which was therefore very much in existence unconsciously. That repression showed through in certain inconsistencies, just as in a neurosis. Jones set out to rescue the Oedipus complex as a universal of humanity. This debate has grumbled on within anthropology to the present (Gillison, 1993; Spiro, 1993), although on the whole psychoanalysts have ignored this debate. One of the highlights of the early debate was the engagement that Freud (1913) and Jones (1926) made with anthropologists, their ideas and their fieldwork. Both weighted their arguments with a depth of understanding of the contemporary issues in anthropology. However, later psychoanalysts have not always avoided a slide into reductionism, taking a psychoanalytic approach in isolation from the issues and essence of the discipline in which they enter. As psychoanalysis tended to move away from simple symbol-interpretation towards analysis of ego and character structure in the 1920s and 1930s, new ideas from individual psychology have been advanced as explanatory concepts in social science. Freud himself commented on this reductionist trend. He did seem to become alert to the problem of society being a collective level of human 'unconsciouses', and not just an individual writ large. This seems to be apparent in his next foray into social science (Freud, 1921):

> From the very first individual psychology... is at the same time social psychology as well (SE 18, p. 69).

Here he is well aware of the individual as being a quite different phenomenon, or a different 'subject', when in a group. In addition much of his work was taken up with how people do come to be a collective:

> If the individuals in the group are combined into a unity, there must surely be something to unite them, and this bond might be precisely the thing that is characteristic of a group (ibid., p. 73).

He based his understanding of this bonding in the concept of 'identification', which he had recently described (Freud, 1917). It was a concept that he had first postulated in connection with the change in the character of melancholic patients. Its importance was that he could begin to see it as the glue that stuck people together, in such a way that they are truly different in the field of social psychology than in individual psychology. Freud was concerned to grasp the mutual influencing that occurred between an individual and those others who were the objects of his libidinal interest. He understood that this was a process which profoundly influenced the psychological functioning of the individual (as in falling in love, or when under hypnosis) (Freud, 1921), and the development of the individual's own mind – through this formation of an identity based on internalisation.[1] These sorts of processes, which he termed 'identification',

---

[1] In 'The ego and the id', Freud (1923) focused particularly on the internalisation of the parents as an internal agency of the child's mind, the superego.

involve a taking in, in some sense, of external objects to become part of the individual's own mental make-up. This is now known as 'introjection'. When Freud was first exploring with this idea he rapidly understood that it was the underlying process which brought groups together and promoted common action amongst the members. Freud's return of these group processes to the normal psychology of the group was a fundamentally important step (Wolfenstein, 1990). It no longer required the collective – the dyad or the mob – to appear as the individual writ large. Nor even did it require the group to be a quasi-family entity. The group in effect became a collectivity inhabited by parts of the personalities of the individuals, and recreating some of the internal dynamics of the individual with himself.

Freud's model focused, too, on leadership. The leader of a group – like a hypnotist – offers functions to the individual, which the individual relinquishes. He stressed the idea of a common figure for the individuals in a group, a form that became a common group ideal – for example, Christ is carried in the heart of all Christians. Or perhaps it is as a common punitive agent – it is well known that an external enemy unites a group. In an army, the leader brings the troops into a coherent body by being the thinking and planning agent for them. Freud's example was the general of the Assyrian army, Holofernes. When he was decapitated by Judith, all the soldiers and members of the army acted in a panicky way, fleeing as if all their heads had all been chopped off too, and they could not think – but only act, by running away.

Freud's third sally into sociology was his late *Civilisation and its Discontents* (Freud, 1930) where, beset by his own persistent decline with cancer, he became equally pessimistic about the world around him. He expressed the thesis that civilisation condemned us to a life, at best, of 'ordinary unhappiness', or at worst, 'neurotic misery'. Civilisation and its internal representative force (repression) inside us permanently frustrate our basic drives, originating in our animal biology. We remain for our lives charged up with unsatisfied energy. Following his description of the death instinct (Freud, 1920), he thought society had the job especially of curtailing the expression of aggression. Our only recourse is to substitute release of energy in culturally acceptable ways. The rigours of sublimation tax us all, and force us from our innocent animal natures into a world of culture – though most of us rarely attain such elevated moments. Freud is drawing attention to a significant point that has to be explained whatever grounding one takes for a social psychology. The human being is born into a biological existence of physical objects and satisfactions, and at some point is required to transfer into a world of ephemeral symbols. Some sort of theory of translation from the biological to the symbolic is essential.

In summary, from briefly reviewing Freud's own work it is possible to grasp some reductionist pitfalls. It seems to us useful to bear in mind three key issues:

- Is the group constituted as a human entity in its own right. at a separate level from the individual?
- How is it conceived that the individuals cohere into this super-ordinate entity?
- What conceptual structure acts as a bridge between individual and society?

Object relations theory

The work by Melanie Klein (1932, 1935, 1945, 1957), Fairbairn (1952) and others represented a conceptual shift from Freud's early work, as it conceptualised human beings as fundamentally object-seeking rather than pleasure-seeking. New primitive mental functions, such as projection, introjection and identification were discovered, which implied a two-way relation with an external and then internal object. A basically interpersonal psychology was being built, which represented a coherent development from Freud's later work (Freud, 1923; 1926; 1933). Klein was only interested in psychoanalytic work, and did not discuss society or groups, but followers (Jaques, 1955a; Menzies, 1959; Bion, 1961; Bott Spillius, 1990 and many others) contributed significantly to the Tavistock tradition. Nor did Fairbairn take an interest in society, although he did write about aesthetics.

With the more recent explosion in understanding of the nature and occurrence of introjection and projection, we have been able to come back to group phenomena with vastly more detailed observations. What Freud was really introducing was an answer to the question: What is it that sticks individuals together to make groups out of them, and how does that bonding create group specific phenomena? This is one approach to the question of levels, and how you move from one level to the other. The stickiness, the glue, is found in the operation of specific mental mechanisms – introjection, projection and identification. The intricacies of introjective and projective phenomena have been outlined roughly in *What Happens in Groups* (Hinshelwood, 1987). The simplistic original theory of repression was later on integrated with a more profound understanding of sublimation (Freud, 1933; Anna Freud, 1923) aesthetics (Kris, 1952) and symbol formation (Segal, 1957; Bion, 1962).

Further developments from within the object relational model explored the use of psychoanalytic ideas applied to social settings. After

World War II the Northfield experiments (see later) were developed further in various places, but in greatest concentration at the Tavistock Cl.r.ic. From there, there was a further international dispersal to Europe and the US. This fertile tradition advanced Freud's initial interest in processes of identification as they occur in groups (Freud, 1921), and in particular it employed notions introduced by Melanie Klein (projective aspects of identification) in her paper on primitive processes (Klein, 1946). Interestingly Klein's descriptions make an important bridge between the intrapsychic world of the individual and the interpersonal world in which he is embedded. Some of the *interpersonal* determinants of self and identity have therefore been described in terms of the *intra*psychic processes. Those influenced by this model have originated in Britain, notably Bion (1961) and Elliott Jaques (1953; 1955a) (see Chapter 6). Eric Trist was a deeply imaginative influence and contributed many ideas to the Tavistock Institute in London (Trist and Murray, 1990b), until he settled in the US. One advantage of this approach is that it gives priority to understanding process. It affords the possibility of understanding individual processes, which are involved at the collective level.

Kurt Lewin and early social psychology

This experimental approach occurred largely in the US during the 1930s. Into that setting Kurt Lewin arrived as a refugee from Germany where he had trained in Gestalt psychology. These two strands came together, and Lewin began to develop a social psychology based on the notion of the *Gestalt*. This resulted in his view of the group-as-a-whole. He regarded the social entity as a field, and this came into the psychoanalytic world in several ways (de Board, 1978). Notably, Lewin set up empirical psychological experiments at his 'laboratory' in Bethel, in the tradition of experimental social psychology in the US. He developed an informed industrial psychology, a study of the workplace, and an instrumental technology aimed at productivity and worker satisfaction and marketing strategies.

Lewin's views, influential in America from the 1930s till after World War II, coincided with another psychoanalytic thrust of interest towards a social psychology. Via Eric Trist, W.R. Bion at Wharncliffe, Northfield and the War Office Selection Boards made a link between Lewin and psychoanalysis. However, Lewin was a direct influence in North America and in Europe after the war (Anzieu, 1986). Gestalt psychology, from which Lewin derived his field theory, was a founding influence on Foulkes. He was connected with the neurologist Kurt Goldstein with whom Foulkes worked as an assistant before his psychoanalytic training (Pines, 1983,

p. 267). Goldstein had developed his own version of Gestalt psychology, which linked Foulkes to the same Gestalt psychology and its applications to social groups.

Lewin and the derived ideas were highly influential in the psychoanalytic thinking about groups and institutions in Britain and North America, and later in Scandinavia and to some extent in France. However, we should bear in mind that whereas psychoanalysis uses the concepts of the unconscious, and of unconscious phantasy, Lewin and other forms of group psychology are based on conscious and cognitive behaviour in groups.

Psychohistory and psycho-biography

In the US the notion of the whole group as one entity married with the developing psychoanalytic theorising about the ego (ego-psychology) (Gould, 1991). The entity of the ego was then seen as the prototype of all developmental processes, engendering the movement of psychohistory in which social phenomena are seen in biographical terms. Freud's ill-fated collaboration with Bullitt on a biography of Woodrow Wilson (Freud and Bullitt, 1967) was the dubious initiating example (Gay, 1989). Later work bloomed with the Institute of Psychohistory (de Mause, 1991).

Systems theory

However, the developmental notion of the ego was also commensurate with the emerging interest in systems and cybernetics (von Bertalanffy, 1968), and communication theory (Watzlawick, Beavin and Jackson, 1967). This new school of thought was based on the assumption that beliefs and behaviour were mainly determined by social and relational rather than intrapsychic factors. They moved away from seeing the individual in isolation with its intrapsychic conflicts, and stressed the interactional dimension of human behaviour, firmly placing communication at the centre of their theory. Its application to social groups and to psychopathology was indicated by Norbert Weiner (1949) and led to the development of a specific theory, the double bind, to explain psychotic phenomena (Bateson, 1972). The family, seen as microcosm of society regulated by specific, often idiosyncratic, rules, was considered to be most influential in shaping personality and behaviour. Hence therapeutic interventions must privilege an understanding of family patterns and dynamics.

The shift from family to understanding larger systems such as schools, institutions and the world of business management occurred as a natural step, both using a pure systemic approach (Selvini-Palazzoli, Anolli and Di

Blasio, 1987) and through the use of ego-psychology ideas in management consultancy with commercial organisations (Shapiro and Carr, 1991; Hirschhorn and Barnett, 1993; Hirschhorn, 1995). In later years the American tradition has absorbed certain characteristics of the Tavistock, group-relations approach and the ideas of object-relations psychoanalysis (Kernberg, 1998a)

Political sphere

A contrasting interest in psychoanalysis as a social psychology came from political interests. This influenced the development of psychology in the new Soviet Union after World War I (Vygotsky, 1934). The notion that psychoanalysis aims to free human beings from internal inhibitions and neurotic misery led to an appraisal of societal sources of external constraints, which militated against more healthy individual development. Awareness of the social implications of psychoanalysis determined a leap into the political arena, to combat conservative or reactionary aspects of how society was structured by the dominant regime. In Vienna Wilhelm Reich became the most significant example. He was the author who most captured the potential revolutionary aspect of psychoanalysis and became actively involved in politics (Reich, 1945). Reich proposed an integration between original marxist ideas with psychodynamic knowledge to explain societal dynamics that would otherwise appear irrational, such as the coming to power of fascism after World War I (Reich, 1946).

As Nazi Germany emerged in the 1930s there was further recourse to psychoanalysis as an explanatory system (the Frankfurt School – Fromm, 1942; Adorno et al., 1950; Marcuse, 1955). We also witnessed attempts to consider a marriage between Sigmund Freud and Karl Marx, although Freud himself expressed considerable scepticism about this project (Freud, 1933). With the dispersion of psychoanalysis as Hitler's grip on Europe expanded, this political strand of interest moved especially to South America.

These grounding influences from the 1930s, together with the evident success stories of social engineering in the Soviet Union and in Nazi Germany, led to an interest, especially within military psychiatry, to harness social psychological understanding to the mobilisation of a nation for war. This occurred on both sides in World War II. However, the most important experiments in the war years occurred in the British Army, and at a military hospital, Northfield, in Birmingham (Bridger, 1985; Harrison, 2000).

In summary, there have been three kinds of impetus to apply psycho-analysis to a social psychology:

- Firstly, to prove psychoanalysis relevant outside the narrow clinical field and as a (or *the*) basic framework for the whole of human sciences, rather as physics claims for natural science.
- Secondly, specifically to enrich industrial psychology and the effec-tiveness of working institutions.
- Thirdly, a political aim of debating the realities of political life, the possibilities of radical (or revolutionary) action and the nature of authority.

There are many writings by sociologists, anthropologists and social psychologists who have attempted to exploit their own reading of Freud and other psychoanalysts. For a brief recent selection see Badcock (1980), Gabriel (1983), Craib (1989) and Prager and Rustin (1993), where further extensive bibliographies are available. However, we have tended to concentrate on those starting from a psychoanalytic position who have looked in the social direction, rather than those who returned the gaze from society towards psychoanalysis, except where those social scientists have had an especially formative influence on psychoanalytic thought about society.

PART ONE
The International Field

Chapter 2 gives an overview of the ideas that have come to the fore over the past 50 years or so, in various regions and language groups.

The subsequent chapters in this part of the book (Chapters 3–7) come from various regions: North America, Italy, France and South America. The task that was given to these contributors was to give some understanding of the developing use of psychoanalytic ideas in that part of the world, and that they may wish to use their own work to exemplify this.

We have decided to make an exception in the case of North America where there is one chapter written on this plan, Larry Hirschhorn's, but we have added a previously published paper by Otto Kernberg, in order to give a degree of balance to a very complex set of themes which comprise the work in the US. As just described, there appear to be at least three sets of contributory ideas, from Freud's early symbol interpretation, the ego-psychology view of the coherence of the institutional organisation, and the assimilation of certain of the Tavistock ideas and practice.

2 INTRODUCTION
A Conceptual Overview of International Contributions

R.D. HINSHELWOOD AND MARCO CHIESA

In this chapter we consider some of the main trends that have occurred outside Britain since World War II, as a context for the four invited chapters in this section.[2]

There have been a number of individuals and centres that have developed this interest – notably in contrasting accounts from North and South America; a vigorous tradition in France; and significant developments in Italy. A compilation of French, Italian and South American papers appeared in French as *L'Institution et les Institutions* (Kaës, 1988).

To some extent the interest in Europe and South America was coloured by the political backdrop of fascism in Europe and the political refugees who went to South America. This contrasts with the developments in Britain and North America where the empirical basis has been as important as ideas (though in very different ways), and where at least one of the sources was the (apparently apolitical) industrial use of psychology. Already, in the 1930s there was a radical psychoanalysis (Jaccoby, 1983) and following the Nazi eradication of psychoanalysis from continental Europe, this was transported to South America rather than the North.

This chapter does not aim to be comprehensive but to provide more of a 'sketch-map' of contemporary ideas that are in currency at present in Europe and in the Americas. The original sources are increasingly appearing in English. The individual chapters in this part of the book will offer more detail on most of the writers considered.

Continental Europe

Aftermath of World War II

In the aftermath of World War II there was massive social reconstruction of continental Europe, which included the recognition of the need in many

---

[2] In Chapter 8, we return to a specific and more detailed focus on the developments in Britain.

15

countries to reconstruct society itself. The application of psychoanalysis to social groups developed as a tradition especially in France and Italy. Exiles from Europe in South America sustained and developed a parallel interest in the social relevance of psychoanalysis from more political motives.

Didier Anzieu reminisced that in 1956 he was able to verify

> I r ud's view, according to which there is only one and the same unconscious at
> work, whether in the individual intimacy of treatment or in a plural situation
> (Anzieu, 1986[1990], p. 90).

In effect individual psychology is a social psychology, and conversely social psychology already exists in individual psychology.

A conference in France, under the Marshall plan for reconstruction in Europe, introduced Lewin's social psychology – the field theory of groups. For a number of years in the early 1960s Anzieu, with a group of colleagues, tried out Lewinian, Lacanian and Sartrean ideas applied to the social field. He was at the centre of a group of analysts, and a presiding figure that blended the work of Klein, Lacan (Anzieu's analyst) and Sartre into a tight synthesis in an attempt to illuminate social dynamics (Anzieu, 1975[1984]). Freud's 1921 essay 'Group psychology and the analysis of the ego' made it possible to talk about group phenomena as such without interpreting them in individual terms. The importance Freud gave to identification was eventually combined with an interest during the 1960s in Melanie Klein. Anzieu was familiar with the development of Klein's ideas in the direction of a social psychology by Ezriel (1950), Jaques (1955) and Turquet (1974).

Whereas analyses offered keys to understand individual and social history after the event, Anzieu as Professor of Psychology at Nanterre had a front seat – or more precisely was on stage – at the onset of the May revolution in 1968. Anzieu was excited by the drama and that 'zone before language', which is the level of activity expressed in groups, institutions and society. The experiences people have in groups are important training arenas for demonstrating this level of the mind. This notion was also very influential for Anzieu as he was interested in the quasi-psychotic level of the mind, which is invested in groups and institutions.

The group, the social body and social action in the French tradition

The primitive level of group behaviour is connected with the psychotic level in the individual. Although he looked at Elliott Jaques' work on the social reaction to persecutory anxiety, Anzieu followed a less usual Kleinian strand of thought. Parallel to Esther Bick's theory of the infant's experience of the skin (Bick, 1968), and its underlying importance for the development of the sense of personal identity, Anzieu's (1985) interest moved to boundaries, and introduced the concept of the 'skin-ego' Phantasies of the surface skin or boundary give a sense of shape to identity, and contrast with the specific influences of the content. Thus the individual has experiences of his mental (and bodily) shape as well as the psychological contents of his mind. Disturbed experiences of the skin lie at the centre of psychotic and borderline patients, while disturbed and conflicted contents of the mind underlie neurosis. He described 'the group represented as a body' (Anzieu, 1975[1984], p. 249), specifically a part of the body, the skin. He referred to Harlow's researches with infant monkeys reared with 'mothers' of various kinds of tactile properties – a 'wire-mother', a 'cloth-mother'. And he also linked his ideas with Turquet's (1974; 1975) description of the experience in a large group in which a member relies upon the 'skin-of-my-neighbour' in order to protect or reinforce a sense of personal identity. These ideas have more recently been described under his concept of the *envelope* (Anzieu, 1987), which was borrowed from a parameter of Rorschach testing (Fisher and Cleveland, 1958). For Anzieu, the 'psychic envelope' functions as a bridging concept between individual and group psychology. Each person and each group process involves the functioning of a protective boundary that retains the sense of identity of the person, and of the group.

Following Durkheim, Anzieu claimed group members developed a 'collective consciousness' based on an illusion, a specific collective imaginative belief:

> the group exists, as a reality that is both immanent and transcends each of
> them, like a good, exacting, and giving mother who only has good children, and
> like an enclosed room whose walls are lined with mirrors that send on to
> infinity the idealised narcissistic reflections of each participant (1984, p. 95).

This collectively experienced illusion functions as the psychic envelope, which gives the individuals a sense of their own boundary and identity. He regarded the illusion as necessary for the formation of a coherent group. He contrasted it with the terrifying unorganised crowd or mass where contrasting 'phantasies of break-up' are stimulated and connected with primary aggressive phantasies, especially envy, as described by Kleinians.

Pontalis (1963) emphasised the group as an object as understood psychoanalytically. Or as Anzieu put it, it 'ceases to be an agglomeration of individuals and becomes a projection' (1984, p. 249). This reflects Sartre s concepts of 'seriality' – a series of unrelated individuals. But he took Sartre a step forward (or down) into the unconscious. The uniting factor of a group that transforms it from a series of individuals is the unconscious collective illusion – the 'group as a body' – mother's body. The illusion serves as a defence against persecutory anxieties – of penetration, of 'breaking-apart'. This dynamic between the uniting narcissistic collective illusion and the phantasies of fragmentation, is the group function as the skin or envelope. And this boundary, coherent or holed, shapely or distorted, is a central feature of group life and of the individual's experience of the group, and collectively of the individuals themselves.

Many of Anzieu's ideas are also re-found in René Kaës, a later contributor to groups who worked closely with Anzieu, but who incorporated South American thinking, as conceptualised by Bleger, into his own. Kaës (1976) conceives of an autonomous entity that is beyond the individual, but which stands upon, is drawn out of, reflects back into, and is separated from the subjectivity of the individual. This he calls the 'trans-subjective' level, a 'shared psychic reality' (p. 224). In so far as the individual personality is constructed from an unconscious populated by memories, the trans-subjective is the role of the social in keeping, giving shape to, or disposing of memories. The individual is not in isolation, but in a trans-subjective medium – like a fish in water. He has an identity through his relationship with this medium.

The trans-subjective level includes a number of formations. The individual's identification with a common ego ideal makes it an agent regulating the subject's relations with the collectivity. The renunciation of instinct is a social demand and a socially organised system that, at the same time, is an individual condition. Individual renunciation underpins social formations, notably the community of law and the possibility of love that is not gratification of instinctual desires. Society channels inhibited instinct into socially provided channels of satisfactions.

The narcissistic contract is another dual psychic formation originally posed by Piera Aulagnier (1975). Individuals are constituted and develop their identity from the outset, as bearers of the parents' expectations and hopes. They are to some greater or lesser extent always to fulfil the parents' dreams and unrealised desires. The primary narcissism of the child, Aulagnier asserts, is formed on that of the parents. The child thus forms a bridge, socially, across the generations. The 'pact of denial' is a specific feature of the collective level in which the whole of the trans-subjective area is itself denied, by collective consent – or collective intimidation:

> . . . every collectivity organises itself positively around mutual cathexis, common identifications, ideals and beliefs, a narcissistic contract, tolerable modes of realising desires, etc. and negatively around common renunciations and sacrifices, around erasures, rejections and repressions, around residues

and what is 'left aside'. The pact of denial contributes to this dual organisation. It creates a non-signifiable, non-transformable element in the collectivity. (p. 240)

Kaës himself has drawn particular attention to these 'zones of silence, pockets of intoxication and dustbin spaces'. He, in turn, has derived the notion of the socially induced silent areas from Rousillon (1987).

These various formations amount to a trans-subjective meta-psychology, one that focuses on the oscillating influence between the individual and the collective level. In particular, Kaës described his view of catastrophic change, when the embedding of individual and group within each other comes apart. Then the individual is radically de-structured. What is denied, the missing, or disappeared, what he calls 'the memorial to the unthinkable' (1976, p. 228), is transmitted through the trans-subjective. And a disruption of the trans-subjective then precipitates a major crisis in that the unthinkable that has gone missing, returns. In situations of crisis the trans-subjective level 'ensures the collective management of the functions of memory and forgetting' (p. 245). Some events leave no trace in experience, except as a hole of a 'non-event', a blank. The hole in the memory itself is alone cathected and can only be represented when it passes into the mental space of another subject. This kind of social deposit is different from the social function of moulding, transforming, giving symbolic currency to individual's experiences, and is more in line with Bleger's notion of the deposit of the 'undifferentiated' into the social entity (see below). In this way the trans-subjective enhances, and even takes over from, the individual subject's function of repression (Enriquez, 1988), with a deep interpenetration of individual and collective memory.

The most significant theoretical contribution of Kaës (1975) is the hypothesis of a group psychic apparatus. This is a trans-subjective reality that has to be constructed. The individual psychic apparatus is intimately bound up with the body, but the group psychic apparatus has no body and consequently must produce substitutes, the reified transpersonal, supra-individual entity. Kaës's work is essentially to try to describe that reified social entity, its formation, its influence on the individuals, and its transmission between them. Though individuals may interpret their inheritance in their own ways as it is branded upon their own experiences, it is reproduced through their own organised perceptions as further transmission to others, and to other generations. The glue of society is thus, in part measure, a process of co-remembering – or co-forgetting. Memories thus make a continual subterranean journey surfacing in individuals in idiosyncratic ways and episodes. This is very different from the phenomenological and ephemeral notion put forward by Berger and Luckman (1966) of the continual reconstruction of roles in society and social institution through the mere performance of those roles, like the keeping aloft of balls by the continual play of a fountain. The transmission of these trans-subjective elements is via the actual identities of the individuals in their immersion in that disembodied trans-subjective medium.

The idea that psychoanalysis is a practice of social action as well as providing a theory of society has developed from the teachings of Lacan. The revolutionary movements of the 1960s, which espoused psycho-analysis and elevated Marcuse, also became the bedrock on which Lacan's popularity has rested. Lacan claimed to study Freud's texts closely. But he did so in a remarkably novel way. He studied the texts as a linguist might and applied the understandings that have developed within linguistic theory since Freud. Since language is the vehicle on which all culture and civilisation depends, Lacan's psychoanalysis is a psychoanalysis of culture, including the culture of the psychoanalytic session. He was interested in the way in which inherent aspects of the human being, starting with the most primitive elements in the baby, come to be represented in given symbols offered, or enforced, by the linguistic community into which the baby emerges. As a result, a great deal of primary experience is reorganised by language (or symbolic systems, of which the verbal system of language is one) in each individual in conformity to the language system itself. A major tension is inherent in the development of the individual arising from the requirement of the symbolic world for the individual to become structured as the language systems, which impose themselves upon him or her. This imposition of a symbolic system is known as the 'law of the father', and Lacan elides this with castration anxiety as described, more concretely, by Freud. In other words, an essential part of the self is removed, or flattened or in some way violated by the crushing effect of having to enter the systems of thought defined by the structure and system of language. This inherent 'social' tension reflects, and expresses, the kind of conflict which Freud described as that between the id and reality – but it is a reality which has a symbolic nature *and structure*. Lacan's originality rests on his view that the ego's devel-opment of itself is through symbolic representations of itself, and he argues this from the inherent importance of the mirror for human beings and society. The symbolising mirror of society defines the person as it reflects him or her. Strictly speaking, Lacan's interest is in the relation between the individual and society, rather than a detailed investigation of organisations themselves, though many followers have applied his ideas to social and political organisations. A distinctively individualistic conception is the individual standing, helplessly, against social forms, which impose themselves. It is a pessimistic individualism. It is characteristic of this genre of thought that organisation is felt to be oppressive, and the mosaic of organisational splits and reformations within the Lacanian movement is legendary. Yet Lacan was never quite as straightforward as to say that social organisation and its symbolic structure is bad and individual self-determination is good. Such a good/bad contrast is mediated by the awareness of the need for organisation itself of some kind. Nevertheless, such ambivalence led to considerable debate about and distrust of the institution of the psychoanalytic setting which organises the symbolic roles of analyst and patient.

The influence of Lacan on various literary and critical studies, history, and women's studies cannot be underestimated. As a system of ideas contributing to the understanding of cultural products it is enormously important. However, as this book concerns more the practical understanding of the way specific organisations work, Lacan's ideas are a parallel rather than central influence.

Developments in Italy: psychotic anxieties

Like Anzieu, the Italian psychoanalyst Franco Fornari was inspired by British psychoanalysis after World War II, especially by the contribution of Glover (1947) and Money-Kyrle (1937; 1951) as well as Jaques (1955). Fornari developed his interest in social processes during the devastation after World War II. He was therefore especially concerned with social processes as they occur in relation to the unconscious dynamics of war and the nuclear threat (Fornari, 1966; 1975). Although there were numerous attempts by psychoanalysts without training in social science to 'explain' war (Glover, 1947; Strachey, 1957), Fornari's ideas reached a high level of sophistication. He was impressed that

> love and sexuality have no need for public display (but on the contrary shun the testimony of society), the pain of mourning, as pain for the loss of the loved person, must manifest itself. The mourner must submit to a public funeral rite, and if he does not, guilt feelings usually arise. (Fornari, 1975, p. 139)

Thus public life is, at least partially, dependent on the unconsciously aggressive side of the person. Often these public rites represent quite unreal beliefs about survival, tumulation, grave goods, etc. Social phenomena gain validity from 'co-participation', not from a secure grasp of external reality. The supremacy in groups of a shared internal reality indicates, following Freud, an alteration of the ego; reality testing is suspended (as in dreams) and replaced by interpersonal relations. This validation of reality only through reference to oneself, he refers to as 'autistic truth', and thus the psychotic dimension of groups. He refers especially to Bion's distinction between the work group (based in some awareness of external reality) and the basic assumption groups; and also with Winnicott's notion of the transitional space, the function of which is to sustain the individual's unrealistic omnipotent illusions. Fornari, like Anzieu, claimed the group as mother's body, attributing this view to Roheim. Then, group formation at its deepest level for the individual is a mystical attempt to restore the dual unity of mother and child, in a peculiar 'coincidence of multiplicity with unity, brought about by the group' (Fornari, 1975, p. 145). He was concerned with the reversion to those states depicted in Melanie Klein's (1946) description of paranoid-schizoid functioning that erupts with such rapidity throughout a whole nation when it gathers itself to mobilise for war. Fornari described this as similar to the public means of dealing with mourning and guilt, and as the kind of oscillations that Bion indicated between the paranoid-schizoid and depressive positions.

Fornari held the Chair of Medical Psychology at Milan University, and from this position he developed a consultative function to institutions based on his theory of institutional functioning (Fornari, Frontori and Riva-Crugnola, 1985). Institutions develop what he called specific 'affective ideology' or 'affective culture', linked to their cultural matrix and history, but above all to the 'prevalent processes of symbolisation' through which the primary task is invested. The affective culture is unconscious but determines a powerful influence on the direction in which planning and decision-making processes take place. The task of the institutional consultant is to devise a strategy in its interaction with the institution that facilitates the discovery of the prevalent affective ideology and its wide-branching effects on institutional behaviour. The similarities with the working model in this area of the Tavistock group are remarkable (Obholzer and Roberts, 1994).

Fornari's colleagues in Rome have continued to mine Bion's work. Neri (1995[1998]) described the paradox (attributed to McDougall, 1920) that in a group the individual can be reduced to very primitive levels of functioning, and at the same time only in groups can he rise to a fully human level. He endorses Bion's characterisation of the work group, which serves to bring out the latter side of the paradox; but he incorporates certain notions of self-psychology. The sense of a group depends, like that of an individual, upon the clarity and consciousness of its unique history, its narrative of development, and thus a sense of the group as an organism with its unique identity of self that must be robust. It is especially the emotional development of the group that enables it to move towards a 'work group' mentality. Antonello Correale (Correale, 1991;

1992) addressed Bion's later writing on groups, exploring the notion of the container (Bion, 1970) as the entire institution. He considers the psychotic dimension of an institution, which admits actually psychotic individuals – mental patients. When a mental hospital admits such patients, it is the field of the whole hospital that must be considered as becoming elaborated to contain the psychotic projections and projective identifications.

South America

Organisation, politics and social action

The Argentinian Psychoanalytical Association was founded in the 1940s partly by émigrés from German-speaking Europe. From the begin.ing it had a profoundly political colour, and included many analysts w'1) had political interests from before World War II (Jacoby, 1983; Langer, 1989). The political interest inevitably led to an interest in social aspects of people gathered in groups and society. This development contrasts with the impetus in Britain and North America that came from the (appaiently apolitical) industrial application of psychology.

One of the founders of the Argentinian Psychoanalytical Society, Pichon Rivière, fought in the Spanish Civil War. He had grown up in a rural part of Argentina,[3] and was a 'man of action'. He began working with groups in 1938, though they were not directly therapeutic groups. He reacted against the large institutional system when he worked at Tomas Borda Neuro-Psychiatric Hospital, in Buenos Aires, which had 4500 male inmates. The majority were kept in isolation, none had visitors or retained contact with the outside world, and they were maltreated by the nurses. He began to train untrained nurses taken from the patient group. He taught a non-traditional view of mental illness; in particular that it was not incurable, though cure entailed the collective effort of everyone. This was the beginning of what came to be called 'operative groups' (grupos operativos), and have some resemblance to the discussion groups that Balint started in the UK (Balint et al., 1966). His training, aimed at changing and revitalising the ward culture, involved a collaborative effort to analyse the stereotyped roles, and he fostered a new kind of leadership that remained involved in the ward group, and culture. The new 'nurses', while helping others, showed a significant change for the better in their own mental health.

---

[3] In fact his parents had originated in Switzerland.

After leaving the mental hospital, Pichon Rivière expanded his work and refined his operative group approach. He conducted similar groups in the University of Rosario (Pichon Rivière et al., 1960), and later in other institutions including a factory.[4]

His work in the late 1930s started as a study of working groups (Pichon Rivière, 1971), and the term 'operative groups' is more comparable to what are now called application groups in Britain and the US. So, quite separately from Bion's ideas, Pichon Rivière described work groups and the processes that affected them. He detailed the phenomena in, and stages of, groups with specified tasks, in contrast to Bion's study of the very specific case of reflexive study groups, those given the task of studying themselves.

The writer and theoretician Jose Bleger took Pichon Rivière's ideas further. Bleger is the other major influential innovator to the psychoanalytic understanding of groups in South America. Originally partly with a political interest, he integrated his psychoanalytic work, deriving from Melanie Klein, with observations on institutions and society. Bleger began to develop a distinctive school in Argentina, with other psychoanalysts,[5] in the 1950s and 1960s. The military dictatorship in the 1970s ended the more political and social activities of the psychoanalytic group. Nevertheless the attempts by psychoanalysts to understand the experience of the terror and oppression during the dictatorship have extended Bleger's ideas. Like Fornari, Bleger was interested in the psychotic part of the personality and in the very early states of the infant (Bleger, 1972). He believed that these are dealt with by public or institutional processes. He introduced a phase that precedes the paranoid-schizoid position described by Klein. He supported Enrique Pichon Rivière's emphasis on the moment before proper object relations. He argued that an autistic phase occurred at the beginning of life as a normal or necessary stage in development; and cited David Liberman's (1958) work on transferential autism, which in turn had depended on Leo Kanner's (1943) description of infantile autism. Bleger regarded Margaret Mahler's laboratory experiments on the symbiotic relations of the newborn with its mother (Mahler, Pine and Bergman, 1975) as corroboration of a period before the object-related paranoid-schizoid position can get going.

---

[4] Pichon Rivière's work remains untranslated into English, and we are grateful to Juan Tubert Oclander for much information in personal communications (see Tubert-Oclander, 1990).

[5] The first generation of psycho-analysts worked there in the 1940s and included Arnaldo Rascovsky, Heinrich Racker and Enrico Pichon Rivière.

Though similar to a phase of primary narcissism, Bleger actually described a distinct *organisation of the personality*. It is not just that differentiation between the self and object is absent, it is a s'?te of *primitive indifferentiation*. It contrasts with the primitive forms of identification based on projection and introjection. He used the term 'symbiosis' and later 'syncretism' to categorise these relations between the self and the world.

> . . . this primitive indifferentiation, with its two most prominent phenomena (symbiosis and ambiguity), is normal, not only by virtue of its frequency but also because of its dynamism; for these reasons it may also mean or imply a pathological picture of moments of pathology some of which are necessary for the normal development of the personality (Bleger, 1989a, p. 4).

However, these moments of re-emergence of the primitive indifferentiation are most noticeably present as the basis of group life. Mental life divided between a psychotic part and a non-psychotic part displays its psychotic part in the formation of social groups and institutions. He called this a syncretic function, or syncretic sociability, institutions and organisations being the vessels for it. Bleger referred to Elliott Jaques' view that part of the need for a social life is the collective support for defences against psychotic anxiety. However, Bleger conceived the involvement of the psychotic part of the personality in social life rather differently. He meant a process in which differences are submerged and differentiation disappears. This is both within the personality and between personalities. At the social level this leads to a *concealed* agglomeration of individuals within the institution. It contrasts, in his view, with the more apparent processes of human interaction between individuals based on differentiation and individuation. The syncretic level is a kind of invisible glue sticking people into the medium of the group or institution. It can be conceived as the sense of belonging. Like Anzieu, Bleger drew on Sartre's description of 'seriality'. The people standing in a bus queue are quite undifferentiated from each other; each is totally self-contained; and yet each is involved in a social entity that accepts and reinforces collective goals and norms. It is not an apparent act, yet on joining a bus queue there is an investment in the activity of waiting in order, etc. The individuals impart a collective recognition of the activity and its form, without ever recognising it. It is not negotiated as an interaction between them, unless they refer to each other about what is happening and a conversation starts up. Looked at objectively people in this form of sociability appear to be unrelated, isolated. But from a subjective point of view they are in a 'state of fusion or non-discrimination' (Bleger, 1989b, p. 111). This aggregation of the persons, or syncretic sociability, is quite different from the organised and integrated level of interaction, predominantly through verbalisation, action, wisdom, reason and thought. A kind of immobilisation of syncretic sociability is needed in order that both the group organisation and the individual personalities may emerge and develop. When the divide between the two forms of sociability is broken down a great deal of fear occurs. There is an invasion of what might be thought of as psychotic elements into the life of the group. Bleger describes this as paranoia, the psychotic part of the personality, erupting in the group, as a terror particularly about the unknown, or as a homogenisation of the individuals. Typically he says this fear occurs when a group first forms, as for instance the first sessions of a therapeutic group, which tend to be extraordinarily tense.

This syncretic aspect of the person is primary in Bleger's view, and is what makes us form groups. Groups are sustained on the basis of this undifferentiated bonding; and at the same time,

> The human being, prior to being a person, is always a group, not in a sense in which they belong to a group, but in the sense in which their personality is a group (Bleger, 1989b, p. 114).

Institutions are thus the organised part of the personalities of the members, and protect them in a sense from the frightening groupiness of the undifferentiated parts of themselves. It is not, as Jaques says, that institutions serve as a defence against psychotic anxiety, induced by institutions, but that they are 'vessels for syncretic sociability or for the psychotic part' (p. 114) of the person, which without institutional organisation would be psychotic. Bleger is also highly critical of organisational activity or arrangements, which blunt or divide off and encapsulate the syncretic function too severely. He calls it 'bureaucracy' and he believes it can function in sharp contradistinction to the spontaneity of the group and of the individuals. He was interested in the therapeutic effects of groups, and recognises the deadening hand of bureaucracy, elaborated to quieten the concerns about that non-differentiation and loss of individuality and identity. The syncretic aspects of individuals are thus the source of psychosis and paranoia, and at the same time are potentially the sources of spontaneity. Imbalance between the interactive and the syncretic functions creates groups (and individuals) that are too rigid or too flimsy.

David Rosenfeld, also Argentinian, and less overtly political, took up Bleger's reference to Sartre, and employed Sartre's dialectical categories of group life (Sartre, 1960). The progress from a collection of essentially isolated individuals (a seriality) towards a permanent group takes various stages involving fusion, oath, organisation, fraternity/terror and institutionalisation. Rosenfeld (1988) emphasised Sartre's opinion that a group is a continual process forever establishing itself, and never finally struc-tured. Each stage requires a group activity to move to the next; and at the final stage there is a return to the first stage, but at a different level. He calls the final one the institution. Rosenfeld blends the Sartrean categories with psychoanalysis. He takes up his own psychoanalytic interest in psychotic experience and, like Anzieu, derives inspiration from Esther Bick. The early infant's experience of falling apart, uncontained by a failing skin, a liquefying of personal identity and substance, is the psychotic's terror (Rosenfeld, 1982). He described this as the 'body image' of the psychotic. Implicitly he is describing the primitive indifferentiation of Bleger, but bringing those ideas of Bleger towards more orthodox Kleinian views and clearly adjacent to Anzieu's writing on the body image and the psychic envelope in groups.

Rosenfeld extended this body image to his understanding of patients' experiences within groups, at least at certain moments within the group, for instance when it is about to disperse. To this extent Rosenfeld's notion of the liquefaction of identity is in line with Bleger's view of the psychotic crisis when syncretic sociability emerges in a group. They are both psychotic experiences of members of groups.

Oppression and psychoanalysis

The particular conditions of South American politics, especially in Argentina, have made oppressive regimes a central focus for a number of people's interest in how to place psychoanalysis within society. During the times of political oppression the survival of psychoanalysis required considerable personal courage. A number of accounts of these difficulties from psychoanalysts and psychoanalytic psychotherapists (e.g. Amati, 1987; Vinar, 1989) were conceptualised particularly in the work of Bleger.

Although working in Argentina during the time of the dictatorship, Puget is French and like Kaës combines the French school with Bleger and the South Americans. She has described a psychoanalyst's experiences under a regime of organised violence that aims at terrorising its population. It cannot simply be described in intrapsychic terms. The task is one of going beyond 'the hitherto insurmountable gap between the socio-cultural and intrapsychic worlds' (Kaës and Puget, 1986). The diffi-culty in such a state is that there can be no debate about the experiences and they remain as an 'unthinkable and indelible area . . . a hole, a void which will have its place in memory' (Kaës and Puget, 1986). The psycho-analyst who does go on thinking about, and debating, these experiences, is making her own revolt against the persecution.

Organised violence (social violence) is intimately connected, recipro-cally, with the capacity for thought. There are certain unthinkable aspects of human experiences, and these need social constructs to give them a form; even, perhaps especially, the form of the unthinkable. Puget here supports herself with Kaës' notion of the trans-subjective, and Bleger's notion of the undifferentiated. As a bounded sense of the unthinkable such experiences are then, in a way, thought. If we can give nameless dread a name – even if it is given the name of 'nameless dread' – it comes partly into the realm of the thinkable. Puget also draws on Piera Aulagnier, using her idea that primordial indefinable experiences can be brought into contact with certain unconscious phantasies, which give them form. This contact constructs the subject as an individual with his own history, with his own experience of himself in history, and with his sense of a continuity and boundary to his own being. However, some of the unthinkable remains in a latent state, as 'searching for a thinker' (Puget, 1986 [1988], p. 127). These are the personal remnants that both Bleger and Kaës have described as being deposited in social groups (Bleger), or disguised behind social interaction as the trans-subjective (Kaës). When the social order sets out to disrupt the individual, as in the organised violence of state oppression, it can unleash disturbance through exposing the unthought residing in the medium of the society. Organised violence is a method, at the social level, for releasing the unthinkable. It disrupts the means of thinking through breaking the links between experience and the socially provided 'names', unconscious phantasies, linguistic symbols, etc.; and dissolves the experience of being a subject at all. The social policy of such a dictatorship is an attack on thinking and being; and one protection that can be mounted against it is to sustain thought and the normal causal links between life and death and between crime and punishment. Puget conveys that psychoanalysis is one means of sustaining thought.

Puget (1991) has been impressed with the overwhelming evidence of the power of the social context, as opposed, for instance, to that of the family. So she argues that it is necessary to define external reality in a broad sense, in order to discriminate

> its different regions, each answering to laws, rules and regulations which establish specific codes for that region (p. 26).

She has investigated this special area of the social, pointing out Freud's ambiguity about the external world and external reality. She brings together Bleger's ideas with those of Kaës and others in France.

Kaës (1976) conceptualised a reified state that is 'outside the intrapsychic world', and described the confronting antithesis between state and individual. Kaës describes this in terms of the Lacanian 'law', or the intrusion of the world of cultural symbols (the symbolic order) into the pre-symbolic (imaginary) world of the individual. However, in the specific instance of the violently oppressive state, it is not just that the individual is massively violated by the extraneous social order, but that it is not a symbolic order at all. Thus the individual exists without the means to imbibe a symbolic function at all. Kaës thus relates Bleger's conceptions of the social setting to Lacan's symbolic order. The point he is making is that the setting in Bleger's terms fails when the social order reverts from being symbolic intrusion to a pre-symbolic, bodily level – or the imaginary can no longer remain merely imagined. It is, he says, the aim of state violence to go beyond murdering the individuals to the murder of the symbolic. Like Puget, Kaës believes there is a need to expand psychoanalysis itself to take account of these levels which are beyond the intrapsychic.

Political radicals

In the 1930s there was a definite strand of psychoanalytic radicalism, which opposed the Nazis. Reich proposed specific 'sexpol' clinics to begin the process of dismantling the social oppression of sexuality, in all its forms, which he believed would relieve intrapsychic repression. A healthy society would ensue composed of liberated people. Reich had to leave Europe and eventually settled in the US. Fenichel too was at the centre of a group of socialist psychoanalysts, who also had to disperse, many to South America, such as Marie Langer (Langer, 1989). They brought psychoanalysis to South America, but also radical politics. Langer formed the Platiforma group in the 1960s, and was eloquent in using psychoanalysis in the women's movement. From the 1960s a new generation of psychoanalysts in German-speaking Europe began to re-find some of their radical roots (Cremerius, 1986; Parin, 1985).

The psychoanalytic radicalism of the 1960s was a new development hardly connected with that of the 1930s. It was above all a popular radicalism to which psychoanalysis lent a crucial pillar of support in the form of the writings of Wilhelm Reich (1945), the Frankfurt School, notably Marcuse (1956), but to some extent Erich Fromm (1942), and in the form of the psychoanalytic existentialism of R.D. Laing (1960).

It is of interest that psychoanalysis has both radical and conservative social impacts, at different places and different times. The conditions which apply when either aspect comes to the fore would warrant some extensive and useful research.

North America

Experimental social psychology and sociology developed prolifically in the US between the wars. Psychoanalysis on the other hand remained primarily a medical activity with individuals, with much less application outside the clinical setting. The notice that psychoanalysts have taken of groups and society has been limited in comparisons with other national cultures. In continental Europe and South America psychoanalytic ideas have often led the conceptions of society and groups; whereas in North America and even in Britain, psychoanalytic ideas have hung on anaclitically to the work of experimental social psychologists.

In the 1920s, Roheim's rigorous symbolic analysis is traditionally Freudian, and takes off from Freud's *Totem and Taboo*. The application of psychoanalysis as symbol interpretation to society was characteristic of psychoanalysis as it developed in its conventional form in North America from the 1930s onwards. So, for example, 'tearing the animal to pieces is a symbolic repetition of the murder of the father' (Roheim, 1922, p. 191), analyses the symbols, as they might appear in a person's dream. And there is not an analysis of the cultural *system* of symbols and symbolisation in which that ritual operates. In America this was reinforced by the rise of 'ego-psychology', an analysis of the defences of the ego, in isolation. This trend differed from that occurring in Britain where dyadic relations became the important focus as an object-relations theory of psychoanalysis. Therefore the concentration on the internal structure of the ego has sucked interest away from social formations, and has perhaps supplied less powerful conceptual tools to form a link between the individual and the collective.

However, the sociological emphasis on formal roles (G.H. Mead, 1934) and on social functions (Parsons, 1951) seemed to infect psychoanalysis and to enhance the formalism of psychoanalysis in its ego-psychology form. In North America, psychoanalysis developed its most conservative form – not only referring back to Freud's work in a religious manner, but also following a political conservatism that supported the status quo, and no doubt contributed to the phenomenal rise in its popularity for a while from the 1950s to the 1980s. This popularity was forged in the McCarthy era, and inevitably set the style of psychoanalysis as an instrument for enabling adaptation to conformity; although American psychoanalysis had always preferred to cling to medical respectability rather than to explore its radical intellectual implications, so important in Europe and South America. No doubt the task of the many immigrant psychoanalysts from Europe was an adaptational one too, as they attempted to assimilate. But importing Freud's well-known suspicions of Americans, the arriving psychoanalysts must have seen their task also as to persuade or browbeat the home-grown analysts into a psychoanalytic conformity (Kirsner, 2000).

An early attempt to blend psychoanalysis with social psychology was the work of Trigant Burrow (1927) who started with the primary social nature of consciousness in man. But this aberrant view in North America has remained marginalised, though not quite extinct. The use of groups as a form of therapy became prevalent earlier in America than elsewhere (Schilder, 1938; Slavson, 1947; Wolf and Schwartz, 1962) as a form of individual psychoanalysis *in* the group. This conformism to classical psychoanalysis seemed to strangle an interest in the group in which the 'psychoanalysis' was taking place. However, during the 1930s and 1940s, the USA was a temporary home for the members of the 'Frankfurt School' (the Institute for Social Research), a group of psychoanalytically informed philosophers who had partly sponsored an Institute of Psychoanalysis in Frankfurt. Fromm, Marcuse and Adorno adapted marxism in order to incorporate classical Freudian psychoanalysis. Much of this was politically inspired due to their exile, for instance Adorno's classical work on authoritarianism (Adorno et al., 1950). Fromm (1941) and Marcuse (1955) debated the social exploitation of Freudian repression of the individual. It too failed to make a significant impact, and the School reformed in Germany again in 1953, although a small remnant has survived in New York (for instance Fraser, 1996; Zaretsky, 1999).

An attempt to marry psychoanalysis to the long-established American anthropology was made by Stanton and Schwartz (1954). Their pioneering work centred on a detailed institutional analysis of Chestnut Lodge, a psychoanalytic hospital for severe mental illness. They discovered the importance of hidden dysfunction in the social network of the hospital environment in triggering highly disturbed behaviour in psychotic and borderline patients. In particular they isolated a prevalence of triangular conflict expressed in various forms between individuals and groups within the institution. They demonstrated the transmission of conflict from one site in the hospital to emerge as disturbance in a quite different place. They concluded that an exclusive focus on individual psychopathology and dyads proved to be wholly inadequate to explain patients' and staff reactions, which could only become understandable when complex interactional and institutional factors were taken into consideration. Their book *The Mental Hospital* became a classic for generations of psychodynamically oriented professionals working in therapeutic communities, psychotherapy hospitals and psychiatric institutions in general.

Devereux (1967) attempted an anthropological marriage with psychoanalysis, with a complicated intellectual device for avoiding reductionism, either sociological or psychological (see Moscovici, 1996).

The ego and the social organisation

As a result of the advance of ego-psychology during the 1940s, social organisation was regarded as the repository of ego function, notably boundaries and conflict-free skills. Thus the social organisation is a kind of auxiliary ego for the individual members. At least this is the ideal model, the role the social organisation should play. The commercial form of applying psychoanalysis to consultancy has therefore been to correct the failings of the organisation, rather than in a more academic way to explore the actual organisational processes. The unconscious identification of ego organisation with the social organisation is a deep theoretical thesis – and tends to be taken on trust rather than adopted as empirically useful practice. The identification is a basis for the experience of personal membership. In the ego-psychology approach it is the higher and non-conflictual aspects of the ego for which the social organisation is a depositcry. There has been a tendency within the tradition to move away from 'the role of the unconscious in group life' (Hirschhorn and Barnett, 1993, p. xvi). Maslow's notion of self-actualisation has been particularly popular in the American culture of individual self-advancement (Gould, 1993). Institutions are regarded within this transition as essentially supp.ortive of individual maturity, and are thus very different from Freud's own doubts about groups as the harbingers of psychotic processes, reducing the human individual to an uncivilised level.

And the field of organisational development, supported by commissions for consultancies from business, focuses on the conditions for optimal functioning of the organisation and of its members. This is a pragmatic aim, not a body of work aiming to develop social theory. To this pragmatic end, the work in North America had been willing to take other traditions – notably that of the Tavistock Institute in London – and to use them when they work. Kernberg (1988a), for instance, has described the defensive potential of aspects of institutional life, notably bureaucracy. He has made a particular contribution to a clarification of the role of leadership, and its interaction with the larger staff/patients group, within organisations and within psychiatric institutions in particular.

Some interest has developed from group psychotherapy and milieu therapy with people whose ego-functions are demonstrably inadequate. Whereas in the 1920s and 1930s group therapy in North America commenced on the basis of a kind of 'psychoanalysis *in* the group', more recently (Greene and Johnson, 1987) the recognition of dynamics in the milieu drew attention to the organisation of the institution as a potential factor in the functioning of the organisation of the personalities of patients cared for within the institution (Semrad and Day, 1966). The idea was that if the organisation was 'strong' then this induced ego-strength in the inmates, and vice versa (Klein, 1981).

This differs quite considerably from the notions of the social as the manifestation of the psychotic dimension of human mental function, which is prevalent in the traditions in Europe and South America. It differs too from the notions of the defence system, which underlies so much of the British tradition (see Chapter 8, and Part Two).

Thus, like the Tavistock Institute, and unlike social psychology developments elsewhere, the American interest has increasingly converged upon commercial interests (Hirschhorn, 1988) rather than political (or radical) ones. There has been a significant influence on organisational development and consultancy work with attempts to establish a bridge between the two fields of activity – psychoanalysis and specifically business management (Hirschhorn and Barnett, 1993). In fact, in the period following World War II, new developments from the British war effort were known early on and experimented with. A special issue of the *Bulletin of the Menninger Clinic* in 1946 reported the British work. As much of this work had been influenced by Lewin's 'laboratory' at Bethel, it was a kind of repatriation. The tradition of object-relations psychoanalysis, which went with it, was less acceptable. Trist, who had been a significant guiding principle in the development of the Tavistock Institute of Human Relations in London, was appointed to the Wright Institute in Berkeley in 1966. There had always been a strong link between the Tavistock Institute, the Kurt Lewin tradition and others in the US, and in the 1960s a series of Tavistock-style experiential conferences under the auspices of the Washington School of Psychiatry led to the establishment by Margaret Rioch of the A.K. Rice Institute in 1969 (Rioch, 1979). In fact there were a number of centres that developed Tavistock-like work in various parts of the US and Canada (Trist and Murray, 1990a). These linked also with the surviving interest at the Menninger Clinic (Menninger, 1985), and a flourishing development of 'Tavistock' groups has grown up.

In latter years the formation of the International Society for the Psychoanalysis of Organisations (ISPO) has provided a gathering of those using psychoanalytic ideas in consultancy work with organisations. Psychoanalysis has been particularly influential as a source of ideas in the advertising industry for the last 50 years.

The emphasis on the ego has by its nature tended to deflate interest in the social, by comparison with the traditions in Europe and South America, where the emphasis on process, characteristic of object-relations psychoanalysis, has tended to give a more detailed perspective on the relations between the individual and his social context. Recent developments in American psychoanalysis, notably self-psychology, have advanced the emphasis on the healthy side of the person and the institution. The US tradition has tended to veer in a different direction from others. If we return to McDougall's paradox, the approach in the US rests on developing organisations that maximise the individuals' capacity to be fully

human. Other approaches seem to dwell on the aspects of social organisation, which pull individuals into states of being that realise their
primitive potential. Such a polarisation may be exaggerated, but its
existence needs recognition in order to repair such splits within the whole
field.

There might therefore be three contrasting, but interweaving strands
in this work in North America. First the interpretation of organisational
phenomena as symbols in isolation; second the ego-psychology emphasis
on the 'ego' of the organisation; and third, the adoption of the Tavistock
idea of a social defence system (see later) supported by the notion of
projection.

3 CONTRIBUTION FROM NORTH AMERICA (1)
The Modern Project and the Feminisation of Men

LARRY HIRSCHHORN

Since the industrial revolution, critics, romantics and revolutionaries have worried that modern life, the modern project, has robbed us of experience even as it increased our comforts. Max Weber described bureaucracy, the hallmark of efficiency, as the 'iron cage'. He argued that work robbed people of their individuality, their right to experience specific relationships with others. Instead, by following rules, the required steps of a process laid down in the 'law', they wound up living in an iron cage. Their experience was rationalised. Today, invoking a similar refrain, we say that people stuck in well-paying but unfulfilling jobs are imprisoned by a 'golden handcuff'. It seems that the more comfortable we are, the more superficial and unsatisfying is our experience. We are led to ask, can we have experiences in depth in the modern world? Can we be surprised by whom we are with each other? Can our institutions promote our ability to relate feelingly to one another and our work can we overcome the compulsion to adjust ourselves to modern life, to rid ourselves of discomfiting desires? Or have we, in the service of securing our comforts and reducing risk, stage managed our lives? Are we reduced to being 'cool', and 'detached'? Are passion and romantic love hopelessly utopian yearnings?

Consider the following two personal experiences. I recently took my fourteen-year-old son Daniel to the Great Adventure amusement park in New Jersey. The rides were suitably horrific, with many roller-coasters, each more treacherous than the last. But there was something unaccountably sterile about the setting. When we ambled over to the area of the park that mimicked the 'boardwalks' or midways of old amusement parks, I understood why. The booths, where you could throw rings on a bottle or balls in a hole, were staffed by scrub-faced teenagers each dressed in the same uniform. This uniformity stimulated my dim

memories of Coney Island amusement park in New York where such
booths were manned by 'characters' – people who looked like they lived at
the fringe of social life making money as 'carnies', often cheating people as
they amused them. This amusement park of my memory and my fantasy
brought to mind the undercurrent of feeling that once made such parks
exciting. They existed at the boundaries of what was permitted; with their
freak shows and whorehouses they provoked taboo thoughts and actions.
They conveyed an element of danger, of risk. Great Adventure, alas, posed
no such risks. Indeed, it seemed to me that one reason modern roller-
coasters, which turn you upside down, have become so wilfully
nauseating is to cover over the absence of the risks and excitement we feel
when living at an edge where sex and crime mingle with normal life. I felt
as if my experience had been staged for me, managed for my own benefit.

I also recently attended a politically correct synagogue service in the
Philadelphia area. The congregation had adapted old prayers and rituals
to fit their own needs and the rhetoric was sensibly compassionate,
tolerant and environmentally sound. People could choose which prayers
to chart, depending on which words made them most comfortable.
However, as I participated in the service I was reminded of a different
tradition of prayer, in which a person could feel awe, danger and mystery
in front of God, and earned the right to consolation only after experi-
encing his vulnerability before God. In this tradition, the Old Testament
notion that God was 'terrible' did not mean that he was cruel, but that his
motives were inaccessible, and that our lives therefore were not under our
control. In this service, however, God was domesticated.

At the same time I was struck by the dress code of the congregants.
Men and women wore loose clothing and dressed more alike than unlike.
Naturally, one expected this in a community where informal dress was the
norm, but the dress code also seemed to spare its congregants the distrac-
tions of sexual experience and of noticing the difference between men
and women. This was reinforced by the fact that men and women participated as equals in leading the services. Like God, sex was domesticated,
brought under the control of the community, and could therefore not
disturb a person's state of mind. In other words, the service was designed
to ensure equanimity, to remove danger. Like the amusement park, the
resulting experience felt flat. Indeed, just as wild rides substituted for
psychic danger in the amusement park, it was my sense that feminism
substituted for religious belief in the synagogue experience. The
wilfulness of gender-neutral rhetoric made it seem as if the women were
confronting a dangerous patriarchy, but it was clear that the men in this
synagogue were completely comfortable and at peace with their now
diminished role. The 'battle' between the sexes seemed staged.

Psychoanalysis and the modern project

I bring up these two experiences because they highlight what many psychoanalytically inclined social scientists are led to ask. Have we created a world which lacks depth, in which all experience is managed, in which our emotional life has been appropriated, by the 'management'? Are the methodologies and world-view we developed to control the natural world, the scientific world-view, being applied as well to the social world, to what the philosopher Jürgen Habermas (1987) has called the 'colonisation of the life world'? In Habermas' conception, the modern life world has been deprived of its spontaneity, its unpredictability, its authenticity, of what the historian Huizinga (1921[1999]), in describing the middle ages, described as the 'enchantment' of l ved experience. Certainly, the two experiences I described here are consistent with this idea.

Psychoanalysis, I suggest, is linked paradoxically to this process of rationalisation and colonisation. On the one side Freud believed that psychoanalysis as a field of study (to be distinguished from psychoanalysis as a practice) deepened and extended our scientific understanding of emotional life. We turned what appeared to be mysterious, e.g. an hysterical conversion, into something rational, something that could be understood through observation and inference, the displacement of a repressed thought into the body. In this same vein, some psychoanalysts such as Jacques Lacan and social critics such as Herbert Marcuse have argued that psychoanalytic practitioners have used their knowledge to help people 'adjust' to the world as it is given to them, to bring their feelings and fantasies under the control of the ego so that they can adju t themselves to their settings. By strengthening the ego, these thinkers argue, psychoanalysis helps people suppress unwanted desires. People participated in the stage management of their own lives. Indeed, many psychoanalysts complain that the model of the 'neutral analyst' untouched by his or her patients' experiences, the analyst who in the popular conception, says little and emotes not at all, creates a therapeutic climate of desiccation. The analyst's world is dry, dried up.

Yet at the same time Freud argued that psychoanalysis posited that the 'ego was not master in its own house'. This is why he regarded psychoanalysis as a narcissistic blow to humanity. People could not and could never control their unconscious lives. Fantasies and desires continuously disturb us, and instead of trying to control them we need to appreciate the power they have to move us, if we are not to suffer the 'return of the repressed'. In this way of thinking, the 'life world' could never be managed. Instead it would be driven underground only to reappear in destructive guise.

To explore the paradoxical position of psychoanalysis in the universe of social science 'discourses', consider Freud's critique of religion. By exposing it as an illusion, by showing that the belief in God results from infantile wishes for protection, he continued the enlightenment project, the modern project, of critiquing religious belief. But at the same time in highlighting how psychological projection results in religious belief, and we project onto God our wish for a loving parent, he also showed how unconscious aims and processes shape thinking, even in the modern world. To be sure, Freud hoped to escape this paradox by assuring us that religious belief would disappear as civilisation itself matured, much as a child escapes magical thinking as it grows. But, looking back, we can be more sceptical. While religious institutions, the institutions that have made their accommodation with the modern world, may be losing their legitimacy, religious fundamentalism is growing and, as evidenced by the popular interest in astrology, magical thinking remains strong. Moreover, the resistance to abortion rights in the US represents, among many things, the belief that people should not control the facts of life and death. Clearly the prospect of human cloning will deepen these currents of feeling. The 'life world' is alive even if it appears, to an enlightenment thinker like Habermas, regressed and dangerous.

Indeed, many have argued that psychoanalysis itself has taken on some of the trappings of a religion. Its practitioners transmit esoteric knowledge accessible only to the initiated, consult holy texts (Freud's work) and are reluctant to subject psychoanalytic theories to scientific testing. The sceptic might turn the tables on Freud and write a book called *Psychoanalysis: The Future of an Illusion*.

In the following essay I want to explore how writers utilise psychoanalysis to come to terms with what I will call the 'modern project', the project of rationalising the social world. They all consider if and how we have inappropriately transferred methods for controlling the natural world to attempts to control our lives with each other. All of these writers work in the rational tradition. They make logical arguments and marshal evidence. But in the process they work to situate, we might say re-situate, feelings states, and the spontaneity and surprise they offer us as an integral element of the human experience. They help to re-enchant the world. We could say that this is indeed one of the functions of a psychoanalytic social science. I draw on the work of Abraham Zaleznik, Christopher Lasch, Sherry Turkle, Howard Schwartz and David Bakan to explore these questions. While this work spans several decades, I make no presumption that it is representative of psychoanalytic social science. Rather, my personal engagement with it has helped me understand some fundamental problems of social organisation, and clarified the locus of my own work. Finally, I approach these authors sympathetically. I am less concerned with determining what is weak in their arguments and more what links them to a common undertaking.

To outline this chapter, in the first section I show how Zaleznik and Lasch each examines how and why social life is managed and manipulated. Each presumes that, having acquired the scientific world-view, we are now applying it dangerously to the social world. In the second section, I show how Sherry Turkle presents a different picture. She suggests that the scientific world-view, which gave us computers, has now paradoxically created a 'post-modern' conception of the social and technological world, in which by contrast to Weber's 'iron cage' we expect serendipity and surprise and can gain access to our fantasies and dreams. I end this section arguing, however, that Turkle is ambivalent about what she has found, and worries that emotional experience in the computer age will in fact prove to be flat and uninspired.

In the third section I consider more directly the issue of why, how and when our emotional life is in fact flattened. In this context I examine the work of Howard Schwartz, who, through his analysis of what he calls 'manichean feminism', argues the modern family has created the neutered male, the man without passion. In the fourth section I suggest that there is another more developmental side to the neutered man, and I suggest that this emerges from the 'feminisation of men'. I develop this concept by drawing on the work of David Bakan who argues that, paradoxically, patriarchy feminised men by leading them to acknowledge their responsibility for their children. In the last section I show how the model of feminisation that Bakan develops helps us see how men who can tolerate despair will be able to acknowledge their dependency on others as well as others' dependence on them. I link this experience of dependency back to the root experience of psychoanalysis, to the process of giving ourselves over to our unconscious, of risking our vulnerability. I suggest that this vulnerability then becomes the basis for experience in depth, for a life full of surprise, for the road to re-enchanting our life in the world.

Finally, I examine how vulnerability itself is becoming a necessary and useful feature of the psychological experience of work in the post-modern world. The new uncertainties and the new technologies, I suggest, make us aware of how dependent we are on others to be effective and competent in our roles. In this sense, I 'turn the tables on modernism'. I suggest, along with Sherry Turkle, that the rationalisation of the social world has reached its limits. Modernism transcends itself and creates settings in which feelings of vulnerability in particular and feelings in general become central to our experience of the world of work. This is at least potential.

Throughout this essay, I suggest that psychoanalysis dramatises the limits of our ability to control our own lives. The modern world has offered us the promise of mastery, but has seduced us into believing that we could master our own experience. Psychoanalysis, by contrast, is a tale of mistaken identity. What we believe we have mastered, our feelings, our fantasies, our desires, we have simply repressed. And the repressed returns oftentimes to our despair. Psychoanalysis counsels that by giving way to the repressed we gain a depth of experience just as we relinquish our mastery over it.

A moral discourse

One reason I was drawn to these particular authors is that each is a moralist, each is animated by a conception of what the good world might look like. For example, Bakan's work is rooted in a psychotheological view of the world, Lasch in a political conception of right and wrong, and even Zaleznik, a management theorist, in a moral critique of the technocratic impulse. In this sense these authors follow a tradition of thinking that, although eschewed by Freud himself, was established by such Freudians as Wilhelm Reich, Erik Erikson, Herbert Marcuse and Norman O. Brown. The practice of psychoanalysis carries with it, of course, an ethical tradition of its own, e.g. protecting the patient's confidentiality or refusing to profit from any opportunities provided by the patient, and Freud's own belief that the truth makes us free carries moral overtones. But in the main Freud himself, hoping to distance psychoanalysis from religion, drew a sharp line between the scientific discourse of psychoanalysis and the moral discourse of religion. I think that this distinction is untenable. Inside psychoanalysis, as Phillip Rieff (1979) has argued, is a moral discourse about love and authority, about how individuals can or cannot find their place in a human community. These authors attract me because each in their own way confronts this question.

Perhaps this explains the interesting stance each author takes in presenting their psychoanalytic faces to the public. It is interesting to note that, with the exception of Howard Schwartz, none of the authors advertise themselves as psychoanalytically informed scholars, though each is deeply embedded in the psychoanalytic world-view. Zaleznik is an emeritus professor of business, Lasch a social historian, Turkle, a sociologist of technology, Bakan a psychologist but also a student of theology and Bible studies. Only Schwartz has identified himself so directly with psychoanalysis, as one of the leading theoreticians of organisational psychoanalysis. Instead, each in some degree has gone 'native', identifying themselves with the disciplines they work in while bringing their psychoanalytic world-view, sometimes subtly, to their scholarship. One interpretation is that each of these authors, aware that psychoanalysis provokes scepticism or hostility, exercises caution, not by withholding insights, but by conveying them gently, or by doing their work without fanfare. They do not announce 'I am doing applied psychoanalysis', but simply do it. But another interpretation is that they distance themselves from mainstream psychoanalysis as a technique or clinical method, in order to exercise their moral imagination.

Manipulation and the decline of spontaneity

The management mystique

Consider Abraham Zaleznik's book (1989), *The Managerial Mystique: Restoring Leadership in Business*. Zaleznik is Professor Emeritus at the Harvard Business School, and was trained as well as a psychoanalyst. He writes from a psychoanalytic heart, but his driving passion throughout his career has been to illuminate the complexities of leadership, and particularly business leadership. Along with Harry Levinson he is one of the founders of the field of organisational psychoanalysis, a school of thought to which I belong as well, and which is centred on the International Society for the Psychoanalytic Study of Organisations (ISPO). Zaleznik writes primarily for business school students, business people and leaders, but his psychoanalytic thinking is far from superficial. He writes with an unerring ear for the cross-currents of experience where leadership meets the unconscious.

The term 'mystique' in the title of his book conveys the idea that management practices conceal something quotidian, something banal, within the aura of something powerful. This something is the modern manager's reliance on processes and methods, rather than people, for getting work done. These methods, whether they be financial accounting or systems thinking, look powerful but they mask the manager's detachment from his real experience. The modern manager, Zaleznik suggests, is a banal person. Behind the facade of coolness and detachment is a person without passion or anger, an empty person.

This manager's character is troubling for two reasons. First, leading a business depends deeply on mobilising one's feelings to create trust and to fire the imagination. The good business leader is a profoundly irrational thinker insofar as he or she hopes to implement a 'vision' which by definition is not yet represented in reality. The management mystique, by contrast, creates the illusion that a person can lead a business 'by the numbers', and by relying less on talented people and more on 'good' processes, such as budgeting, planning and even participative management. This illusion spares the business leader the anxiety both of collaborating with others and of drawing on his own fantasy life to supply him with ideas and ambitions. Instead, the manager becomes the master-architect of stage managed processes, meetings that are entirely scripted, decision-making sessions where the results are 'cooked', and internal public relations documents in which the real-life drama of hirings and firings is described without any reference to the conflicts that stimulated them. ('We are so sad to see John X leave. He gave us many years of service . . . '.)

Harold Geneen and ITT

Second, the repressed always returns. When anger is denied or passion disclaimed they may re-emerge destructively as sadism, or more benignly, as boredom and alienation. Zaleznik provides the interesting example of Harold Geneen, the one-time head of ITT, a conglomerate he built two decades ago. Geneen governed by the numbers. He divided the company into 250 profits centres and held 15-hour-long meetings in which each profit centre manager explained if and why they had failed to reach certain financial goals. The meetings were brutal and consumed 35 weeks of his and his managers' time. Rather than delegating authority to his managers, giving them goals and letting them achieve them in ways they thought most effective, he wanted to get in on the inside of their lives, he wanted to get under their skin. His apparent focus on the facts, in Zaleznik's view, revealed underlying dependency needs. By virtue of his method of managing, Geneen was never alone. But his needs for others were masked by the dominating way in which he forced others to share their time and experience with him. This process led to business failures, as Geneen acquired far too many companies. He was out of control (Zaleznik, 1989, p. 168).

Examining Geneen's autobiography, Zaleznik notes how early on he developed the ability to be alone. As Geneen tells it

> I have a vivid memory of myself at age six, sitting at a desk alone in a large empty classroom reading a book. The Mother Superior came by and concerned over my apparent loneliness, asked me what I was doing. I told her simply that I was reading a book. She smiled at me sympathetically. Perhaps I noticed the pity in her expression. What remains with me is the feeling that she was wrong, that I never felt uncomfortable being alone. I thought I could always find something to do even at that tender age. Perhaps the isolation back then taught me to be independent, to be able to think through my small daily problems and to achieve a sense self-confidence. (Zaleznik, 1989)

Zaleznik's argument is quintessentially psychoanalytic. As Geneen's later behaviour suggests, he had dependency needs which created conflict for him, because they re-evoke his vulnerability as a schoolchild. While repressed, these needs 'returned' in the form of his wish to force others to be with him, hence his interminable meetings. But since he could not consciously acknowledge his need for others, he was instead, as the passage from his autobiography suggests, proud of his self-sufficiency, he brought his subordinates into meetings only to depersonalise his relationships to them. By hitchhiking on the control that managing by the numbers affords – after all, profits and costs are either up or down – he controlled his subordinates psychologically. Thus the ostensibly rational management of business – watching the numbers closely – was deployed in the service of an unconscious conflict, a clash between a wish for and fear of closeness.

Similarly, Zaleznik tells the story of a CEO who found that her subordinates were meticulous in preparing budgets and compliant in following the rules, but were unconnected emotionally to the whole process. The driving rhythms of the budget cycle and the abstract language of numbers and tables made it difficult for the team to talk about the core issues of technology and markets that preoccupied managers day to day. Understanding this situation, the CEO noted 'I need the numbers, but more importantly, I need executives with fire in their bellies to accomplish something in their business that will make them and their people proud'. (Zaleznik, 1989, p. 95) Later, Zaleznik adds that

> the hidden danger for managers, a danger that they only dimly perceive against the background of their structured life is boredom. Managers evade the messages boredom communicates that goals are too narrowly drawn, that relationships are without depth and that the self imposed routines cannot sustain the illusion that compulsive work is the equivalent of productive work. (Zaleznik, 1989, p. 275)

Zaleznik's critique of the management mystique echoes Karl Mannheim's extension of Weber's work. Mannheim (1936) distinguished between substantive and functional rationality, and suggested that the latter could grow and was growing at the expense of the former. The business process, which flourishes only when people exercise their feelings and their imagination, in Zaleznik's view, lacks substantive rationality. Its hallmark is obsession rather than creativity. In this sense Zaleznik reaffirms the insight developed by Norman O. Brown (1959), in *Life Against Death*, that the modern project, the project of applying scientific method to social life, is obsessive if not 'anal' in its character.

The revolt of the elites

Christopher Lasch, the historian, arrives at a similar conclusion from a completely different route. Consider his last book (Lasch, 1995), *The Revolt of the Elites and the Betrayal of Democracy*. (Lasch died in 1994.) In the 1960s and 1970s Lasch was an historian of the 'new left' in the US, working to find roots of radical thought in US history. In this sense he stood in an uneasy relationship to other scholar activists of the new left who sought inspiration from European marxism. Beginning in the 1980s, and until his death, he increasingly separated himself from left-wing scholarship, feeling that its feminist and multicultural turn made it increasingly irrelevant to most of the electorate in the US. Writing essays of cultural criticism for the *New York Review of Books* over this period, he developed a distinctive psychoanalytic voice, though he was first and last an historian. This work culminated in his highly regarded *The Culture of Narcissism* (Lasch, 1979), in which he argued that the modern culture of capitalism created a 'minimal' self, a person with little inner life, superficial ambitions and a feeling of emptiness that was matched only by his sense of entitlement.

His last book continues this argument. It is a passionate diatribe against the new cosmopolitan elites who dominate the global economy. Transforming the title of Ortega's classic work, *The Revolt of the Masses*, Lasch argues that the elites threaten democracy. They are rootless, detached from the common life and do not take traditions seriously. Having lost all contact with real work, they manipulate symbols, shuffle papers, and do work that has no purpose; they believe deeply that social life can be engineered. Reality is as transparent to them, as fungible to them as the letters on a computer screen. Lasch emphasises in particular the changing role of experts. He believes that since the progressive period, circa 1900, experts in education, social work and industrial relations have come to dominate the ways in which we engage in such practical activities as parenting, teaching and leading. Children, for example, used to play together without adult supervision and regulation. But, beginning with the building of city parks, the foundation of the Boy Scouts, the establishment of Little League baseball, childhood play has become increasingly regulated. Today, the elites manage their children's time to ensure that they spend it productively, in extra schooling, band practice and soccer leagues. Absent is the spontaneous life of children. Expert thinking now governs such practical activities as parenting, teaching and leading.

Similarly, evoking the work of Richard Sennet (1992) in *The Fall of Public Man*, Lasch's thinking is also consistent with the idea that we have lost our public spaces. Shopping malls, designed by private companies for a profit, substitute for city streets; television has replaced serendipitous encounters with strangers in the town square. The mall, Lasch suggests, is just one example of the rise of social engineering. As an example of the latter, Lasch is particularly enraged by the forced bussing of black children to white schools. This method of forcing integration undermined the integrity of white ethnic neighbourhoods and simply led white parents to send their children to private schools or leave the inner city entirely. As a consequence, inner city schools have never been so segregated and the public space of the inner city has been criminalised.

Lasch assesses the elites' ethic of diversity through these same lenses. In favouring multiculturalism, Lasch argues, elites sacrifice respect for tolerance. They see the social world as a marketplace where every culture occupies its stall, setting out its wares for others' amusement. Every culture is equal and no member of one culture can judge the behaviour or beliefs of the member of another. But this seeming tolerance masks an underlying contempt for all culture. Elites value differences because they do not take them seriously. Dulled to the actual experience of the 'common people', elites imagine that the trauma of social dislocation and structural unemployment can be overcome if people are simply helped to recover their lost self-esteem. This results, in Lasch's view, in seriously flawed schooling programmes in which children are pumped up with messages of self-esteem at the expense of learning real skills. Teachers no longer judge performance. In this cultural setting, elites substitute the ethic of compassion for the ethic of respect. People who no longer have the skills and traditions they need to feel productive are to be pitied. This means that political and social programmes, such as affirmative action and neighbourhood development, are window dressing, pathetic attempts at co-optation which mask the despair enveloping people whose social roles are vanishing. While Lasch does not say this explicitly it is as if compassion, once motivated by love, is now motivated by guilt. Through social policy the elites salve their own conscience.

A vision of the nineteenth century

Lasch imagines a counter-world, the world as he believes people experienced it in nineteenth-century America when democratic movements were vital. Public life thrived, people had pride in their communities, and patriotism was the natural outgrowth of love of place. This world rested on the integrity of the household, the economic strength of skilled craftsmen and the vitality of political debates. Young people mingled with adults at the workplace, in the church, in the bar, and acquired skills and abilities by observing their elders at work and play. As evidence of his argument, Lasch points to a political event that could never be replicated today; thousands of common people showing up to hear a considered and long debate between Abraham Lincoln and Stephen Douglas on the future of the 'union'. Instead, presidential debates today are entirely scripted, with journalists primed to ask embarrassing questions and candidates searching for ways to convey the image of mastery.

We may dismiss Lasch's vision of the nineteenth century as overly romantic, but before doing so it is important to note that Lasch does not equate social mobility and material comfort with democracy. Lasch is not impressed by affluence, if, as he believes, it means that we sacrifice our democratic temperament. By the latter, he means the disdain for inherited wealth, for unproductive work (such as currency speculation), for hierarchy that bears no relationship to competence. The world he imagines may have plenty of privation but it also supports the democratisation of competence, scepticism about experts and a commitment to pragmatism.

In his rendering of the nineteenth century he evokes a culture in which working class Americans and farmers had a deep appreciation for science and practical knowledge. Lasch (1995) reminds us that Europeans visiting the US in the nineteenth century were struck by the population's habits of free thinking and disregard for ceremony:

> For Michael Chevalier, in many ways the most astute of all visitors from abroad, it was the key to the whole democratic experiment. In America, the 'great discoveries of science and art were exposed to the vulgar gaze and placed within the reach of all'. The mind of the French peasant, according to Chevalier was full of 'biblical parables', and 'gross superstition', whereas the American farmer had been 'initiated into the conquests of the human mind', that began with the Reformation.

The superego

Lasch's vision of the present is consistent with Zaleznik's conception of modern management. Social life is manipulated, staged, and we have been deprived of the ability and the right to create order in our lives spontaneously. What is the psychoanalytic basis for Lasch's thinking? It lies, I believe, in the way in which he creates a seemingly paradoxical connection between a strong superego and social spontaneity.

When the superego, as a culture affords it, is strong – and this means that it is the source of ideals as well as sanctions – children and parents relate spontaneously with one another. The father, confident in the standards of performance he has internalised as his own, feels free to represent them to his children. Children internalise these standards, and because they are not experienced as arbitrary or over-personalised – indeed, they have standing, precisely because they are impersonal – a child who rebels against them may still love and respect his parents. The impersonal roots of the superego paradoxically confer freedom. This does not mean that the child will be rewarded for rebelling, or even loved for showing initiative, but that sanctions and rewards are not arbitrarily distributed. 'Child guidance' then follows spontaneously from the respect that children feel for their fathers, and from the confidence that fathers feel in imposing their standards on children. Experts are not needed. Education in turn is based on the bedrock of the child's internalisation of the father. This is why the child can learn from teachers and other adults.

By contrast, when the superego is weak, and Lasch develops this argument in an earlier book *The Culture of Narcissism* (1979), parents feel they must manipulate their children to ensure their proper behaviour. The child, however, is frightened by the father's apparent weakness, and consequently his own power, and thus develops a harsh and cruel superego, simply to regulate his own impulses. Paradoxically, children feel less free, less protected, as parents in the guise of behaving permissively impose no standards of performance.

Lasch's vision is dystopian, and he presents it with the passion of a biblical prophet. I don't want to evaluate its truth value here, though I believe that Lasch has described aspects of the dark side of a post-modern culture. It is interesting to observe how Lasch ends his diatribe. His last chapter is entitled 'The soul of man under secularism', a play on the title of Oscar Wilde's book, *The Soul of Man under Socialism*. Wilde argued that under socialism, which he identified with the end of drudgery, people would once again experience a childlike enthusiasm for the world. Lasch rejects such utopian thinking. He goes on to argue that our historical conception that in primitive times we were more childlike, more naive, and that modern life exacts the price of scepticism if not cynicism, does not stand up to the facts.

> Nostalgia (for the past) is superficially loving in its re-creation of the past, but it evokes the past only to bury it alive. It shared with the belief in progress, to which it is only superficially opposed, an eagerness to proclaim the death of the past and to deny history's hold on the present. (Lasch, 1995, p. 242)

In this sense he rejects Freud's supposition that we can read human history as the passage of man from childhood to parenthood. If ancient man was more feelingful, he was certainly not naive. One need only recall the book of Job. Freud's supposition, Lasch argues, led him to misunderstand religion as a consoling illusion rather than as a challenge to belief. Religious practice, Lasch suggests, pulls people to ask the ultimate question, 'why am I here?', whose only answer is the necessity of mystery itself. Religion in Lasch's sense is an opening into the unknown and that is why people who come to believe in God have so often struggled with despair. He cites the interesting example of the 'collection of songs written by medieval students preparing for the priesthood, *Carmina Burana*' (though apparently there is controversy about the authorship of these songs.) These songs, he argues, dispel the notion that religion is consoling. Instead they 'give rise to the age-old suspicion that the universe is ruled by Fortune not Providence, that life has no higher purpose at all, and that the better part of moral wisdom is enjoy it while you can' (p. 243). Indeed, it is well known that faith, if not killed by doubt, is always strengthened by it. Religious belief won through struggle is then based on the conviction that God designed the world for his own purposes, not for ours.

Like Zaleznik, Lasch believes that elites have emptied the world of substantive meaning, represented for Lasch in real work, meaningful authority, standards of performance, political dialogue and public life. Zaleznik argues that elites have substituted the management mystique for business performance, and Lasch argues by analogy, that the elites have substituted social manipulation for the practical activities of leading, governing and teaching. But while Zaleznik turns to psychoanalysis, the science of feelings, as the framework for 'restoring leadership to business', Lasch, who believes that the psychoanalytic enterprise is on its last legs, turns instead to religion. Yet each hopes to counter the modern project, the project of rationalising the world, with what can never be fully known or understood and is thus the source of spontaneity and mystery. Zaleznik focuses on the unconscious as the source of feelings, which after all lie beyond our conscious control and oftentimes surprise us with their intensity and the direction they provide, while Lasch focuses on God as the source of continuous mystery.

Beyond the modern project

Life on the screen

Sherry Turkle (1995), in *Life on the Screen*, comes into a dialogue with the modern project in a different way. Turkle, a professor at MIT, has studied the impact of technology on identity, first in her book *The Second Self* (Turkle, 1984) and now in *Life on the Screen*. She is deeply versed in psychoanalysis and published her first book, *Psychoanalytic Politics: Jacques Lacan and Freud's French Revolution (Critical Perspectives)* (Turkle, 1978), on the intersection of Lacan's work and revolutionary currents of 1968 France. This first book is integrally linked to her later work on technology. In both she hoped to explore the dimensions of post-modern identity. Indeed, the Lacanian school of psychoanalysis in France is associated with the problem of how psychoanalysis can help restore desire to patients' lives. In this sense we can understand it as one response to the problem of empty living, of living without feelings. In *Life on the Screen*, psychoanalytic thinking, while in the background, nonetheless colours her text. At one point she notes that psychoanalysis is a 'survivor' psychology; it helps us live after re-working the trauma of becoming human. In her later work, psychoanalysis is a survivor discipline in two senses. It survives in the background of her work and it can help us survive what may be a traumatic transition to the world made by computers.

Life on the Screen is a rich case study of how people, particularly college students, experience the computer, and is also a disquisition on the relationship of computer science to 'science' as the modern project conceives it. Turkle argues that computers show a different face of technology and science. The old computer science was based on what she calls the 'culture of calculation'. This culture, which she identifies with the spirit of modernism, breaks down wholes into parts to uncover root causes. It is the basis for modern systems analysis and has influenced deeply how social scientists and managers think about social process. While Turkle does not explore this connection, systems analysis was heir to the hope, first expressed by positivism, that social scientists could use the exact methods of science to predict and control social behaviour. She argues that a new, or what she calls a post-modern, computer science is emerging that is based on the 'culture of simulation'. Her use of the term 'culture' is appropriate because she is trying to characterise two distinct world-views.

Working in the culture of calculation, a social scientist, systems analyst or artificial intelligence practitioner creates models of reality which approach the 'truth' and therefore permit increasingly better prediction. Working within a culture of simulation the systems analyst creates pictures of reality, which, while presenting a necessarily partial view, can deepen a person's appreciation of the social world's complexity. In the culture of calculation a person completes a model: in the culture of simulation a person plays with a model. In a culture of calculation a person resolves apparent complexity by highlighting the underlying elements that create it. This is the culture's programme of 'reductionism'. By contrast, in the culture of simulation a person focuses on what are called the 'emergent' properties of a model, that is those properties that emerge as a result of the interaction of the parts and which cannot be predicted from simply understanding the basic elements and their properties. These emergent features are discovered when people 'play' with their models. Here the operative word is 'play'. In conveying the difference between world-views, Turkle wants to emphasise that the culture of simulation stimulates playfulness.

Living with computers

Turkle believes that playfulness also characterises how people relate to computers in general, and throughout much of her book, she presents case studies of people interacting with computers (perhaps 'living with' would be a better term). For example, she argues that through the World Wide Web we have created a new kind of virtual reality on the Internet, 'multi-user dungeons' or MUDs in which people take on pretend identities. A man might appear as a woman, and 'marry' a woman (who might in truth be a man), according to the rules of a particular game. Turkle explores these games and the people who play them at great length. She recounts her own virtual date with Tony at Dread's bar, a 'watering hole MUDLambda Moo'. They enter the bar, order drinks, Tony throws salt over his shoulder and is later confused when Turkle, lifting her virtual glass, says 'L'chaim'. They then dance and later retire to a private booth for more conversation (Turkle, 1995, p. 233). While acknowledging that such fantasising can be a substitute for lived experience, she suggests that virtual reality may also create a 'transitional space' between reality and private phantasm in which people can in fact develop their competence and enlarge upon their sense of identity. In other words, computer technology, the most advanced artifact that the modern world offers us, has or may become an instrument of play, surprise and development.

Turkle in this sense turns Weber on his head and she does so by looking at computers with a psychoanalytic eye. Psychoanalysis works by creating what the psychoanalyst D.W. Winnicott called a 'transitional space'. The relationship of the patient to the analyst has both real and unreal properties. It is real insofar as patient and analyst relate to one another as helper to one seeking help. It is unreal insofar as the patient projects onto the analyst the feelings and anxieties associated with his or her relationship to a parent. For example, the patient may treat the analyst as if the latter were her father, while at the same time her 'observing ego' knows that the analyst is not her father. As long as the patient can sustain this contradictory response to the analyst, the conditions for healing are in place. By working through her feelings towards the analyst, she simultaneously re-works her feelings towards her father. In this sense, history can be 'undone'. When this process works, the relationship between patient and analyst is affectively charged. The patient, who by virtue of her ambivalent relationships to her father has suppressed her feelings, comes alive in the psychoanalytic encounter. She retrieves her desires for love and recognition, as well as her anger for failing to fulfil them.

Sexuality

Turkle also argues that the Internet and its MUD games give individuals insights into their sexuality. It is a tenet of psychoanalysis that everyone has bisexual tendencies, Every man has a woman in him and every woman a man in her. This is often reflected in a man's desire to turn passive, and a woman's desire to turn aggressive. Many patients in psychoanalysis get stuck because they find it hard to accept their bisexual tendencies, fearing that it means that they are homosexual. People in MUD games are acutely sensitive to gender; when two players meet, their first order of business is to discover each other's gender. But at the same time people use the game to become for a moment a person of the other gender. As Turkle writes,

> Gender swapping on MUDs is not a small part of the game action. By some estimates, Habitat, a Japanese MUD, has 1.5 million member users. Habitat is a MUD operated for profit. Among the registered members of Habitat there is a ratio of four real-life men to each real-life woman. But inside the MUD the ratio is only three male characters to one female character. In other words, a significant number of players, many tens of thousands of them, are virtually cross-dressing. (Turkle, 1995, p. 212)

Habitat thus allows people to try on the psychological garments of the opposite sex, presumably putting them into touch with the excitement of becoming the gender forbidden to them. Consciousness is expanded.

Finally, touching on the issue central to Lasch and Zaleznik, she suggests that the Internet may enable people to come out from under the mass media, the public relations specialists and create 'indigenous' images. 'We can look at MUDs as places of resistance to many forms of alienation and to the silences they impose.' (Turkle, 1995, p. 242) People regain control over their own identities and have the tools to develop themselves as they see fit.

Ambivalence

Turkle acknowledges some ambivalence, however. When she enters a MUD site to play, she types 'emote feels a complicated mixture of expectation and desire' and then 'all screens (of the other players) flash – "ST (her screen name) feels a complicated mixture of expectation and desire"'. But Turkle goes on to ask,

> When we get our MUD persona to 'emote' something and observe the effect, do we gain a better understanding of our real emotions which can't be switched on and off so easily, and which we may not even be able to describe? Or is the emote command and all that is stands for a reflection of what Fredric Jameson calls the flattening of affect in post-modern life? (Turkle, 1995, p. 254)

In others, the playfulness she applauds may indicate simply that people are engaged in superficial activities, that the culture of simulation is ultimately disconnected from the real world, and that its games constitute psychological bread and circuses. We are thrown the bones of pretend identities, of pretend creativity to mask the emptiness of our experience.

The man without passion

Turkle's ambivalence about our experience with computers, her worry that it simply 'flattens affect', connects her to the work of both Zaleznik and Lasch. As we noted, Zaleznik too describes the manager as a person with flattened affect, as someone who is bored by work, whose relationships are superficial and goals narrow. Similarly, Turkle's prototypical computer user is also like Lasch's father, the man without standards, who represents nothing that is important, who lives entirely within a world of symbols. Thinking psychodynamically, what kind of man is this, what are the developmental roots of his character?

There is a tradition of social thought, as represented in the work of Kenneth Keniston (1965), David Riseman (1961), Richard Sennet, Edgar Friedenberg (1964), Uri Bronfenbrenner and others that characterises this man not simply as cold or detached but also passive, if not actually impotent. His edge has been blunted. As Bronfenbrenner argues, today parents manage children by withdrawing their love, rather than disciplining them. In this context the father turns passive and is no longer able to represent the authority of the social world to the child. Similarly, Sennet argues that after 1900 when class conflict displaced civic life, many men withdrew from participating in the 'public space' into the privacy of their own lives. This induced in them a certain passivity, and they lost their ability to act as entrepreneurs (Friedenberg, 1964). Instead, this new man became instead the quintessential bureaucrat who works compulsively, and is, in Hannah Arendt's terminology, 'banal'. Because he has no passion he turns his psyche over to the organisation and becomes the perfect conformist. He is a far cry from the patriarch, who dominated through the expressions of his passions, the imposition of his ideals, the enforcement of impersonal standards of performance. Instead he is the obsessive 'boy scout', squeaky clean, a good citizen, but seemingly empty on the inside. If we had him on the couch we might discover his grandiosity and his rage but this layer of experience is very, very suppressed. At most, it shows up as his fragile narcissism, his weakness, and his unquenchable need for reassurance and love. We can hardly respect him, though we may feel compelled to protect his self-esteem.

The psychodynamics of political correctness

Howard Schwartz has examined the psychodynamics of this man, and the
woman who experiences him, in a series of very provocative articles.
Schwartz is a leading theoretician in the field of organisational psychoanalysis and is a founding member of ISPO. Building on the psychoanalytic
concept of the ego ideal, he developed the notion of the 'organisational
ideal'. In his book, *Narcissistic Process and Corporate Decay: The Theory
of the Organization Ideal* (Schwartz, 1990) he showed how, when
managers internalise the organisation as their ideal, the organisation itself
is subject to decay. He has in the last few years developed a new and rich
vein of work based on a psychodynamic reading of certain feminist
currents, and on the impact of 'political correctness' on institutional life,
for example in universities and the army. In a series of articles he takes as
his fundamental problem the analysis of what he calls 'manichean
feminism'. By 'manichean feminism' he means the tendency that some
feminist scholars have to attack men as if they were all seducers, and to
belittle their actual accomplishments. Behind this attack is the
presumption that social reality itself is not 'real' and that consequently
men do not do real work. Manichean feminists, Schwartz argues, think
that male dominance is illegitimate, for it has been constructed, not to
deliver goods and services but simply to create pleasure for men.
Extending his critique, Schwartz goes on to note:

> thus the whole question turns on the nature of reality. If there is no self-
> subsistent reality with which we must cope then [the manichean feminists] are
> correct. All is fantasy and pleasure, and the only question is whose fantasy and
> pleasure. (Schwartz, 1995, p. 269)

For Schwartz this is the cul-de-sac of manichean feminism These feminists,
he argues, are trying to repeal what Freud called the 'reality principle'.
This is the notion that social life is recalcitrant, that we meet with its resistance when we try to fulfil our wishes, and that to gain pleasure we have to
engage in real work. Since there is something outrageous about denying
'self-subsistent reality' Schwarz is led to ask what experiences, what
particular history can give rise to this kind of thinking.

The sin of the father

In a companion article 'The sin of the father: reflections on the roles of the
corporation man, the suburban housewife, their son and their daughter in
the deconstruction of the patriarch', Schwartz (1996) links manichean
feminism to the rise of the 'conformist' man in modern bureaucracies, a
man not unlike the manager Zaleznik describes. He suggests that what

manichean feminists have contempt for is this new man, the man without passions or ideals, not all men. Like Lasch, he suggests that post-modern man is no longer engaged in productive work, but instead sacrifices his desire for accomplishment to the blandishments of the organisation that promises him status and security. In the place of the ego ideal, which his father once supplied and which might pull him toward craftsmanship and creativity, he substitutes the 'organisation ideal' which pulls him towards good citizenship and the wish to simply 'go along to get along'.

This man, Schwartz argues, unwittingly created a new family constellation around him. Drawing particularly on the work of Kenneth Keniston (who in the 1960s and 1970s studied both alienated as well as rebellious young people in college) Schwartz argues that the suburban housewife and her children developed a contempt for their unproductive father. The son in particular identified with his mother rather than his father. The wife, caught in a world where she had no productive role, but finding no appeal, nothing to emulate in her husband's world, was drawn instead to the image of the primordial mother, the mother who created a home in which she was entirely self-sufficient and all providing. This was the basis for what Betty Friedan, the intellectual founder of the modern women's movement, called the 'feminine mystique'. It was the mystique of the all-giving mother, and was supported by companies, who through advertising created the fantasy of the self-sufficient household to sell their appliances. The problem with this fantasy was that is was based on illusion. Housework could hardly provide meaning.

> External reality, for the housewife, had indeed been pushed away. There was nothing that she had to do, nothing she had to see as a constraint. All she had to do was express her feminine essence, to permit the free flow of desire and spontaneity. (Schwartz, 1996, p. 1029)

The son, because he could not identify with the work his father did, was drawn to the world of fantasy in which the phantasised primordial mother could meet all his needs. Psychoanalytic theory suggests that when the father is held in contempt, and the mother in turn favours her son, the son has won a hollow victory. Far from emerging triumphant, the son instead becomes overly dependent on his mother. Because he cannot identify with his father he fails to acquire the confidence and the skills he needs to compete with others at school and ultimately at work. He is in some sense feminised.

In short, the trouble with the feminine mystique, as Schwartz points out, was that it not only oppressed women, but was built on everyone's contempt for the father, for his lack of courage and individuality. In this sense Zaleznik's management mystique and Schwartz's analysis of the feminine mystique are two sides of the same coin. The former disguises pseudo-work as real work, while the latter, recognising this disguise, creates the fantasy of the primordial mother as a substitute for a world of real work and real men. One imagines that this may be the boy Turkle worries about, the boy who gets 'pseudo-sex' on the Internet rather than the real thing.

The feminisation of men

The meaning of patriarchy

I believe that the issue of the feminisation of men is a central question for any psychoanalytic social science. It lies at the heart of recent social criticism; it is reflected in the mourning for 'real' men, and is inextricably linked to the cultural meanings of feminism. It is commonplace to note that while parents have a clear idea of how to raise the post-modern girl – she should be allowed to tap into her ambitions and drives, her phallic nature should not be as suppressed as it once was – parents are mystified about how to bring up boys. They remain frightened by the prospect that if they encourage their son's passivity he might turn homosexual. Indeed, homophobia as well as manichean feminism might be seen as distorted responses to the prospects of male feminisation. Psychoanalysis is familiar with this issue. Freud noted that at the root of a male patient's resistance to psychoanalysis is his reluctance to acknowledge his own passive trends, his wish to submit to his father. We might say that psychoanalysis itself offered to feminise the male patient. After all the man would lie prone on a couch, submit to the analyst and give himself over to the process of free association, in other words, suspend the operations of his ego.

I suggest that we need to look at feminisation as a developmental process, in which earlier phases set the stage for later ones. Along with the social critics cited above we can say that in the twentieth century, because they were deprived of productive work roles, men became more passive. But I want to suggest that this passivity has in turn set the stage for a different kind of feminisation, where the passive turn leads paradoxically to more vitality and more passion. Feminisation is the escape route from a life of emotional superficiality. The concept of the feminine as passive has always played counterpoint to the concept of the feminine as the 'life force'. Indeed, this was part of the 'mystique' which Friedan criticised. In other words, I think that our conventional ideas of feminisation are inadequate.

David Bakan, in a series of books, has developed a very different conception of the feminisation of man. For example, in an idiosyncratic but brilliant text, *And They Took Themselves Wives: The Emergence of*

Patriarchy in Western Civilization (1979), he argues that patriarchy itself represented a feminisation of man. This appears deeply paradoxical, but if we can unpack the meaning of this historical paradox, we can understand the feminisation of men today as representing something much more than their neutered quality.

The matrilineal culture

Bakan began his career as a psychologist and methodologist and actually wrote some essays on mathematical statistics. He was one of the earliest critics of the '*t* test' as the overused test of significance in psychological experiments. Following this early methodological work, and already anticipated in it, he developed a more manifest psychoanalytic frame of thought. This culminated in a very popular book, *The Duality of Human Existence: Isolation and Communion in Western Man* (Bakan, 1966). After this he progressively turned to biblical and rabbinical sources for examining what still were psychoanalytic themes. This has lent his work a certain obscurity; for example his last book (Bakan, 1991) was a careful explication of Maimonedes' 'A Guide to the Perplexed', in which he argues that the 'hidden' message is about the treatment of sexuality in the Bible and how the rabbis believed it should be handled interpretatively. *And They Took Themselves Wives* lies in between his earlier psychoanalytic work and his most recent turn to rabbinical studies. In this book Bakan argues that we can examine the Old Testament as a text that has both manifest and latent content. This results from the fact that it evolved over time but that successive scribes were very careful when, to reflect particular political realities of the time, they changed the text. It is after all a holy book. This means that the text contains traces of older ideas and stories which, through a careful reading and through reference to other rabbinical sources, can be re-discovered.

In the spirit of this kind of interpretative framework, Bakan argues that the Bible reflects a tension between a matrilineal and a patrilineal conception of the human order.

> Unquestionably, the general impact of the [Bible] text is to promote patrocentrism and the associated patrilineality and patriarchy. This feature of the text has come to special prominence with the growth of the women's liberation movement. . . . However, there are strong traces of a prior matrocentrism, with matrilineality and perhaps even matriarchy in the text. While later writers may have 'written over' earlier texts, the traces exist. Since they exist, we might also allow that strong forces prevailed to keep the traces in the text. (p. 66)

The Bible, he says, is preoccupied with the problem of child sacrifice, which was closely linked to idol worship. The story of Abraham's near sacrifice of his son Isaac, 'his only son', a story which is re-evoked in the story of Jesus' crucifixion, should be read as a dream in which an impulse is both acknowledged and then displaced, i.e. Abraham sacrifices a ram instead of a child. Indeed, this is one reason why the Bible focuses so much on the conditions for sacrificing animals, to pull people away from sacrificing children. Similarly, circumcision may be understood as a displacement from the act of killing the child to the act of cutting him.

Paternity and matrilineal culture

Bakan argues that in biblical times men could sacrifice children, particularly when food was scarce, because the culture was matrilineal and fathers felt less accountable for the children's welfare. (He notes in passing that among Jews today, 'Jewishness' is still passed down through the mother.) In turn, the roots of a matrilineal culture, he says, are linked to the ancient peoples' uncertainty about the role of the father in procreation. There is no doubt that a child comes from a woman, but, Bakan argues, there was a time in our own prehistory when people did not comprehend the facts of paternity. Indeed, even after understanding paternity, men did not necessarily understand that nine months separated conception from birth, that it took only one act of intercourse to fertilise the woman with a man's seed, or that one man alone could contribute to the growth of the fetus. Indeed, Margaret Mead, reflecting on her own understanding of conception when she was young, writes that 'the father's role in conception was essentially a feeding role, for many acts of intercourse were believed to be necessary to build up the baby, which was compounded of father's semen and mother's blood' (quoted in Bernstein, 1994, p. 30).

Bakan suggests that the Bible is a record of human civilisation coming to terms with paternity.[6]

---

[6] Bakan does not participate in the more classical debate about whether or not children in matrilineal societies go through an oedipal phase. Briefly, some anthropologists argued that because the uncle rather than the father was the child's protector in matrilineal societies, the Oedipus complex could not be universal. Other analysts suggested that the uncle could in fact substitute for the father, though it seems less likely that under these conditions the boy could see the uncle as a sexual rival. As Robert Hinshelwood pointed out to me in an earlier draft of this essay, Ernest Jones argued that ignorance about paternity, which may appear to be one corollary of a matrilineal society, may in fact reflect repression or denial of the sexual couple. How does Bakan stay away from this argument? Partly by focusing less on the Oedipus complex and more on what he called in *The Duality of Human Existence* the 'Laius complex', that is the tendency of the father to in fact wish to kill the child. In the Oedipus myth, Laius after all does twice try to kill Oedipus before Oedipus kills him.

The Bible may be interpreted as a document representing the crisis of paternalisation all the changes involved in the male's assumption of the various obligations of fatherhood. This crisis is not only associated with some historical period in which males took on the social status of fatherhood as a common expectation, it is also a crisis repeated in the individual life history of many males who become fathers. Historically, the composition of the biblical text corresponds to a period following the discovery of the role of the male in conception and simultaneous with the development of the patriarchal ideas of marriage and their social integration . . . (Bernstein, 1994, p. 13)

Through patriarchy a man takes responsibility for the children under his care *and this constitutes his feminisation*. Indeed, Bakan notes that in the story of Isaac's near sacrifice, God refers to Isaac as Abraham's 'only son', when in fact Abraham was the father of Ishmael as well. In fact, Isaac is *Sarah's* only son, but the scribes have changed this reference thus placing the father where the mother was. This account also helps explain other dimensions of patriarchy. A man promises to care for his children, only with the proviso that his women not sleep with other men. This is why patriarchy supports chastity. If a woman slept with a man before she was married, there was no guarantee that her first child was his own. Indeed, this is why to this day, orthodox Jews perform the ritual of 'redemption of the first born', since in ancient times, before the facts of paternity had been fully internalised, men would kill the first-born child rather than risk raising another man's child. The Bible represents then a moral vision for patriarchal culture, one that is focused on children and a man's obligation to care for them. This is the sense in which patriarchy represents the feminisation of men.

Sarah

To support his argument Bakan presents, among many other detailed discussions, a fascinating interpretation of the story of the three angels who visit Sarah announcing that she will give birth to a son (again one sees how this central story prefigures the story of Jesus). Through a careful textual analysis he suggests that the repressed or latent story is one in which the angels actually sleep with Sara and therefore impregnate her, or contribute to her impregnation. Bakan argues that before people understood man's role in paternity they in fact believed that gods mingling with women created children. This, he says, explains one of the most peculiar passages in the entire Bible, from the sixth chapter of Genesis:

And it came to pass when men began to multiply on the face of the earth and daughters were born to them. And the sons of god saw the daughters of men, that they were good and they took themselves wives, whomsoever they choose. And WHW said' 'My spirit shall not abide in man forever, because he is flesh;

and his days will be a hundred and twenty years. The Nephilim were in the earth in those days and also after that when the sons of God came in to the daughters of men, and they bore children to them. The same were the valorous one of old. The men of fame.

This is a passage about the sexual relationship between God and man. Bakan argues that the fact that this passage was retained, despite the way in which it contradicts the Old Testament's fundamental conception of God as without a body, signals that its content was too important to be entirely eliminated. The passage records the trauma, so to speak, of man coming to terms with the male's role in paternity and the resulting transformation of his moral vision and practical guidelines for living.

Psychoanalysis and post-modern man

How is this relevant to our current understanding of the role of men in family life and at work? How does it help us understand the central theme of this essay – can modern man have experiences in depth? We can answer these questions and bring the work of the authors discussed here under one overarching theme, by connecting four terms, 'sacrifice', 'despair', 'repression' and 'vulnerability'. Essentially, to avoid despair people sacrifice parts of themselves or others. Now we say that a person who sacrifices part of their makeup, their God-given characteristics, has undergone repression. But it is repression which leads to dull affect, to superficiality. We can overcome repression, however, only by acknowledging our despair and thus coming into touch with our vulnerability. It is the experience of our vulnerability, our dependence on others and on a world we cannot control, that enables us to experience ourselves and others in depth. I want to identity this process of feeling vulnerable, of surrendering ourselves to others, *as our feminisation*. Let me unpack this argument.

Sacrifice

In several other works, most notably *The Duality of Human Existence* (1966) and *Disease, Pain and Sacrifice* (1968), Bakan argues that in times of privation or difficulty ancient man was tempted to kill his children. Indeed, Bakan argues that the story of Jesus' virgin birth (or Mary's divine impregnation) and his subsequent crucifixion, the killing of the child, had particular resonance for Jews and the early Christians because the political situation of the Israelis was so despairing. When ancient man felt despair, he hoped to regain control of his environment by appeasing the gods through the sacrifice of children. This had three consequences. On the economic level it meant that adults had more food, on the proto-scientific level it meant that the man was manipulating his environment to change it, and on the psychological level it provided an outlet for the man's rage. The rage helped him overcome his despair.

Despair in psychoanalysis

Despair plays a very important role in psychoanalysis. It is inextricably linked to resistance. Why does a patient hold on to a defence that causes him unhappiness? One reason is that he has not yet 'hit bottom'. He has not yet reached the point of despair. But what makes it difficult to hit bottom? The defence itself is a protection against psychic pain. Thus to relinquish the defence the patient must come to believe, to experience really, that the pain caused by the defence is greater than the pain masked by it. Moreover, when that latter pain is too great, it is projected on to the analyst and becomes the basis for what Freud called 'the negative thera- peutic reaction'. The patient cannot hit bottom because he has come to believe that the analyst has become the source of his pain. There is no gain to relinquishing his defence, since his analyst will continue to persecute him. Indeed, the defence, once the cause of his unhappiness, now becomes his protection against the analyst. But of course he needs the analyst to project his pain on to someone else. Hence the analysis becomes, as Freud remarked in a famous essay, 'interminable'.

In despair because he could not secure food for himself and his family, ancient man hoped to remain in control of his environment by sacrificing his children to God. He could appease the gods in this way while projecting his rage at his condition on to the child. In this sense we can say that by sacrificing children ancient man could avoid 'hitting bottom'. The Bible is then a psychological counsel to in fact hit bottom, to cease trying to control one's situation and to accept God's direction no matter where it leads. This represents a passive turn, but has the moral power of protecting children in particular and the defenceless in general when times are difficult.

Repression

The is a general name for this entire process. Psychoanalysis refers to it as 'lifting a repression'. When we repress an impulse we create the fantasy that we can control our unconscious life, that the repressed will not return. But it does, creating unhappiness in its wake. We sacrifice a part of our own makeup, to protect our illusion that we are in control. The sacrifice of children and the process of repression are thus psychodynamic equivalents. Psychoanalysis can in this sense be seen as a series of texts that modernises the biblical message, that counsels relinquishing control over our unconscious life, by acknowledging that our ego is not 'master in its own house'. This helps us contain our destructiveness. But to do this we acknowledge that our vulnerability is in the end less painful to us than the consequence of resisting our vulnerability.

Feminisation and vulnerability

Let me propose that we need to use Bakan's conception of patriarchy, and its links to the feminisation of man, to modify the analyses that Zaleznik, Lasch and Schwartz propose, while expanding on Turkle's conception. Psychoanalysis gave mankind the gift and plague of the unconscious. To accept it, we must at critical points turn passive, trusting that our resulting feelings of vulnerability while leading us into despair can also lead us out of it. As we have seen, the modern project promises us that we can control the social world around us. Psychodynamically, this promise is the ego's conceit, its assurance to us that we are not the subject of forces beyond our control, that we can control others, and so be the independent authors of all of our experience. Since psychoanalysis undermines the ego's conceit, we can say that it challenges the modern project. It does so by asking us to lift our repression, suspend action, which after all is the ego's province, and accept what is not rational, our feelings. I want to call this feminisation process, in the sense that it represents a passive turn in our psychic life, a process of surrender.

I think this account helps us round out and correct Zaleznik's and Lasch's account of the psychodynamics of manipulation and control. While Zaleznik hopes to 'restore leadership to business', by restoring feelings to leadership, he is too one-sided in his conception of feeling states. He ignores the passive turn and consequently refers primarily to anger and passion. He does not acknowledge enough the productive uses of dependency, and the sense of community that emerges when we surrender ourselves to others. Indeed, anger itself is a feeling state that connects us to others. Repressed anger, by contrast, may result in feelings of cruelty or indifference which separate us from others. Similarly, Lasch places great emphasis on the role that the father plays in representing impersonal standards of performance. The concept of the father as standard bearer accentuates the father's capacity for control rather than his capacity for love. Lasch is contemptuous of the father who tries to be his children's friend. But surely, there is much to be gained if fathers become more intimate, more loving with their children. They need not sacrifice respect to win the love of their children, particularly if they garner self-respect from their own work. Similarly, we can join Howard Schwartz in critiquing the fantasy of the primordial mother which he argues lies behind a manichean feminism. But, as Schwartz himself acknowledges, this does not preclude men from coming more into touch with their feelings.

Reworking authority

I want to refer here to some of my own work. In *Reworking Authority: Leading and Following in the Post-Modern Organization* (Hirschhorn, 1997), I argue that the post-modern economic order creates a new set of demands on our sense of identity. If there is a limit common to the work of the writers I discuss in this essay, particularly that of Lasch, Schwartz and Zaleznik, it is situated particularly in their rather un-worked or implicit arguments about the economy. Each takes as a model the conception of the independent tradesman or craftsman, who, they argue, has all but been replaced by corporate man, the 'man in the grey flannel suit' as Vance Packard so ably put it. While Schwartz argues that the organisation ideal has substituted for the ego ideal, there is also much evidence to suggest that large organisations are hardly considered ideal any longer. There has emerged a counter-ethic of entrepreneurship, reflected in the large number of start-up companies that are now offering their shares on the stock market, which in turn is reshaping the culture of the large corporation. This counter-ethic values risk-taking over conformity and may provide both a new source of feeling and passion as well as a new source of self-respect. Moreover, in contrast to the stereotype of the entrepreneur, much experience suggests that successful entrepreneurs are not loners, but are instead connected deeply to large numbers of people. They are successful because, in addition to their passion, they feel free to rely on others.

In my own work, I show how executives' and managers' failure to take a stance of vulnerability actually limits their effectiveness. Today there is, paradoxically, 'power' in vulnerability. This happens for at least two reasons. First, as corporate competition intensifies executives face issues of strategy with greater frequency. But while executives, and the consultants who help them, may hope that they can develop strategies by doing market research and dispassionately examining the facts, experience suggests to the contrary. A strategy worth its salt, one that can be pursued to its limits and without equivocation, must arise from the passions and vision of individual leaders and followers. The executive who hopes to lead others must 'lay his heart on the table' and take the risk of communicating his very personal vision for a product or market that may in the end simply prove wrong. Indeed, in my consulting work I have been consistently struck by how enervating and disheartening formal strategic planning processes actually are. People tire of them so quickly. But they persist in using them because they are afraid of putting their passions on the table, and risking either ridicule or failure.

Second, as leaders take up issues of strategy they have to delegate increasing amounts of responsibility to their subordinates. They cannot succeed in both managing and developing the enterprise by monopolising control. But this means that they need to acknowledge their dependency on their subordinates. Again, while consultants might promise them that a 'perfect' compensation system can ensure that their subordinates will act in the organisation's interests, in the end, good dependency relationships require trust. But trust emerges only when people discover that in revealing their vulnerabilities or doubts to another, they gain the other's respectful attention rather than contempt. In *Reworking Authority* I show that when passion and vulnerability are suppressed, an organisation's performance suffers.

In this sense, my argument is similar to Turkle's, though I cast it on a different plane. I also make the case, sometimes in as indirect a way as she does, that psychoanalysis is uniquely positioned to help us understand the post-modern temper and to provide a corrective to the modern project. As vulnerability becomes necessary we need a psychoanalytic temperament to find our way through the thickets of passion and trust. Yiannis Gabriel (personal communication) reminds us here of the myth of Achilles, the greatest hero of antiquity. His mother tried to make him invulnerable, forgetting to protect him at the heel. While he was the bravest of heroes, he was also the most effeminate. He dressed as a girl and was admired for his looks as much as for his deeds.

We can argue dialectically here. The modern project has created the conditions for its own transcendence. We need to restore a fuller meaning of rationality to our work and institutions, one that incorporates feeling, if we are to design institutions appropriate to the post-modern age. Psychoanalysis, the science of feeling, which has always stood in an uneasy relationship to the modern project, is uniquely positioned to help us accomplish this task.

I noted at the start of this essay that since the industrial revolution, critics, romantics and revolutionaries have worried that modern life, the modern project, has robbed us of experience even as it increased our comforts. The romantic critique has taken many forms over the centuries: the elevation of nature over culture, artistic expression, revolutionary movements, philosophies that offered us a way to transcend our alienation from our own subjectivities. Psychoanalysis occupies an important place in the romantic critique of modernism, particularly because it does so by appropriating scientific discourse. It criticises modernism from within. Today, standing at the post-modern divide, stirrings intimate that, through the feminisation of men, we can transcend modernism not just in theory but in practice. Psychoanalysis provides us with an invaluable guide in this passage.

4 CONTRIBUTION FROM NORTH AMERICA (2)
The Couch at Sea[7]

OTTO KERNBERG

Psychoanalytic contributions to the theory of group and organisational psychology have a puzzling quality. A few of the key theoretical contributions in this area occupy a territory that is somewhat peripheral to the mainstream of psychoanalysis, and most psychoanalysts tend to shy from them. These contributions have nevertheless had a significant impact on the intellectual, scientific, and even political scenes. Their impact, however, has been limited in the field of organisational intervention, and there are good reasons for that. More about this later.

In what follows I present a brief overview of this field, with an emphasis on an area that seems to have received less attention than it merits – that of leaders of groups and organisations. The title of my chapter is intended to convey the sense of uncertainty and even danger that I have come to associate with attempts to apply psychoanalytically gained knowledge to large groups and organisations.

Freud and leadership

Freud (1921) initiated the psychoanalytic study of group processes, explaining them in terms of his then newly developed ego-psychology. In illustrating his theories of group psychology, he used the organisation of the Church and the army as examples of the group or, rather, of the whole organisation, to its leader. But, as François Roustang reminds us in *Dire Mastery* (1987), Freud was never actually in the army, nor was he a member of any church. His personal experience of leadership came from the psychoanalytic movement. Roustang notes the paradox that Freud, who critically described the irrational relations between leaders and followers in organised institutions, should have been the author of 'On the history of the psychoanalytic movement,' written in 1914. Freud's

---

[7] Reprinted from Kernberg (1998)

paper clearly indicates, according to Roustang, his conviction that a truly scientific commitment to psychoanalysis must coincide with loyalty to his, Freud's, ideas, whereas any questioning of key psychoanalytic concepts represents determined resistance to truth. The *ad hominem* nature of Freud's arguments against Jung and Adler is painful reading for any admirer of Freud's genius. One could dismiss Freud's relationships with his immediate followers as an irrelevant historical curiosity, were it not so intimately linked with subsequent psychoanalytic history. Roustang, in his study of the relation between master and disciple, calls attention to a contradiction inherent in all psychoanalytic societies. The goal of psychoanalysis is to resolve the transference. But psychoanalytic education attempts to maintain the transference that psychoanalysis tries to resolve. If fidelity to Freud, the charismatic founder of psychoanalysis, were required, the members of the societies could not become scientifically independent. This tradition has persisted, as Roustang makes clear in his discussion of Lacan.

Was Freud describing his psychoanalytic movement or unconsciously using it as a model while writing 'Group psychology and the analysis of the ego' (1921)? And how can one explain his lack of interest in examining the personality of the organisational leader? Freud seems to consider the nature of the leader mostly in terms of his symbolic function as the youngest son of the symbolically murdered father. Freud simply attributes to the leader, characteristics of self-assuredness and narcissistic self-investment, in contrast to the libido the group invests in him.

Bion and leadership

Bion's findings concerning small-group processes, summarised in his *Experiences in Groups* (1961), are the most important single contribution psychoanalysis has made to small-group psychology. But, whereas Bion's method of exploring primitive defences, object relations and anxieties in small, unstructured groups may be of great value in learning about small-group psychology and group processes or even about large organisations and large unstructured groups, the therapeutic value of his technique is questionable.

In fact, inherent in Bion's method is the refusal of the leader to participate in the group. The leader observes and interprets all transactions, even those directed towards himself, in terms of group processes as though he were a cipher. This strategy reduces the ordinary role relation between the members and the leader. The attempt to eliminate the leader as a distinct personality not only prevents the ordinary structuring of the group situation by means of socially accepted and reassuring roles and interactions, it creates – when applied to group psychotherapy – an artificiality in the posture of the leader. It results in the psychoanalyst seated unobserved behind the couch.

Confusing the psychoanalyst's technical neutrality with 'disgruntled indifference,' to which Freud himself (1927) objected, is a problem that is still prevalent. Some analysts think that to be technically neutral one not only must not share one's inner life with the patient (which is entirely appropriate) but must create the illusion that the analyst has no personality at all, which is hardly realistic. I doubt whether it could have been said of Freud that he appeared to his patients as a 'man without qualities'.

This issue is related to the current analytic controversy regarding the extent to which transference is based on the reality of what the patient observes in the analyst or belongs to the patient's past. This discussion neglects the fact that the transference usually crystallises around realistic aspects of the analyst's personality, which are exaggerated and distorted as a consequence of the patient's unconscious transfer from the experiences in the past. To differentiate the reality of the stimulus for the transference from the transference *per se* as a distortion or an exaggeration of that stimulus has always been a primary technical task. My point is that the fantasy or wish to erase *any* reality stimulus derived from the analyst only serves the patient's unconscious need for idealisation.

There are advantages and dangers in Bion's technique. Among the advantages are the sharp highlighting of primitive modes of mental operations and the possibility of examining unconscious processes that influence group behaviour. On the negative side, questions have been raised (Scheidlinger, 1960; Malan et al., 1976) concerning the extent to which the artificial distancing of the group leader, the elimination of ordinary supportive features of group interactions, and the failure to provide cognitive instruments for self-understanding to individual patients regarding their particular psychopathology may be too demanding on the individual patient and thus be therapeutically counter-productive. Bion's technique may also artificially foster the idealisation of the therapist.

Bion stresses that the basic-assumptions-group leaders are sucked into their leadership role by the very nature of the regression in the group. Hence, Bion's leader is really a prisoner of the group atmosphere or, rather, the group uses his personality characteristics for its own purposes. In contrast, the leader of the work group has a rational approach to reality and an awareness of the boundaries of the group. This rational leader has a capacity for reality testing, an awareness of time, and the ability to stand up to the hatred of rationality activated under basic-assumptions conditions. The distinctions Bion draws between the two types of leaders offer seminal concepts for the understanding of the ascendancy of narcissistic and paranoid personalities under basic-assumptions-group conditions; but they also convey a strange failure to consider the reality of the person who is the work-group leader. Did Bion assume that his own extremely powerful personality (which was apparent to everyone who met him) was submerged by his refusal to fulfil the ordinary role expectations in the group?

Again, this might appear to be a trivial issue, were it not that, after many years of silence regarding group issues, Bion again introduces the theme of the group and its leadership in *Attention and Interpretation* (1970). Here he refers to the 'exceptional individual' who may be a genius, a messiah, a mystic, or a scientist. Bion offers Isaac Newton as an outstanding example, pointing to Newton's mystical and religious preoccupations as the matrix from which his mathematical formulations evolved. It is hard to avoid the impression that Bion is referring here not only to the work-group leader and his creativity, but also to a special type of leader whose convictions have a religious core, and whose behaviour, as indicated by the collective term *mystic* (with which Bion frames this category), implies the secrecy of the initiated, an obscure or occult character, someone mysterious or enigmatic.

Bion here, I believe, is referring to himself, and the question of whether he was aware of that resonates with the question of whether Freud was aware of the nature of the model of the unmentioned leaders of the army or the Church. Be that as it may, Bion conveys a sense of the impotence of rationality, the fragility of the creative mystic, who is endangered by the envious, paranoid, pedestrian, conventional, and limited nature of what Bion calls the establishment. Bion describes three types of interactions between mystic and establishment: a mutually enriching, or 'symbiotic,' one, a mutually destructive, or 'parasitic' one, and a mutual ignoring or 'commensal' one. His emphasis is on the risk that the mystic who cannot be 'contained' by the establishment will be destroyed by it, or, vice versa, on the risk that the disruptive creativity of the mystic will destroy the establishment.

Kenneth Rice's school

Kenneth Rice's systems theory of organisations treats the individual, the group, and the social organisation as each being a continuum of open systems. Rice (1965) integrates Bion's theories of small-group functioning with his own and with Turquet's (1975) understanding of large-group functioning and an open systems theory of social organisations.

Within this model, psychopathology may be conceptualised as a breakdown of the control function, a failure to carry out the primary task, and a threat to the survival of the system. In the individual, we see breakdown of the ego and emotional regression; in the group, breakdown of leadership and paralysis in basic assumptions; and in the institution, breakdown of the administration, failure to carry out the institutional tasks, and loss of morale. Breakdown of boundary control is the principal manifestation of breakdown in the control function.

In my experience with both large and small groups, including group-relations conferences, the following phenomena emerge rapidly with impressive regularity and intensity: first, the activation of intense anxieties and primitive fantasies in the small study groups, and second, the activation of a primitive quality to both group functioning and potential individual aggression in the large group. The rapid development of *ad hoc* myths about the leadership or about the conference, and the search for a comprehensive and simplistic ideology in contrast to discriminating reasoning, illustrate in one stroke what happens during breakdown of organisational functioning. The crucial function of boundary control and of the role of task-oriented leadership in task performance emerges in contrast to the temptation, at points of regressions, to elevate the most dysfunctional members of subgroups to basic-assumptions-group leadership and to blur all boundaries in the emotional turmoil that pervades the group.

One important drawback to group-relations conferences is the relative failure on the part of the corresponding theory to consider the effects of their temporary nature. Katz and Kahn (1966) pointed out that when the staffs of social and industrial organisations try to learn new attitudes in the context of exploring the irrational aspects of group processes in an experiential setting, they frequently fail. This failure comes from their neglecting to analyse the stable features of the organisational structure and the relation between that structure and the real (in contrast to fantasised or irrational) conflicts of interests that such organisational structures mediate.

Short-term learning experiences in groups do not give the group members time to study the impact of personality structures on members of organisations, particularly the personality of key leaders.

Here we are touching again, now at the level of the relation between large groups and organisational structures, on the same barely perceptible neglect of the impact of the personality of the leader on organisational conflicts. Rice has the enormous merit of having fully developed a theory of organisational functioning that permits the diagnosis of both organisational regression – 'loss of morale' – and the administrative distortions that facilitate such regressive group processes, in a theoretically elegant and eminently practical approach to organisational dynamics. But, once again, the effects of the distorted personality on stable social organisations are missing here. It is almost as though the optimal, rational leader were a person without qualities or perhaps *should be* a person without qualities.

The more severe the leader's personality pathology and the tighter the organisational structure, the greater the destructive effects of the leader on the organisation. It may be that under extreme circumstances, the paranoid regression of an entire society maintains the sanity of the tyrant and that when his control over that society breaks down he becomes psychotic: Hitler's final months point to this possibility.

Under less extreme circumstances, the effort to correct organisational distortions by changing the behaviour of the leader may have disastrous consequences for her as well as for those at the next level. If the organisation has to live with a characterologically dysfunctional leader, it may become preferable to adapt the administrative structure to an optimal balance between task requirements and the leader's needs – a solution that is the opposite of Rice's.

But how is one to know where to draw the line between restructuring the organisation to protect it from the leader's pathology and acknowledging that the organisation requires a different leader?

The application of a combined psychoanalytic and open-systems-theory model of institutional functioning to therapeutic community models (see Main, 1946) illustrates the limits of the therapeutic use of large-group analysis. (For a critique of therapeutic community models, see Chapter 11 of Kernberg, 1988a.)

There is an enormous danger within a therapeutic community setting. The open exploration of the entire social field, wherein patients and staff interact by analysing the content of the communications that emerge in the community meeting, may be transformed into a messianic denial of reality should the group come under the sway of a leader with a narcissistic and paranoid personality. It is exciting and potentially helpful to view the content of large-group meetings as a reflection of the unconscious of the organisation and to trace the origin of distortions in the social system to its administrative structure, the psychopathology of individual patients, or conflicts at the boundary between patients and staff. By the same token, the transformation of trust and openness into the messianic spirit of the dependent or pairing group or, rather, the large group that has found a narcissistic leader and a soothing, simplistic ideology is a great and constant temptation for group and leader alike. The threat to rational evaluation of task boundaries and constraints and to the ordinary political negotiation around boundaries is enormous. The proverbial disillusionment and burning out of the staff involved in this process, who overextend themselves in a messianic over-evaluation of what can and should be accomplished, needs no illustration.

Here we find a paradoxical effect of the psychoanalytic illumination of the unconscious in institutions: the deepest, hidden agendas of the institution appear at the surface in verbal communication at large-group meetings. But this is an illusion. The immediate availability of understanding of basic issues is no guarantee that they will be resolved. Unlike individual psychoanalysis, there is no direct link between emotional reality in groups and conflict resolution by actual institutional mechanisms of change. The neglect of the personality of the leader in the psychoanalytic contributions to group and organisational functioning mentioned before is compounded by the underestimation of the risk that all rational functioning will be disrupted by the snowballing effects of expanding small-group and large-group regressions in the process of self-exploration. The diagnostic instrument self-destructs, the collective patient becomes psychotic.

Rational leadership

Combining psychoanalytic observations of mobs, large groups and small groups, I proposed in Kernberg (1983) that group processes pose a basic threat to personal identity, a threat that is linked to a proclivity in group situations for the activation of primitive object relations, primitive defensive operations, and primitive aggression with predominantly pregenital features. For me, Turquet's description of what happens in large groups constitutes the basic situation against which (1) the idealisation of the leader in the horde, described by Freud; (2) the idealisation of the group ideology and of leadership that promotes narcissistic self-aggrandisement of the group, described by Anzieu (1981) and Chasseguet-Smirgel (1975); and (3) the small-group processes described by Bion (1961) are all defending.

Large-group processes also highlight the intimate connection between threats to one's identity and the participants' fear that primitive aggression and aggressively infiltrated sexuality will emerge (see Kernberg, 1988b). I made the point earlier that an important part of non-integrated and unsublimated aggression is expressed in vicarious ways throughout group and organisational processes. The exercise of power in organisational and institutional life constitutes an important channel for the expression in group processes of an aggression that would ordinarily be under control in dyadic or triadic relations.

I shall now modify and expand these formulations. I still maintain that large-group processes threaten individual identity and therefore activate defences against identity diffusion and a defensive idealisation of the leader. But this formulation underestimates the primary gratification to be found in dissolving in fantasy the boundaries between the self and the primitive forerunners of the ego ideal, in what Freud (1921) – referring to falling in love – called the fusion of ego and ego ideal in mania, in hypnosis and in the excitement of identifying with others in the group. Anzieu and Chasseguet-Smirgel clarified this illusion of merger when they noted its pre-oedipal nature, which is in contrast to the illusion of merger with a cruel but morally sophisticated superego that characterises Freud's group member. To put it differently, the messianic characteristic of small- and large-group regression, with its pregenital features and its denial of intra-group aggression, must be differentiated from the spirit of the mob, which satisfies every member's need to overcome a sense of separateness by participating in a common, powerfully self-righteous, emotionally laden movement forward, a movement that becomes the destructive expansion of a rioting mob (Canetti, 1960).

But these two levels of regressive temptation (of the small and large group as opposed to that of the crowd) also call for two layers of regressive leadership. At one extreme we find the self-indulgent narcissist who can lead the small, dependent, assumption group or pacify the large group with a simplistic ideology that soothes while preventing envy of the leader ϳr, in a more sophisticated combination, the sexually liberated narciϳrist who preaches sexual liberation in the group's (symbolic or actuaʰ) bathtub and condenses polymorphous, pre-oedipal sexuality with messianic merger. At the other extreme, and more disturbingly, we find the sadistic psychopath, who with a well-rationalized cruelty energises the mob into destructive action against a common enemy and frees it from responsibility for murder.

In Kernberg (1979), I described the effects on organisational regression of various personality characteristics of the leader, with particular reference to schizoid, obsessive, paranoid, and narcissistic personalities. I limited my observations to small organisations, such as psychiatric hospitals and university departments, however, where there are usually no more than three hierarchical levels and where it is still likely that the leader and the followers know one another.

The question now is the extent to which such small, self-contained types of social organisation surround the leader's position with a structure of rationality that would avoid the takeover by a sadistic or narcissistic leader or neutralise his regressive effects over an extended period. The possibility that the leader will be personally acquainted with everyone in the organisation protects the realistic nature of the leadership of the institution. But larger organisations, such as national bureaucracies or international corporations, where four to seven hierarchic levels of leadership are the rule, may no longer offer the possibility of ordinary social control. In such large organisations, any direct contact between the different levels of staff becomes impossible or unrealistic, and the replacement of reality by projective mechanisms increases.

Jaques (1976) made a systematic study of bureaucracy. He found that well-functioning bureaucracies have merit. They provide the social system with rationally determined hierarchies, public delineation of responsibility and accountability, stable delegation of authority and an overall accountability of the organisation to its social environment by both legal and political means and through a parallel organisation of employees or labour unions. Bureaucracies may thus provide an optimal balance between the potentially regressive consequences of hierarchically determined relations between individuals, on the one hand, and the redress of grievances and protection from arbitrariness, on the other.

Jaques's assumption is that the leaders of large social institutions are accountable to or controlled by the state. The implicit counterpart to this assumption is that when such social controls do not exist, the distortions at the top will go unchecked and will spread throughout the entire organisation. A well-functioning bureaucracy in a democratic system may be an ideal model of organisational structure. In contrast, a tightly organized bureaucracy, controlled by a totalitarian state with a paranoid psychotic or a sadistic psychopath at its head, would represent a social nightmare into which the regression of all included groups would easily fit, without any possibility of rational correction. The totalitarian bureaucracies of Nazi Germany and the Soviet Union were able to murder millions of people without causing internal convulsions. These examples suggest that the authoritarian power generated within organisations, which stems from both individual psychopathology and organisational regression, not to mention the ordinary discharge into the organisation of the unacknowledged narcissistic and aggressive needs of all its individuals, may rapidly increase, given certain social and political conditions, and transform into socially sanctioned cruelty and dehumanisation. The distinction between an ordinary dictatorship in which the right to privacy is preserved as long as no direct action is taken against the regime and a totalitarian system in which all social interactions are regulated by an imposed ideology may be one of the painful discoveries of our time.

Canetti (1960), in *Masse und Macht* (Crowds and Power), describes the universal temptation to become part of a crowd and to ensure personal survival and immortality by killing others as a basic unconscious motive for desiring the leadership of the crowd. The psychoanalytic study of a particular subgroup of narcissistic patients with aggressive infiltration of their pathological grandiose self elaborated by Rosenfeld (1971) provides a counterpart to Canetti's description.

Psychoanalytically oriented consultants for institutional problems, whether they follow the model of Rice, Jaques, Levinson (1972), or Zaleznik (1989), assume that regressive manifestations in group processes indicate institutional malfunctioning and that these group processes potentially point to the nature of the conflicts affecting the system. The consultant's usual procedure is to study the primary tasks of the organisation, its administrative structure, how authority is distributed and delegated, whether its system has checks and balances and whether it provides for redress of grievances. With the possible exception of Levinson's, all these approaches focus on the leadership only after other factors have been explored, arriving there by the process, as it were, of elimination.

Personality problems always appear at first in the foreground, but they can be diagnosed as causal features only after all the other institutional issues have been analysed and discarded.

Jaques's (1976, 1982) findings regarding an individual's capacity for work as measured by his capacity to estimate the time it will take to accomplish certain tasks and his ability to organize and carry out such tasks (the maximum time span of decision making in his work) offer an important contribution to organisational psychology and to selection criteria for leadership. Yet the psychoanalytically oriented consultant may be averse or reluctant to take this factor into consideration and would more likely think in terms of psychopathology than of the leader's unequal capacity to perform various tasks. In fact, it may be more difficult to assess this quality than to assess or even identify the aspects of personality that produce optimal leadership functioning. The leader of an organisation, as well as the consultant, must be constantly alert to the danger of giving rein to his own narcissism and aggression and therefore may have difficulty acknowledging that managerial leaders do differ in administrative capabilities. The leader (and the consultant) must also resist any tendency to allow himself to be influenced by fears of arousing unconscious envy by exposing these differences. The leader's task is to judge. Perhaps the best he can do is remain alert to the implications of standing in judgement on others.

On the basis of my experience as a psychoanalyst, leader of groups (including therapeutic communities), medical director of psychiatric hospitals and consultant to mental health institutions, I offer a list of the personality characteristics most conducive to rational task leadership.

Intelligence, which is necessary for strategic conceptual thinking, is the most important, followed by honesty and incorruptibility, the capacity to establish and maintain object relations in depth (which is essential for evaluating others realistically), a healthy narcissism (in the sense of being self-assertive rather than self-effacing) and, finally, a sense of caution and alertness to the world – what someone I once knew called justifiable anticipatory paranoia.

The importance of intelligence that is expressed in the capacity for strategic conceptual thinking and probably also in creative imagination is self-evident. The value of honesty and incorruptibility is also self-evident, but these qualities must be tested under conditions of stress and political constraints. In practice, many leaders can be fair and just to people they know personally; but to be fair and just to unknown subordinates is the test of disinterested integrity. The leader's fairness to the entire staff will necessarily appear as rigidity to the few in her immediate entourage; her incorruptibility in the face of the temptations of leadership will be experienced as sadistic rejection by the tempters, as may her maintenance of fair rules for all. Here the narcissistic investment in moral righteousness, together with paranoid distrust of temptation, may protect rational leadership. These functions require a well-integrated and mature superego, which assumes the sublimatory nature of ideals and value systems and signifies the preconditions for normal (in contrast to pathological) narcissism.

Under optimal conditions, the leader's narcissistic and paranoid features may each neutralise the other's potentially negative effects on the organisation and on the leader herself. The paranoid implications of suspiciousness towards subordinate kowtowing may prevent the disastrous consequences of a narcissistic leader's needs to be obeyed *and* loved at the same time. The narcissistic enjoyment of success in leadership may prevent the erosion of self-confidence that derives from paranoid fears about potential attack or criticism from others. In contrast to these optimal combinations, a severe character pathology in the leader in the form of pathological narcissism complicated by paranoid features may prove disastrous (see Kernberg, 1988a, Chapter 13).

What is the 'correct' balance of normal narcissism and paianoia required for rational leadership? Is it firmness without sadism, incorruptibility without rigidity, warmth without manipulativeness or emotional depth without the loss of distance required to focus on the Gestalt of the group, and on the task rather than its human constraints? The ideal leader of an organisation may have to ignore the impact of his own personality on the organisation if he is to address the needs of the group, but he must not thereby lose his capacity to exploit his personality in the leadership role.

A small amount of narcissism and paranoia may reinforce the power of rationality and honesty, and a small amount of sadism may protect the task systems from regression. Yet an excess of these traits can trigger regression in leaders: a sense of justice and fairness may become self-righteousness and sadistic control. Regression in the leader can in turn trigger regression in the organisation.

In the psychoanalytic situation, the psychoanalyst has sufficient boundary control to help a patient discover his unconscious and permit the development and potential resolution of the patient's unconscious conflicts over sexuality and aggression in the transference. In transferring the psychoanalytic investigation to group processes, an easy activation of primitive processes may occur which would immediately exceed the boundary control of the exploring psychoanalyst. By the same token, the psychoanalytic consultant, in exploring organisational issues that deal with the personality of the leader, may trigger a violent reaction that would destroy not only the consultative process but the capacity of the organisation to tolerate this confrontation. The complexities of communicating organisational dynamics may be one factor limiting the consultant's task. But it is not the dominant one. The discrepancy between analytic instrument that is used to evaluate group-shared unconscious fantasies and basic-assumptions groups and apply a system theory of organisations, on the one hand, and the capacity for containment by the institution, on the other, may be a more important, perhaps intimidating barrier to advances in this field.

Ambiguity pervades the subject of leadership in Freud, Bion and others. My metaphoric title, 'The couch at sea', should communicate some of the excitement I find in exploring the social unconscious, even if the uncertainties still facing us mean that we must navigate in troubled waters – and on the couch rather than behind it.

5 CONTRIBUTION FROM ITALY
Psychoanalytical Approaches to the Study of Institutions in Italy

ANTONELLO CORREALE AND GIUSEPPE DI LEONE

The history of the psychoanalytical study of institutions in Italy has been very complex. This complexity is mostly due to the strong cultural and heavily political movement that developed within psychiatry, leading to legislative changes which in the end decreed the closing down of psychiatric hospitals and the introduction of a network of psychiatric services within the community. In addition, many psychoanalysts deemed it important to get involved in the public sector and to introduce the wealth of psychoanalytical thought into the mainstream of everyday psychiatric work. Consequently, the debate on institutions and their status has been very problematic in Italy, based as it was on discussions pertaining to the day-to-day management of services, resulting in a very heated and complex debate. In order to keep things simple, in this chapter, which is dedicated to social psychology in Italy, we will proceed by consecutive stages.

We begin with a short introduction offering a bird's eye view of the main schools of thought in this area, and then focus on individual authors, illustrating their thought in greater detail. Finally, the general perspective of the 'institutional field' is presented, which illustrates the authors' own ideas regarding this area. We hope that this approach will allow the reader to gain insight into the work of individual authors and to get a clearer idea as to the areas of convergence and divergence.

Italian schools of thought

It is possible to identify in the Italian scene three main schools of thought that could be defined as the Basaglia school, the Roman school and the Milanese school.

The Basaglia school

The Basaglia school, which takes its name from its founder Franco Basaglia, represents the Italian core of the anti-institutional movement and is linked, though not closely, with the English anti-psychiatry movement of Laing and Cooper and with the so-called 'institutional psychotherapy movement' in France.

The movement founded by Franco Basaglia, which aggregated into an association called 'Psichiatria Democratica', was based on the assumption that mental illness must be viewed within the context in which the patient lives, which usually tends to aggravate suffering and loneliness. A central aspect was represented by the struggle against the psychiatric hospital, mistakenly considered as the ultimate solution for mental illness, based on separation, regression, custodialism and long-term stay. The main assumption is that the institution is there first and foremost for the 'sane', to protect them from the sick. According to Basaglia, the mental institution was essentially an agency, alongside others (jails, special schools, etc.), built for the purpose of controlling a category of people, defined as the 'outcasts'. The essentially organic orientation of Italian psychiatry had demarcated, through diagnostic categorisations, a differentiation created by society between what is normal and what is abnormal.

> The problem of psychiatric assistance is not just technical, insofar as it is a technique used to defend the norms which do not and cannot have an objective value.... No-one argues that mental illness does not exist, but the true abstraction is not in the illness as it is manifested, but in the scientific concepts that define it without dealing with our lack of comprehension of the contradiction that is in us and in the illness. (Basaglia, 1968)

The control imposed by society in conformity with the level of development reached has to adapt to the changing social and economic context. The general concept of 'deviancy' fits in with society's logic based on control. The institutionalised patient is stripped of all forms of subjectivity and comprehensibility. In order to understand him, it is necessary to move backwards to the context he belonged to, and to the roots of his exclusion from society. This implies that the institution must challenge the mandate based on control and open up to the social sphere, review the rigid roles, dismantle itself progressively and eliminate the reason for its existence. The aim is to allow patients to have a say and to remove the inhibiting layers that the institution has put on them. To accomplish the task of true rehabilitation it is necessary to put the illness 'between brackets' and deal with what revolves around it, opening up the narrow field of action of psychiatry by attending to the social underpinnings that support a so-called science (Basaglia, 1968).

Abolishing the mental institution would lead to an evolving and uncertain situation – the subsequent step cannot be foreseen, in line with Basaglia's position to set his work without any pre-existing plan.

It is too easy for the psychiatric establishment to define our work as not serious and respectable, scientifically speaking. Such a judgment cannot but flatter us, since it associates us to the lack of seriousness and respectability which has always been attributed to the mentally ill and to all outcasts. (Basaglia, 1968)

Basaglia developed a milieu that tried to reverse the exclusion and isolation of the mentally ill. The daily community meeting, involving both patients and staff, was the key activity, which aimed to restore status and subjectivity to all the members of the institution. It became a spontaneous and free event that one could join and leave at will. One or two inpatients who introduced topics and coordinated the debate chaired the community meeting. The atmosphere was characterised by mutual sympathy, by the recognition of the fundamental importance of mutual relationships, and frictions and tensions caused by disturbed behaviour by patients was settled on the basis of those values. The topics addressed by the assembly were often of a practical nature, such as bureaucratic procedures, outside activities, etc. Group activities steered institutional life; there were meetings of nurses, doctors, social workers and sisters (nuns). After the general assembly for the whole staff, there were follow-up meetings with patients' leaders during which the issues raised at the general assembly were discussed. Basaglia did not consider these meetings as a form of group therapy; he was not interested in grasping and interpreting the psychodynamic aspect. Although he was aware of the activation of group dynamics, he believed that the meetings were there to help the patients find alternatives to their condition and favour participation in institutional life by confronting and acknowledging one another. The meetings became the place where the rigid aspects of the institution, the hierarchies, statuses, outcasts and outcasters, were dialectically reviewed and softened, which generated enthusiasm. If it is true that it v,as possible to identify anxieties present in the inner world of the participants, such anxieties were never ascribed to the presence of the group but to the concrete condition of institutional life as a world that denies individual rights.

Basaglia conducted the groups, trying to grasp the tension, unhappiness and decline in enthusiasm in the whole patients and staff group. In contrast with the institutional system, he tried to bring forth and amplify the emotions present under the institutional layer of each person (Basaglia, 1968), particularly in relation to the issues of exclusion and of the dignity of every individual.

The way in which the mental institution deprives the individual of his subjectivity is described in his book *L'Istituzione Negata* (1968) through an oriental tale about a snake that crawled into the mouth of a sleeping man and crept down into his stomach, depriving him of his freedom.

When eventually the snake left, the man had become so accustomed to its presence, to tuning his desires to those of the snake, that he no longer knew what to do with his freedom and felt the void, having lost, with the snake, his entire new 'essence'.

The Basaglia school was sceptical about psychoanalysis as it concentrates entirely on the individual, while they believed that the focus should be on what the collectivity denies to the sick person.

Such an approach gave a crucial contribution to setting up of a network of services, which placed the relationship with the patient without the mediation of the hospital as central and consequently placed greater responsibility upon the caregivers. The disadvantage lies in the fact that it has shifted the focus of the debate on to external reality (the material needs of the patients, home, work, health) to the detriment of taking into account the private and subjective suffering.

The Milan school

We could define the Milan school as being particularly close to the thought of Foulkes, strongly influenced by the contributions of Jaques and by contributions from the Kleinian tradition. The concepts of matrix, net of relationships and mirroring, enriched by and integrated with the concepts of projective identifications and splitting, are central to the founders.

This view emphasises the defensive functions of institutions. They are places where the individual unconsciously hopes to be helped to deal with splitting or projective identification, which, in turn, protect the individual from depressive and persecutory anxieties. The concepts of network and matrix represent the developmental aspect of the institution. The more the institution functions as a network, the less likely it is to operate as a rigid apparatus dominated by projections and splitting, which create 'areas' where the affective life of the institution concentrates.

This approach conceptualises the institution as a self-perpetuating entity, a shifting place where needs of the individual are met, but endowed with a rigid shell. The identification of the phantasmatic cores that operate in the institution counters this dangerous tendency. The institution is conceived as a container, a frame, a shell, in other words its boundaries and limits are taken into account more than the inner vital aspect, the wealth of ideas and history, the group biography and time.

Franco Fornari is considered as the main founder of the Milan school. He trained as a psychiatrist and a psychoanalyst. The work with psychotics put him in contact with unconscious destructive forces and spurred him to deal with the destructiveness mobilised in war. In the Anti-H group, to which he belonged, he stressed that the management of one's destructiveness is delegated to the state, thus leaving individuals apathetic and sceptical. He recognised the difficulty, in the atomic era, of adopting attitudes connected to the depressive position rooted in the vision 'vita tua, vita mea', instead of the paranoid-schizoid vision that guides the various armed forces. Years later, thanks to his work in this field, he was sent to the United Nations to co-operate with the preparation of the Program for Peace.

He was influenced by Klein's work on projective and introjective identification, part-object, sadism and depressive position. According to Fornari, institutions should have the same function as the ego has with respect to the individual's unconscious. The ideal institution allows mediation between depressive and persecutory conflicts, according to a distance resembling that of the porcupines in the fable cited by Freud (Fornari, 1971). Institutions are seen in terms of facilities, cultural mechanisms, people and defensive functions against anxieties. These considerations helped him to build up the alpha diagram. According to this diagram, the institution is like a tetrad consisting in the interaction between subject, rules, roles and the alpha factor, the latter being a world different from the social and individual sphere (Fornari, 1971, 1976).

A stands for the subject, B for rules, C for roles. The social aspect consists in the triangle ABC; the meta-social one is the triangle BCA of which the side BC represents repression. The BC rules and roles of the institution serve as defence mechanisms against unconscious anxieties. The subject is the link connecting hierarchy, roles, social level and meta-social and meta-individual alpha factors, and thanks to this connection it is possible to get an idea of the institutions of the collectivity.

It is possible to apply the alpha diagram to the family, in that the prohibition of incest, as a fundamental rule, is based on the latent fantasy of incest as it is illustrated in the Oedipus myth.

The mentally ill person in a psychiatric institution represents the other world with his madness, towards which institutions function in a triadic, that is to say, phallocentric manner, directly addressing the alienated part and obliterating the conscious part of the subject. Institutions are charged with this task by the family and by society, which are concerned by the emergence of the alpha element.

Institutions can borrow from psychoanalysis an omphalocentric-type treatment method (Greek *omphalos*, umbilical cord), recovering the alpha dimension contained in the childhood of the subject. Socio-analysis aims to reveal the defensive constructions of institutions against the other world – which, however, is also one's own, insofar as it is part of every individual – in order to evolve towards a better functioning of the organisation.

One of the steps in bringing about the change, both on the institutional and on the individual level, according to Fornari (1976), consists in shifting from a private symbolisation to a public one. He identified a 'traffic-light' function that governs the circulation of affects in institutions, allowing the identifying of the interference of ideological processes with decision-making processes.

Gustavo Pietropolli-Charmet, a psychiatrist and psychotherapist, professor of dynamic psychology at the University of Milan, was the author who developed Fornari's work after his death. He initiated a most influential research project, conducted with a group of professors, researchers and external collaborators of the Psychology Institute of University of Milan's Literature and Philosophy Department, on a training programme for healthcare workers at Milan Vittore Buzzi General Hospital (Pietropolli-Charmet, 1987). The project aimed to study the effects on the hospital of a merger with the university, which entailed a shift in institutional primary task, from a paediatric to a general hospital. In addition, the university also imposed a shift in medical culture on the institution. The research group focused on the dangers that clinical psychologists face in work within the institution, which may turn them away from their task. First, they may be tempted to comply with the stereotype of the psychoanalytical trainer who offers discussion groups in a setting not motivated for that kind of work. Second, sanctioned by the dominant institutional culture they may be forced to provide a clinical counselling service, which addresses individual cases and will deter them from exploring more central issues concerning institutional culture. The question facing the research team was how motivated the hospital, as an institution symbolising medical culture, was to face the long and painful process of re-elaborating its medical and affective culture. A further central question facing the research team was to discover the language of the institutions (general hospital and university), or of every institution that mirrors the free associations of individual work. The task of finding and disclosing the natural institutional communication connected to the work functions allows us to go beyond the operative language of the organisation and of its roles. This represents the specific institutional unconscious code.

According to Charmet, the theoretical model of the institution delivering training and the institution hosting it are seen as 'two families' that enter into a contract of 'cultural union'. The affective institution, as a family, must have an 'affective culture' of its own tied especially to the processes of symbolisation with which it invests its work and various roles. In the case of the Buzzi hospital, the specific task, that is 'caring for sick children', was at the basis of the processes of affective symbolisation that represent the ideology of the institution as a whole.

If, for instance, the child is represented as a tiny and defenceless creature standing helplessly against the death threats of an alien persecutory entity, the entire hospital will mobilise and activate military-like procedures aimed to keep the enemy away to protect the child. In this case the task has activated a symbolic function endowed with an affective culture belonging to the entire group which can be identified with the paternal one, for the father is the family member who must fight the enemy that threatens the other family members. The first phase of the project, therefore, needed to probe the type of affective culture present in the various medical and surgical wards of the hospital and was conducted on the basis of interviews on a significant sample of healthcare workers and administrators.

It was found that specific ward cultures existed. For example, the symbolisation of the child in the obstetrics ward was different from that in the neonatal ward, which in turn was considerably different from that in the paediatric ward, and so on. The training group was set up in such a way as to represent all the professional categories operating in the wards concerned and was led by two psychologists, one functioning as 'code analyst' and the other in charge of coordinating the group's activities. The group was given a manual written by Fornari, with examples of transactions regarding the life of couple and family life, through the characteristic expressions of the Parent, the Child and the Adult. The purpose was to put as the object of cathexis a cultural object like the handbook in the place of group leaders, thus shifting from a type of training based on identification, like that envisaged in the psychoanalytic tradition, to a type of training focused on the transparency and verifiability of data.

The group leader, besides animating and containing the activity of the group, has the specific function of 'providing adequate code interpretations' with the aim of revealing the scene concealed in the manifest representation. This has to do with enucleating a 'central meaning that cannot be reduced further' of the group's web of associations, and tracing it back to the values of the father, mother, child and siblings. The group then can ponder whether the spontaneous resolution is the one that is geared towards survival.

Charmet holds that there are no interpretations regarding either the relationship between the group and the conductor or the resistance to the training work; rather, what is 'transferred' through language is interpreted by means of a reversed re-reading, from the manifest scene to the concealed scene of the group.

The material was subsequently elaborated by the supervisory group and was then returned to the group in a summary form at the meetings that followed, according to a 'transparent society' model.

Another important moment was the conference of the psychology service chaired by the director, at which all the data was communicated; the conference was open to all the workers of the hospital, thus offering an opportunity to celebrate the inter-institutional encounter.

Charmet believes that the purpose of this type of training is the 'practice of the unconscious', not as a practice that prepares collectively within the group to grasp the conflicts expressed by the individual, nor those of the group through its dynamics, with projective and introjective phenomena, but the meta-historic and meta-individual unconscious, 'that inborn disposition to symbolise that is released by some genetic mechanisms'.

An important goal is the 'education to peace'; this does not mean concealing conflicts, rather it means that instead of being interpreted as the expression of destructive forces according to the Eros–Thanatos contrast, they are to be seen as a need for integrating natural codes present in the family.

The Roman school

The Roman school identifies with Bion and tends to develop the idea that group phenomena are so pervasive and powerful they deserve special attention, even more attention than is devoted to single individuals. Basic assumptions – the polarity between work-group and basic group, the enhancement and development of some ideas that generate and activate affects – represent the fundamental concepts. The institution is believed to serve the function of essentially containing and developing fundamental affects. This approach has the merit of having pinpointed the power of group phenomena. However, a possible shortcoming may be the .endency not to give adequate consideration to the individual within the institutional context. We could say that the Milanese school is more focused on the individual, whereas the Roman school privileges the group level – affect space – partly finding the individual dimension.

Within the psychoanalytic tradition, external reality, which may concern the patient but which may be external to the analytic relationship, has always been considered as a disturbance or an undesired interference. These elements could be taken into consideration only if they were somehow filtered inside the relation and transfigured, as it were, by fantasy during analytic work. Consequently, medical and pharmacological interventions, the influence of the family context, possible admission to hospital and, in general, all external elements that influenced the analytic relationship were considered as potential sources of confusion and were not directly subject to analytical study. In other words, every time an analytic patient needed additional institutional help, the institution was never considered as the subject of study but rather as a necessary evil, an inevitable recourse to a reality, that remained almost exclusively as a backdrop or a limitation that could not be analysed.

This perspective has slowly changed in time. Psychoanalysis has widened its treatment aims and has considered the possibility of taking care of difficult patients with unstable boundaries of the self who need more substantial, broad and real support than less difficult patients do. There is also a growing awareness that specialist institutional programmes for severe disorders (hospital and partial hospital-based, residential communities) may lead to changes in mental functioning that cannot be ascribed exclusively to the dynamics of the therapist–patient relationship, but are the result of powerful group affective forces (Correale, 1991). Hence institutions have gradually acquired an increasingly complex function that has become an important area of study. It was therefore necessary to engage in deeper and more detailed analysis of the ways in which institutions operate to understand how the institutional context and the psychoanalytical process integrated in a fruitful dialogue rather than be viewed as mutually impenetrable and incoherent opposites. In order to carry out such a study, it was necessary that the tools of investigation of the psychoanalytical method and those for the study of institutions be homogeneous. This entails methodological consistency founded on common basic conceptual tools (Tagliacozzo, 1986). The aim is to reach an understanding of how institutions work and to comprehend how institutional life, dual relationship and mental functioning of the individual intertwine.

The institutional field model

In this section we try to describe an all-inclusive model of how institutional functioning based on the previously stated considerations. The model w:ll emerge gradually from the analysis of a series of concepts elaborated within the framework of different but converging research studies. This global psychoanalytically oriented model, called the institutional field model, will then be compared with other similar models produced by research conducted in Italy with a view to identifying advantages, features and specific developments.

Bion

Bion (1970), who sees the institution as a container (Hinshelwood, 1987) provides a first model, particularly useful for the study of institutions. This model extends and broadens the concept of projective identification (Klein, 1946), based on the idea that human behaviour may be designed to make another human being experience particular emotions and fantasies in order to relieve one's own psychic life of psychic elements that are distressing or intolerable. Bion (1962[1967]) extended this idea by enhancing the aspect of communication, in addition to that of evacuation, served by projective identification and extended the concept to show that one contains in one's mind the affective and phantasmatic aspects that are present in the other's mind. The key aspect is that psychic life can take place only if psychic experiences are shared with another person. However, some psychic experiences need to be contained in the mind of another person to be transformed, and only then can they be returned to the original owner. Bion (1970) did not simply deepen the relational model present in the container concept, but actually extended it to group life. Bion stated that the group must equip itself to contain, preserve and develop new thoughts suggested by productive and intelligent individuals. According to Bion, institutional life can be seen as the answer to the primordial human need of perpetuating truths or innovations produced by an individual as the wealth of a group whose objective is to preserve what someone produced in the past through a periodical revival.

A further aspect of Bion's model is concerned with thinking. In fact, according to Bion (1962[1967]), containing does not just consist in the elaboration of the projective identification and does not exclusively involve perpetuating intellectual and affective wealth in a group; rather it constitutes a universal process of thinking. In order for psychic elements to exercise their function they must first be placed next to each other, as it were. In other words, Bion hypothesised that all thinking activities require a preliminary phase in which the elements of thinking are placed within a space that contains them; in this first stage the elements of thinking are simply placed next to each other, with no active connection among them (Bion, 1965). The significant aspect of this stage consists in the notion of a space of preliminary arrangement. Psychic activity becomes impossible if the human being cannot benefit from the fantasy of having a mental place where his psychic elements can be thought and arranged. A particularly distressing experience, in many psychic disorders, consists in the frightful feeling that one's psychic products flow into an unlimited space, without first being contained within a framework.

The institution can be conceived as a container in which affective and phantasmatic aspects of the patient begin to be preliminarily arranged (Correale, 1991). In this first stage the patient can picture the institution as a place with boundaries, in which his psychic life can finally find form, which has a positive and therapeutic effect. Thus the institution represents a preliminary form of mental space in which the patient can begin to arrange his fragmented and scattered mental world. If the institution is conceived as a container, all the events that take place within the institution itself gain importance as they all pertain to aspects of the mental life of the individual, placed within aspect of institutional life. From this perspective, the dual relation is increasingly seen as an element of integration and of conscious elaboration of an experience that involves the entire group framework, rather than as a separate element.

Winnicott

Winnicott (1958), through the extension of his key concept of 'holding environment', offers another significant model of how institutions function. Winnicott hypothesised that a fundamental experience for the small child's development consisted in the feeling – and not just the fantasy – of being 'held' by the mother. Winnicott included in the concept of 'holding' a series of physical experiences such as being fed, cuddled, watched over, relieved, warmed, entertained – a series of experiences aimed to modify the bodily state of the small child. A harmonious integration of the various experiences and parts of the self could be achieved only by devoting constant attention to the body, its temperature, pain, and kinaesthetic variations. Only in this way can the child gradually begin to feel he is living inside his body rather than experience it as something that is foreign to him, or that serves merely to support his mind. Winnicott's idea was further enriched by the introduction of the transitional object model (Winnicott, 1958). Winnicott uses this expression to indicate objects – people, pieces of furniture, toys, sounds, images – that convey to the child the feeling that the reality that surrounds him is both foreign and familiar to him. In other words, each transitional object contains, at once, something of the self and something of the outside world. The area of play of fantasy, of illusion, therefore takes on the value of a space that is of crucial importance for the formation of an integrated sense of the self. It is possible to apply to the institutional framework the two concepts (holding and transitional object). Indeed, it is possible to imagine that the entire institutional group works as a holding environment. In fact, the inpatient experiences significant physical sensations in it such as eating together, spending part of the day in a group, and other significant aspects of the life of residential institutions such as watching television with a group of people, cleaning the rooms, running the cafeteria. Often anyone who enters an institution gets the strong feeling that it is a place characterised by powerful physical sensations, smells, lights, sounds, atmospheres that are immediately perceived either as bitter or sweet, stiff or soft, heavy or light. Many interactions that occur within institutions can be considered as designed to try out new possible aspects of one's way of being, to implement fantasies or desires, fears or habits, anxieties or libidinal cathexis. Winnicott's concepts allow us to envisage the entire institution as a theatre in which the performer feels a number of significant physical experiences at once and has the possibility of staging different behaviours and interactions, each connected with a potential area of the self. This concept is especially important for difficult patients who, because of the fragility of their self, are forced to adopt compulsory behaviours, strict habits and rigid ways of relating. Thanks to the existence of a wide range of interactional options provided by an institution, it is possible for such individuals to activate more private and concealed parts of their self, in a multitude of possible exchanges. The institution represents a widely equipped space where the patient can enact different and often disconnected parts of the self. The containing function of the institution allows focusing on the vicissitudes of thinking and on the capacity gradually to transform the elements of thinking. The emphasis of the holding environment is on the physical-bodily aspect of being in this space and on the possibility for this space to function as a theatre of enactment or behaviours that the patient has never experienced before.

Anzieu

In his studies on the group, Anzieu (1983) has highlighted the recurring phenomenon that the group tends to organise its psychic life around basic thematic cores, which permeate the entire affective life of the group. A whole set of group life phenomena, seemingly scattered and disconnected, become comprehensible if they are considered as belonging to just one organiser, that is one basic thematic core, which carries out the important functions of connection and homogenisation. One such organiser is the membrane. The group tends to activate the phantasy, shared to a greater or lesser extent by all its members, that there exists a boundary of sorts between the inside and the outside, between what happens within the group and what happens elsewhere. A polarity forms between the inside and the outside, which, in turn, becomes a polarity between what is familiar and what is unknown, between orderly and chaotic, personal and foreign, and, in some cases, between good and bad. At times, the boundary seems to be experienced by the group as a semipermeable membrane, that is as a space to be crossed, a living organism, comparable to the cell membrane, where significant phenomena for the survival of the organism take place, connected with the exchanges between the inside and the outside. This entails the aspect of group identity to be powerfully stressed: the group becomes my group, my story becomes our story, I becomes We, uncertain and confused feelings of the self become clear and consistent because they are strengthened by participation in the life of a supra-individual and collective identity. The definition of the organiser as a membrane allows attention to focus on the limit itself as a living and physiologically active element, not just as an inert no-man's-land between two neighbouring countries. In fact, the membrane is a place that is crossed by constant affects and fantasies, expressed as movements of identifications and projections, attributions of mental states inside or outside, where the identity of the group undergoes constant remodelling and development.

Neri

It is useful to associate this concept with Neri's (1998) idea of 'area of belonging'. Neri formulates that the fantasy and feeling of belonging form quite rapidly in a group. Such belonging is viewed as a mental space where fantasies and emotions stemming from the sense of belonging to that group are strongly active. Belonging is understood as the conviction that a part of one's own identity is deposited in the group and that the image of ourselves that we offer to the outside cannot be independent from our belonging to that group. The feeling of belonging may lead to an intense affective investment in the group, which one gradually begins to experience as the matrix of vital emotions that are comparable, for instance, to one's homeland or childhood. In Roman times every house had small structures devoted to the worship of the household gods (the Lares and Penates). The Romans believed that every place, even the most solitary and secret, was always inhabited by a god, wild but loving towards it; they called this god the *genius loci*, who could be known only by those who respected that place (Neri, 1993, 1998). By attending regularly a place where significant events for one's life occur, characterised by group life, it inevitably makes the individual feel emotions of an almost sacred nature towards the affective matrix of that very place.

It is possible to apply these concepts to institutional life. Anyone who works in an institution knows from experience how strong the feelings of belonging are and how much an individual's sense of identity is fed by the institution they belong to (Correale, 1992). This may lead to inter-institutional, inter-group competition that, if contained, is a physiological and healthy occurrence. If the strong bond that ties every individual to his institution were to be broken, one of the most important sources of enthusiasm and vitality, which the individual can draw from institutional life, would be extinguished.

An institution can be viewed not just as a powerful machine that performs a task, and not even as a group with strong affective bonds, but as a place with layers of a common memory. Powerful emotions of kinship and enthusiasm are entailed in sharing common memories with other people belonging to the same group. Having a common past represents an important guarantee that there exists an antidote to passage of time and that not all that happens is crushed in the inevitable flowing of events. In other words, every institution tends to establish itself as a historical field where the past or history are felt as a humus, a common ground, an area of collective affects and memories, which will continue to generate energy and evolutionary impulses for the future.

It is possible to hypothesise that the obsessive degeneration, bureaucratic involution and institutional formality, which may characterise institutional life and which make it difficult to stay in an institution, are caused by not taking into due account this fundamental channel of vitality that each institution activates.

The institutional field model – a synthesis

We now try to combine the three models described: the container, the holding environment, the membrane organiser and area of belonging. Each of these models tends to underline one particularly important aspect of institutional life, but none of them alone can contain the wealth of events that characterise institutional life, which is an expression of a synthesis of the models. It is useful to build a supra-model that can somehow combine the main tools provided by the other models, within the framework of a global and unifying perspective. This model will give us a global outlook, that is an approach that may allow us to give value to all the events taking place in institutions and connect them, on the one hand, with the life of the institution and, on the other hand, with the vicissitudes of the relationship between the individual patient and the institution. I would like to suggest that the field concept is especially suitable for this purpose.

The field concept was born within the Gestalt psychology of form, precisely with the aim of grasping the totality of group phenomena, just as form psychology had the aim to grasp the structural lines that unified perceptive activity rather than a sum of separate events. Lewin (1952), who introduced this concept for the first time, conceived of the affects that are activated in a group as physical forces, which operate, for instance, within an electromagnetic field, precisely to indicate this total and global aspect. The concept was then taken up again by Bion (1961), when he underlined the need to study the group as a whole and not as a sum of separate parts. In psychoanalysis, the concept was reintroduced by the Barangers who underlined that at times the analytic couple produces common fantasies (functional aggregates) where there is no longer a distinction between what is produced by the patient and what is produced by the analyst (Barangers and Barangers, 1961). In these cases, it is useful to see the relationship no longer as a dialogue between two people, but as a common area occupied by common material. According to the perspective that we intend to propose, we understand the field simply as a vast equipped space corresponding to the institution itself where all affective, phantasmatic, perceptive events of the institution take place. In other words, the field is, at once, a container, a holding environment, and an area of belonging. However, considering it a field offers at least three main advantages.

This concept of the field allows us to adopt a very important and specific approach. In fact, it is possible to focus our attention with equal curiosity and dedication on all the events that take place in institutions; this makes it possible to understand facts that would otherwise remain unexplored. If we take the shape–backdrop perspective, we may say that the institution is the backdrop against which the therapy relation stands as the shape. However, we may also state that the institution is the shape and the therapy relation can serve as a backdrop. If we look at this from another point of view, we could start out with the idea that splitting represents a constant element in the psychic life of a difficult patient. Such splitting, however, is not always the result of an active attack against thinking. More often than not, it is the result of an embryonic functioning of the mind, of unintegrated aspects of the self, of shapeless parts of the personality, of elements that are too concrete and barely thought out, liveable but not knowable. In these cases, the simple dual relation is not able to bring these elements back to unity because too much of the life of the patient occurs outside the relation and cannot but occur outside it.

Adopting a global field approach allows us to overcome this limitation, considering the life of the patient in an institution outside the relation as the possible expression of parts of the self that would otherwise remain in the dark.

A second great advantage offered by the field concept is that it represents a bridge between group psychology and individual psychology. In fact, it is not a matter of privileging the group over the individual or the individual over the group. Rather, one must constantly ask ourselves: how does the psychic life of this individual influence that of the entire group, and how does the life of the group influence that of the individual? In other words, each individual contributes, more or less, to creating a global field.

A third advantage of the field model is that it allows us to investigate trans-individual phenomena (Neri, 1995). We refer to events characterised by emotions or phantasies which, though originating from an individual, seem endowed with a particularly pervasive capacity to spread within the group. These emotions are connected with life and death, love, hate and survival, or are also typical of the basic states of the self – vitality, energy, enthusiasm, pleasure, oppression, sterility – that spread in a powerful but unexpected way and contribute to the creation of group moods or atmospheres whose causes are not always easy to grasp. The field approach allows us to realise at the outset that there exists a phantasy or an emotion that occupies the group, and only at a later stage, once the phantasy has been identified, is it possible to comprehend the ways in which it spread and its source.

A first significant layer of the field can be defined as the sensorial field. Bleger (1967) offers a remarkably accurate definition of what we understand by this expression. He stated that in psychoanalytical experience a series of events takes place which, though they are not recognised directly and consciously by the protagonists, contribute considerably to characterise the experience itself. The events that he spoke of are mainly sensorial experiences – the light in the room, smells, noises, the pitch of the voice, the consistency of the sofa, in summary the sum of the feelings felt in the room. The most significant aspect is found not in the quality of the sensations but in their continuity, that is to say they represent a sort of uninterrupted sensorial flow, into which the individual plunges when he resumes his analysis and from which he surfaces at the end of the session. Such a flow is almost entirely unnoticed and manifests its existence prevalently when the flow is interrupted, that is when a separation, a sudden event, an unexpected rupture of affective harmony occurs. Bleger defined this area of analytic experience as the syncretic area, to indicate that it is at the same time the sum of different sensations and the undifferentiated result, as it were, of this very sum. Bleger also defined the analytic setting as a vast deposit of undifferentiated but powerful sensations that the patient unconsciously finds again and which he tends to fantasise as being located in a specific place and time. In severe mental disorders and, in particular, all the situations in which the cohesion of the self is damaged, Bleger's syncretic deposit acquires special importance. Indeed, under these circumstances, the patient does not seek the verbal meaning of what is being said but the specific sensorial experience, characterised by a particular continuity and emotional drive, which has a powerful containing effect. It is particularly important to consider how Bleger (1966a, 1980) extended this concept to institutions. In fact, he stated that in the institutional group a deposit of sensorial experience gradually forms. These sensorial experiences constitute a sort of undifferentiated common ground, a shared bodily and almost physical foundation, which involves all the workers. The sensorial field is an essential component of the total field: if it is excessively curbed, the members of the institution experience the group as dry, devitalised and sterile. Too much sensorial input is felt as overwhelming and intrusive. The interruption of the continuum represented by such a field can explain many individual reactions that would otherwise remain mysterious and obscure.

A second layer consists of the emotional field. In order to understand this concept, we need to refer to Bion's theory of basic assumptions. Bion (1961) postulated that if group life is taken over by intense emotional waves, all individuals are captured by these emotions, as it were, and can experience an intense conflict between their own individual way of being and the basic assumption that prevails in the group. Later on Bion (1970) gave a positive and benign interpretation of basic assumptions. In order to have a complete and full emotional life, the individual needs to live out intense experiences that can be obtained exclusively in a group. Experiences such as dependence, faith, hope, defence of the territory, preservation of one's cultural heritage, defence of one's identity, faith in a better world, mysticism, utopia acquire depth and full meaning only if they are experienced in a group. If the basic assumption is initially considered only as a defence, an escape from emotions and a flight from reality, at a later stage it takes on a benign tone and even becomes an emotional experience that is necessary for the psychic life of the individual. The attachment of the individual to an institution, the anger and frustration generated by affective events within the institution, means that the individual seeks a constant emotional supply, as it were, a sort of affective and perpetual spring that he can feed from. Bion placed great emphasis on this important aspect of emotional nourishment that the group offers to individuals.

According to this perspective, the institution is a field crossed and intersected by powerful collective emotions that have to do with the security that institutions offer by strengthening the identity that also results from a comparison with other institutions, the pleasure that comes from mastering one's task, the confidence that comes from broadening one's field of knowledge.

If we want to understand an institution, therefore, we must always ask ourselves what are the basic emotions that define and characterise it, how are they connected with its history and how do they develop towards a collective shared future (Correale, 1991).

This third layer is connected with the phenomenon that Foulkes (1975) defined as polarisation and Kleinian analysts accurately understood as based on the projective identification model. Once an individual enters a group he projects parts of himself, aspects of his psychic life, phantasies and mental functions into the other people in the group who may be suitable as recipients of such projections. The group can be considered as a place where the mental world of the individual is submitted to a powerful kaleidoscopic process: the various projections come from all directions and every individual can either recognise or not recognise parts of himself in the other members of the group. This phenomenon is particularly evident when the atmosphere becomes persecutory or simply not conducive to emotional exchanges, thus dampening every individual's reflective function. When the persecuting atmosphere of the group threatens the self, the group tends to counter the distress with intense projective identification, in order to avoid the pain of acknowledging the prevailing emotional situation. In institutions the official and bureaucratic hierarchies favour the creation of roles, subgroups, delegation s, and so on. Although such subdivision meets, to a large extent, actual needs for effective planning and management, it facilitates renouncing and delegating parts of the self to other groups and avoidance of individual responsibility. Polarisation meets a twofold need: on the one hand, it allows individuals to better distribute burdens and responsibilities, but, on the other hand, it can favour processes leading to emotional rigidity.

The institutional field can be conceived as a theatre where events of particular explicative value occur. The dramatisation of these events can be considered as a form of externalisation of inner relations by patients or professionals, which cannot find expression through verbalisation. Some relations can be understood only if they are first staged and enacted (Correale and Celli, 1995). This happens not only when phenomena of splitting and denial predominate, but also when embryonic emotional factors, indistinct yet powerful, generate a group atmosphere that facilitates partial obliteration of reflective capacities. In these cases, institutional life offers a truly valuable resource: what is not said can nevertheless be represented actively in daily life. What happens takes on the characteristics of a painting in which every detail has a specific meaning and there is no contrast between the content of the picture and the landscape that contains it. It is important that all the members of an institution can, at given times, move away from the flow of daily life in order to observe the pictures that they have painted.

What has been said thus far provides us with guidelines that allow us to investigate what occurs inside institutions. Indeed, the individual needs institutions both for his bodily identity and for his affective life, both as a grid for the projection of the self and as a theatre of possible shared scenarios. The institution is a container of emotions and bodily experiences as well as a self-object and a living area of relation and relationships. The pragmatic implication inherent in this model for those who run institutional life is to bear in mind these requirements and vital functions which are present in institutions. Indeed, many institutions have become sterile and exhausted, not because this is the inevitable fate of all institutions, but because these vital functions have not been adequately acknowledged and taken into account. Those in charge of institutions must constantly listen to the emotional space present and regularly appraise the quality of the institutional space, its permeability, vitality, affective tonality, and promote through reflection and initiative the constant vitalisation and enrichment of such a space.

Conclusion

The recent history of Italian approaches to institutional life is linked to the struggle initiated in the 1960s by Basaglia (1968) and his followers, which resulted in the closing down of psychiatric hospitals and the concentration of psychiatric assistance in daycare and rehabilitation facilities within the community. The work of Basaglia, which deserves credit for having profoundly renewed psychiatric facilities in Italy, gave rise to a suspicious attitude towards any institutional work. This was considered as hostile to the growth of individual identity, as stiffening human relations, and potentially hostile to important functions such as phantasy and, more generally, individual originality and creativity. In contrast, the Milanese and Roman schools hold that it is not helpful to discuss in abstract terms whether institutions are good or bad, but stress that institutions meet fundamental emotional and real needs for the individual and for society. The problem is how to operate within institutions to ensure that they can actually fulfil their function. A purely sociological approach would consider the institution as a machine aimed to execute a task, hence consider only the mechanical aspect of the institution, but would miss the key function of container of emotions and phantasies it fulfils. By integrating a sociological and a psychoanalytic approach to form new models, the two schools give us important conceptual tools to improve our understanding of the often-intricate workings of institutions.

6 CONTRIBUTION FROM FRANCE
Psychoanalysis and Institutions in France

RENÉ KAËS

In France, psychoanalysis and institutions have a history of connectedness in the context of successive transformations in psychiatric institutions, the conceptualisation of mental illness, especially psychosis, and the emergence of psychotherapies, especially group psychotherapies. The psychoanalytic movement has inspired practice in and thinking about psychiatric institutions in two main areas: 'institutional psychotherapy' and 'psychoanalysis applied to institutions for psychiatric care', to quote a formulation suggested by P.-C. Racamier (1970). Psychoanalytic research has also been extended to other sorts of institution (e.g. for training, service and production) and this in turn has given rise to further work.

The historical context of connections between psychoanalysis and institutions: principal trends

Three distinct phases can be identified in the history of relations between psychoanalysis and psychiatric institutions. The first began in the final years of World War II and ended with the implementation of psychiatric sector policies in 1960. The second period covers arrangements made on the basis of these voluntarist policies. Then, in 1968, conditions were ripe for a transformation that ushered in the third period, characterised by a socio-political critique of psychiatry, sector policies and psychoanalysis, and by rather detailed psychoanalytic research into the psychic processes at work in groups and institutions.

This introduction could have focused on the epistemological problems raised by the relationship between psychoanalysis and institutions. There is a highly characteristic French way of dealing with these connections, by investigating the conditions that might make psychoanalytic theory and practice possible in institutions or make psychoanalytic thinking about institutions possible at all. This is bound up with the

97

national cultural context in which psychoanalysis began to emerge on the eve of World War II. Until then, psychoanalysis had been resisted in society at large and especially by the majority of psychiatrists, while it was being embraced enthusiastically by creative writers and people in the plastic arts.

During and after the war itself, both psychiatrists and psychoanalysts found their practice and ethics being rudely challenged by the living conditions and fate that had been inflicted on the mentally ill: human experimentation, systematic extermination of some categories of patient, and administratively orchestrated famine (40,000 mental patients died of starvation, while others died of dysentery and tuberculosis). During the war, psychiatrists like Paul Balvet in Montpellier in 1942 denounced the wretched state of psychiatric aid in France and proposed that there should be an immediate revival of the Esquirol principle of running institutions as instruments for care. Doctors who had been imprisoned and experienced the world of the concentration camps saw a number of parallels with the totalitarian conditions in psychiatric asylums. With liberation, different models for understanding mental illness and therapeutic practice were called for as a new society was being built, there was wider access to care with the introduction of social security in 1945, and caregiving institutions were restructured.

In the course of this 'war work' some psychiatrist-psychoanalysts, in a quandary about the care that was available to psychotic patients, began to consider psychoanalysis as offering a possible frame of reference to place institutions at the service of caregiving, explore their therapeutic resources and limits, transform them and identify the anti-care arrangements that beset them. It is important to note to what extent research in this area is both empirical and speculative: its theoretical reference points are still established by trial and error, while fundamental debate, still relevant today, centres upon major problems of method and the definition of the sphere of competence of psychoanalysis and psychoanalysts who, with neither couches nor armchairs, are attempting to grapple with the workings of the unconscious in settings that are radically different from that of the classical cure.

The drive to transform psychiatric institutions may have lent stimulus and support to psychoanalytic interest in institutions and in psychosis, but would not have done so had it not been for the development of child psychiatry, nosography and the psychotherapies. Psychoanalysis is a serious contender in the same field, presenting an alternative to drastic treatment (Cardiazol-induced shock therapy, ECT, psychosurgery, insulin therapy), and in return receives a broad measure of psychiatric support. Several psychiatrists went on to form a group of second-generation psychoanalysts (Diatkine, Lebovici, Lacan, Racamier, etc.) who played a decisive part in transforming institutions for psychiatric care.[8]

First period: psychoanalysis, institutional psychotherapy, and sector psychiatry policies

Some introductory remarks are in order to describe what went before the shift towards institutional psychotherapy, itself a component of social psychiatry.[9]

Movement in this direction probably began at Saint-Alban, a small commune in the Cévennes, in the work of Tosquelles (1966), a Spanish republican psychiatrist who had taken refuge in France, P. Palvet and L. Bonnafé. From 1942 to 1944 they formed the groupe du Gévaudan and implemented the active therapeutic approach of H. Simon in the departmental hospital, turning the asylum into a place of high-level sociability in the very midst of the war. The Journées psychiatriques de Sainte-Anne, held in Paris in March 1945, initiated the shift towards institutional psychotherapy, and work began on the organising principles of sector psychiatry that came to fruition in 1960. At the Paris conference, F. Bernard proposed the use of group psychotherapy as a basis for the therapeutic organisation of social life in psychiatric hospitals.

After the trauma of occupation, the urge for renewal that seized the country encouraged pilot experiments promoted by the newly formed social security from 1945 onwards. CTRSs – centres for treatment and reintegration through work – used every means at their disposal to care for and resocialise the patients they accepted. Sivadon at the CTRS in Ville-Evrard and Le Guillant in Villejuif showed the important therapeutic function both of occupational therapy and the institutional setting, with positive results. Situated somewhere between expressive methods and professional re-education, occupational therapy requires patients' cooperation: for this reason Sivadon saw it as a first step towards social readaptation through work.

Other psychiatrists grouped together to make experimental suggestions that were to prove of lasting value. Daumezon, for instance, and Koechline at Fleury-les-Aubrais, supported the idea that recovery was

---

[8] On the contribution of psychoanalytic theory to the understanding of mental illness, see Diatkine's 1968 paper to the 2nd Congrès des psychanalystes de langue romanes, published in Racamier (1970), pp. 15–42.

[9] On the development of French trends in social psychiatry and institutional therapies, see Béquart in Racamier (1970), pp. 138–195; Bléandonu and Despinoy (1974), Bléandonu (1976) and Beauchesne (1986), pp. 216–221.

possible only if a network of authentic communications could be restored. From the outset, they placed emphasis on the transformation of nursing.

Between 1945 and 1947 a working group of psychiatrists with various different viewpoints assembled at the hospital in Bonneval under the direction of Ey to think about the conditions and results of these continuing experiments in terms of psychoanalytic, sociological and political, especially marxist, theories. Ajuriaguerra, Bernard, Bonnafé, Daumezon, Duchêne, Ey, Follin, Fouquet, Lacan, Le Guillant and Tosquelles adopted the collective name 'Doctor Batia', to sustain hope for a second psychiatric revolution. In this pre-psychoanalytic period the main aim was to create living conditions at the hospital that were as close to 'normal' family and social life as was possible. Psychiatrists attended to the functional aspects of mental illness and tried to resocialise patients through a wide range of 'occupational' activities (occupational therapy, clubs, circles, cooperatives and theatre).[10]

In 1948 G. Daumezon introduced a range of psychoanalytic ideas to account for the effects of therapeutic activities in hospital (cathexes, identifications, transference, etc.). Psychoanalysis was initially invoked as an explanatory theory that might help to describe institutional reality, rather than being mobilised as a therapeutic technique adapted to that specific situation. It was applied by borrowing concepts from a metapsychology based on individual treatment: thought had not yet been given to the formulation of concepts to explain the psychic processes at work in hospitals.

The symposium on collective psychotherapy at Bonneval in 1951[11] highlighted discrepancies between a number of different conceptions of therapeutic work: should doctors conduct their therapeutic work on patients' real, concrete activities or, as psychoanalysis would demand, on their worlds of fantasy? Daumezon, who cast the issue in these terms, chose the first option, gaining the support of those who were in favour of readaptation and resocialisation, though he drew criticism from others, like Le Guillant, who refused to transform hospitals – artificial, imposed and transitory places – into factories or villages. F. Tosquelles supported the second alternative, which implied a potential for gathering and analysing transferences within the setting and for devising techniques for collective psychotherapy. For him, institutions were places where unconscious 'dramas', in which everyone is a player, can unfold, be confronted,

---

[10] This was developed especially by Tosquelles at Saint-Alban, marking one of the 'beginnings' of psychodrama in France. Later on it started the debate between Morenian and psychoanalytic psychodrama.

[11] Its proceedings were published in 1952 in *L'Évolution psychiatrique*, volume 3.

and be treated under certain conditions, including team work. Concepts were borrowed from psychoanalysis and phenomenology (identifications, mirror image, the ego, roles, and the dialectics of We, exchange and giving, and of I and Thou) in an effort to establish some theoretical reference points to account for the components of social groups and for their effects within an institution. Lebovici and Diatkine limited collective therapy to psychoanalytic psychodrama, since it allowed analysts to make classical interventions in the treatment of unconscious conflict.

In the year after the meeting at Bonneval, Daumezon and Koechlin proposed using the term 'institutional psychotherapy' to describe 'the whole spectrum of activities that are arranged for therapeutic ends, using the features of the setting within which patients live'.

Institutional psychotherapy can be understood in two principal senses: to describe the task of organising institutions in such a way as to make individual psychotherapies possible within them (Tosquelles, 1966), and to describe the task of making them function in such a way as to lend therapeutic value to institutional life. This would locate institutional psychotherapy within the current of French psychiatry that affirms the therapeutic value of institutions.

The driving force behind the pioneers of the second psychiatric revolution in France (Daumezon, Oury, Paumelle, Racamier, Tosquelles) was the idea that caregiving institutions do have therapeutic potential for chronic psychotic patients and that it is possible to devise treatment that mobilises and employs institutional processes. Communication must be structured and space and time must be organised to support the therapeutic process. Taking a lead from Simon (1929; 'l'hôpital est une personnalité qu'il faut soigner'), they also revealed institutions' capacity for developing a specific pathology connected with treatments, conditions and the institutional setting itself:[12] chronicisation, massive psychosocial deficit, apathy, an impoverishment akin to dementia and uniformity in symptomatology. From then on many discoveries were made about the pathogenic function of institutions, with their dissociations and splits mirroring psychotic pathology. Thinking began about institutional pathology. Nonetheless, the time was not yet ripe to specify the conditions under which institutional settings might promote such processes, whether therapeutic or pathogenic. Psychoanalytic input would prove to be necessary before this could happen, but during this first period, even if psychoanalysis provided important terms of reference, it did not furnish the dominant concepts and practices of social psychiatry; neither was it

---

[12] Daumezon proclaimed, 'we must cure asylums if we are to cure the sick' and several years later Oury said that it was essential to 'treat the establishment'.

the source of inspiration for the shift towards institutional psychotherapy. Instead, this still relied heavily upon the tenets of the psychosociology of communications, role theory and a sort of social behaviourism.

Sector psychiatry, the involvement of psychoanalysts in institutions for psychiatric care, and the second phase of institutional psychotherapy

Building on this work, especially the pre-sector experiments at the CTRSs in Sivadon and Le Guillant, in 1957 and 1958 a working group called the Groupe de Sèvres brought psychiatrists, psychoanalysts and nursing staff together to work out ground-rules for sector psychiatry.[13] Their aim was to arrange for psychiatric care outside asylum walls, providing continuity with a single caregiving team, in the patient's own everyday surroundings, thus avoiding the added alienation of placement in an asylum. An important part of this thinking bore on the involvement of nursing staff in psychiatry: they were to play a decisive role in the realisation of this project, since they ensured the duration and continuity of the underlying dynamic structure of caregiving units. All the same, efforts to conduct shared work with psychiatrists, psychoanalysts and nursing staff ran into serious difficulties, raising the issue of therapeutic qualifications for specific roles, and especially the problem of training for nursing staff: there was awareness that this problem had been identified at the outset by Daumezon. Diatkine stressed the risk or even danger attendant upon introducing an understanding of unconscious mechanisms to nursing staff, as he felt that it would provoke reaction formations and make their work unbearable. At this point, Oury was able to show that whatever mode of relationship existed between doctors and nursing staff as discrete groups, its quality would transmit between them and their patients as a group, so that it was important to set up training and dialogue in order to understand the meaning of such symptoms in depth.

A report presented by H. Duchêne at the Congrès de Neuropsychiatrie de Langue française at Tours in 1959 focused on a new definition for psychiatric and outpatient services, and was to become one of the major reference points for sector psychiatry.

Bléandonu (1976) defined the expression 'sector psychiatry' as denoting the mental health policy officially advocated in France since the circular of 15 March 1960. It could be regarded as one of the most

---

[13] Its work was published in 1958 in *L'information psychiatrique*, 5 and 10.

thoroughgoing examples of social psychiatry, whose principles were as follows. Emphasis was placed upon active prevention and the provision of care at the earliest possible stage. Displacement of the actual sites that brought patients, their caregivers and their environment together was the principle that informed the outpatient practice that was to alter the organisation and therefore the aims of psychiatric hospitals. From then on, psychiatrists' efforts were to be confined within a patient catchment area. Treatment would be conducted in the community, with the result that patients would not be distanced from their natural surroundings. Psychiatrists were to circulate within a network where a wide range of different treatments and relationships would be on offer: they were not to work in a single place, and the realisation of this policy presupposed team work, or an 'institutional ensemble who coordinate inside with outside' (Sivadon, cited by Bléandonu, 1987).

Day hospitals and the more differentiated structures at mental health centres were major elements in sector psychiatry,[14] and the fact that they shared in the development both of community psychiatry and of psychoanalysis gave these experiments a prime place in institutional innovation. The notion of the frame, in Bleger's sense (Bleger, 1966b, 1967), seems to have been in the forefront of psychoanalytic thinking, concerned as it was to define a field of interpretation that would not collapse into what Napolitani (1967) dubbed 'panatanalysis'. Taking into account theoretical and methodological developments in the psychoanalytic approach to groups seems to have been helpful in thinking about the therapeutic process and the conditions for analysis of 'intertransferential' relationships amongst caregivers.[15]

An experiment in the 13th arrondissement of Paris, which began in 1954 with Paumelle, Lebovici, Diatkine, Racamier, Azoulay and a co-opted team, quickly became the showcase and emblem of sector psychiatry, providing a vast range of structures for outpatient care, from consultation to therapeutic readaptation workshops and from hospitalisation at home to day hospitals for adults and children. Inspired by the principles of Freudian psychoanalysis, its therapeutic doctrine made a scrupulous distinction between the institutional field and the psychoanalytic

---

[14] See Bléandonu and Despinoy (1974). On community psychiatry, see the work of J. Hochmann (1971).

[15] I have suggested using the concept of intertransferential analysis to account for the effect that the transferences of a group's members tend to have both upon the transferential links amongst psychoanalysts and upon their respective counter-transferences. I have myself tested out the usefulness of this model in work to develop the practice of caregiving teams, especially in day hospitals.

situation: it clarified the way in which institutions can mobilise a psycho-dynamic with which caregivers can work, providing continuity of care, and with team cohesion supporting investments and identifications and mediating between inside and outside. Here, as in other experiments of its sort, the concern was not so much to set up institutional psychotherapy as to apply certain psychoanalytic principles to caregiving institutions and ensure a better correspondence between therapeutic activity and the functioning of psychotic patients.

Le psychanalyste sans divan: psychoanalysis and institutions for psychiatric care

P.-C. Racamier's work, *Le psychanalyste sans divan* (1970), had a strong impact upon the French psychoanalytic scene. With rigorous argument, he broached a line of thinking about the potential for widening the scope both of caregiving and of psychotherapy that had been created by psycho-analysts who had left their armchairs without abandoning their functions as psychoanalysts. This work is an excellent synthesis of psychoanalysis applied to institutional care. The author undertakes the task of describing the presence, viewpoint and activities of psychiatrist-psychoanalysts in bodies caring for the mentally ill, i.e. 'in a situation defined by not being psychoanalytic'. The notion of a specifically institutional field made it possible to understand that admission simultaneously involved patients, their families, their caregivers and the institution itself as an organised grouping. Racamier is especially sensitive to the fact that, in the institu-tional field, psychoanalysts do not create their own sphere of activity, as they had been doing since Freud with the technique of the classical cure. Instead, they are entering a pre-existing field with which they must become familiar if they are to succeed in working in an entirely psychoan-alytic way within a non-psychoanalytic situation.

Racamier made a very detailed analysis of the turmoil and need for fresh work that a psychoanalyst's presence tends to bring to an institution, and began by cautioning against any illusory belief in the automatically therapeutic nature of institutions. On the contrary, he demonstrated, as Bleger had also thought, that caregiving institutions are subject to a process of reversal of their therapeutic purposes, and that they have a tendency to adapt to the mental pathology they undertake to care for, thereby preserving and perpetuating it. He drew attention to the fact that caregiving institutions are always conflict-ridden by virtue of the very nature of the psychic processes they deal with: how conflictuality is handled determines the structure of the institution, its own future and that of its patients. It is therefore necessary to recognise and tackle conflictuality in order to facilitate treatment.

Psychoanalysis brings renewal and transformation into institutional psychiatric practice in these two characteristic areas as well as others. It requires

> monitored authenticity in relating to patients and in relationships amongst those caring for them. In so doing, far from simplifying practice, it actu il´y reinstates its complexity: bodies with therapeutic aims are probably the most delicate because they are more highly evolved. (pp. 62–63)

Racamier adheres to a proposition that is fundamental to the whole institutionalist movement: that institutions can fall ill, and that some go on to die. There are potentially pathological and pathogenic structures which reveal themselves as such when they put up collectively organised forms of defensive response to the multiple and massive transferences of their patients and the anxiety mobilised by them, or when they produce impersonal, apathetic organisations deficient in libidinal investments and communication, or when they split apart in mimicry of psychotic defences. He took on board research by colleagues in France and elsewhere who had worked on psychiatric hospitalisation, incontinence, stereotypes and agitation, showing very precisely how schizophrenic dissociation and environmental dissociation together form a sociopathologically resonant phenomenon. He concluded that psychoanalysts must pay constant attention to the state of caregiving bodies.

Racamier therefore examined the conditions for and limits of institutional action by psychoanalysts. While Mannoni (1975) saw psychoanalysts as being either inside or outside, Geahchan (1958) proposed three ways in which psychoanalysts might engage with institutions: externally, by treating a number of patients outside; by taking part in specific institutional activities while maintaining a degree of extraterritoriality; or by being an integral part of the caregiving team. Racamier suggested a fourth way: by being included in a caregiving team as its leader.

On this point he connected with the stance of the institutional psychotherapy movement, whose contribution to awareness of institutional processes he acknowledged while remaining perplexed by many of their conceptions, especially the idea that all caregiving staff have an analytic function. He was critical of this non-differentiation of roles which denatures the meaning of relationships, but supported team work and the practice of discussion groups such as Schneider set up in Lausanne. He defended a precise conception of caregiving work in institutions, for example by supporting the principle of therapeutic continuity in the name of the psychoanalytic understanding of the psychoses: the same members of a team should remain in unbroken relationship with the same patients, and this *open* continuity would include diversity, presence and availability towards each patient.

Sector psychiatry aimed to provide wider and more open access to care, to develop efforts in prevention and screening, to seek a better adjustment of treatments to pathologies and to support therapeutic action on patients' environments. However, these choices and their outcomes drew criticism for their drawbacks. Political criticism came from Althusserian marxists who were afraid that public psychiatry was developing into an 'ideological state apparatus'; institutionalist criticism was directed at the power of psychiatrists and their administrative and social control over a 'sector' of the population; and finally there was criticism of the quest for economic profitability in the provision of health facilities.

More or less connected with this criticism, the debates and controversies that informed institutional doctrines, especially regarding the place and function of psychoanalysis, went on to inspire new experiments, of which La Verrière, Laborde and Bonneuil were amongst the better known, and the second phase of institutional psychiatry opened in 1965 with the creation of the Société de psychothérapie institutionnelle. This society's theoretical views were essentially inspired by the works of J. Lacan – who was a psychiatrist in the Bonneval group – and found its first application at the Laborde clinic in Cour-Cheverny in 1975 with Oury, Guattari and Michaud. J. Oury formulated the new guiding principles of institutional psychotherapy:

> It is not confined simply to the development of the necessary conditions for psychotherapy to be conducted. Instead, it takes account of each and every person that comes into its purview in order to facilitate the creation of spheres of multifocal transference and a veritable institutional fabric. (Oury, 1965)

The essential aim was to undo patients' alienation, seen as inseparable from undoing institutional alienation. Individual intervention only made sense if located within a grouping which possessed symbolic laws. J. Oury ascribed an essential function to institutionalisation, which he understood as a therapeutic process achieved by reinventing an institution through the agency, especially, of intrahospital clubs. Use was also made more generally of anything that ensured plurality and mobility inside institutions and thereby furthered the process of institutionalisation (Tosquelles spoke of 'polygroups'). Freedom of movement, reviewable contracts for admission and discharge, availability of concretely structured sites, and permanent accommodation: all these elements were seen as combining to produce an institution with rules that supported the therapeutic process in such a way that psychotic patients could create their own ways forward and find, or fail to find, their historicity.

These experiments clearly contributed to an understanding of institutions and psychotic patients. They also attracted criticism, which Bléandonu summed up as follows: most took place outside large urban centres and depended on local socio-economic conditions, while enclosure (Saint-Alban) and long-stay hospitalisation (Laborde) promoted chronicity. Hochmann (1971) saw this as a legacy of asylum psychiatry and deplored the lack of work by the institutional psychotherapy movement on experiments in hospitalisation on a part-time or community basis (see Fustier, 1989). Some psychoanalysts were sensitive to the recurrent problem of training for nursing staff who are informed about unconscious mechanisms without being really trained in handling them, something that risked raising their anxiety and provoking countertransference reaction formations. This criticism promoted a need to draw distinctions between psychoanalytic understanding and interpretation, and between the psychoanalytic and institutional fields.

The experiment at Bonneuil conducted by Mannoni opted for extreme minimalism in its institutional base: what she described as an 'exploded institution' contrasted not only with Bettelheim's (1974) but with Oury's conception, even though she shared Oury's Lacanian outlook. The Bonneuil experiment was inspired both by the English anti-psychiatry movement of Laing (1960) and Cooper (1967)[16] – which meant exposing absolutely everyone's alienation in the imaginary world of institutions – and by Lacanian theories about psychosis. Thus, the institution was not organised as a place for treating psychosis or as a meeting-point where each individual had a specific relationship with others. Before this could happen, and subjective individuals appear on the scene, destructiveness had to be unleashed against the institutional setting. The concept of an 'exploded institution' came from this project, and systematic arrangements were made for psychoanalytic treatment outside the institution. Patients therefore encountered a range of different 'interpretative positions', although the same theoretical terms of reference were shared by analysts inside and outside the institution. The latter was ultimately reduced to a mere assemblage of individual subjectivities, since the fundamental theoretical option was that institutions cannot function except as alienating imaginary units that are by nature only persecuting or divisive.

---

[16] Anti-psychiatry emerged in England at much the same time as sector psychiatry began in France. It contributed to criticism both of asylum-type institutions and of sector psychiatry, and was the sounding-board in a public debate about 'madness' that reached a wider audience in France after 1968 because of it.

In point of fact, 'exploded' institutions, like their psychotic patients, are wide open to the repetition of fragmentation. Psychotic splitting risks being reflected in institutional splits and in hardened oppositions between institution (indeed, any form of grouping) and individual. This model falters precisely on attempts to think about intermediate and transitional phenomena, despite the fact that Winnicott was one of Bonneuil's touchstones.

Models for patient care in psychiatric institutions

It would perhaps be useful to review various models for patient care in psychiatric institutions from a psychoanalytic point of view. Fustier (1989) identified two underlying theoretical models, which he described as 'living with' and 'technical action'. The first refers to a system of steady relationships between caregivers and patients in a project of shared living and global togetherness. In Fustier's view, this model is most powerful if an institution tends towards community functioning in an in-patient situation, a model perfectly realised in the residential re-education projects of 1943–1955, where institutions were organised to meet all needs and a 'good' institutional environment replaced a 'bad' pathogenic one. In this situation all distinction between inside and outside and between professional and private living was abolished. The dominant regime was characterised by non-separation and by chronicisation sustained by the effects of group illusion. This model for patient care is shaped by the features of an omnipotent maternal imago. From 1968 onwards experiments at residential sites were designed and conducted on this utopian model of an anti-society, with the institution representing the reverse of bad caregiving institutions and therefore of society as a whole, and we saw some therapeutic innovations being inverted to conform with the very model that they were supposed to counteract.

The second model propounded partial patient care, structured around precise objectives and on a limited timescale. Internal and external were differentiated and separate; caregivers and patients were distinguished; neither 'reality' nor the communal washrooms were deemed curative 'in themselves': work on the meaning of situations was demanded as much from patients as from caregivers, and the latter could not make headway unless they had gained knowledge and competence. This second model was structured around the symbolic gains of Oedipal organisation.

Inspired by the works of Hochmann, P. Fustier proposed a third model, one of dual patient care, a sort of compromise or a system in tension between the two previous models. It simultaneously distinguished between and associated care and treatment, and had to contain and work through contradictions between the other two models.

Further contrasts may be found amongst psychoanalytically inspired models for patient care in institutions exemplified by three prototypical configurations: institutional structures set up in ideal isolation, sheltered from alienating social factors, with the institution so organised as to reproduce an analytical setting comparable *mutatis mutandis* with that of the classical cure; the minimal institutional organisation of 'exploded' institutions that supposedly avoid falling into the trap of creating an alienating illusory unity; and more pragmatic settings that tolerate ambiguity, inspired in a more classical sense by applied psychoanalysis, in which providing continuity of care involves neither enclosure nor 'explosion'.

Broadening of connections between psychoanalysis and institutions

The third phase in the history of relations between psychoanalysis and institutions was characterised by an increase in their areas of overlap and by more precise theoretical conceptualisation of the institutional sphere as a composite reality with psychic, social, economic and political dimensions.

Mendel's sociopsychoanalysis

In this context, the initiatives of Mendel and the sociopsychoanalytic movement made a decisive contribution. In 1968, the psychoanalyst Mendel embarked upon a critique of psychoanalysis[17] when he was faced with the socio-political dimension of institutions. Since psychoanalysis offered only a single psycho-familial schema in the logic of an unconscious structured by the Oedipus complex and its corresponding identifications, it mistook the ways in which the organising forces in society obey economic and political logics. If institutions – and psychiatric institutions above all – were to be analysed using psychoanalytic tools, it would be necessary to include as a dimension of the analysis the fact that every organisation with several different levels of divided labour is a fertile place for the study of the interconnectedness between the logic of the unconscious and that of economic and political phenomena. A method of separate treatment for salaried staff would become imperative if they were to achieve a sufficient sense of distance from the psycho-familial structure

---

[17] See his first work, *La révolte contre le père* (1968), which inspired later work in sociopsychoanalysis.

inherent in such institutions, to arrive at a better understanding of relationships with parental imagoes as embodied in the director of the specific institutional functions. But this level of analysis was incomplete because it left no room for analysis of yet another level of institutional reality, one structured by work activity, professional specialisations and their influence on salaried staff.

With these fundamental tenets, the socio-psychoanalytic movement was distinct both from group psychoanalysis (Rouchy, 1978; Anzieu, 1985; Kaës, 1993), which stressed access to unconscious formations, and from institutional analysis[18] (Lapassade, Lourau, Hess – see Hess and Savoye, 1981), which made analytical use of key features of an institution's political structures.

The sociopsychoanalytic project developed further. In its first phase, one of its principal aims was to analyse power within institutions, which validated a project for socialist self-management that Mendel very courageously espoused as one of his main platforms, introducing a political dimension into the sphere of psychoanalytic thought. His attempt to analyse the regression of the political dimension in institutions towards the psycho-familial and to work upon archaic and Oedipal strata in institutions in order to bring about political democracy was founded on the idea that the structure of the political dimension is a specific organisational force, different and opposed to the psychic dimension.

In a second phase, Mendel located the sociopsychoanalytic project more specifically within the psychic dimension of what he termed 'psychosociality', which emphasised the idea of '*actepouvoir*':

> this dimension of the personality [psychosociality] comes into play in relating to external reality (collective, organisational, institutional) through the actions it produces. Development of the psychosocial dimension tends to be blocked by the organisation of labour. If he is to appropriate some degree of power over his activity, an individual must make contacts in contradiction with the situations and people around him, which have their own actepouvoir.[19]

In this sense the aims of the sociopsychoanalytic movement converge with those of institutional psychotherapy, and in caregiving institutions both

---

[18] Or socianalysis, to use a concept introduced by Moreno (1960). The socianalytic movement has very little connection with psychoanalysis, and is indeed critical of it, affirming its own project as sociological, and taking the concept of a social or political unconscious to mean whatever falls outside conscious awareness.

[19] The quotation is from a personal communication, further developed in his work and in a recent article (1996).

are concerned to relieve mental patients of their double psychic and political alienation.

Contemporary research

Research on institutions in France since 1968 builds on a considerable extension of the sphere of psychoanalytic thinking and practice beyond institutions for psychiatric care to include hospital services (medicine, surgery, emergencies, neonatology, cancer, palliative care, gerontology, etc.) and institutions for education, training,[20] industry and administration (prison administration, the army, churches, etc.). But in all these new fields, psychoanalysts have tended to serve either in a consultative capacity, or within the framework of supervisory functions or by accompanying other practitioners or analysing team relationships.

This research has benefited from a growing awareness of Argentinian and Anglo-Saxon lines of thought, including the concepts of the setting, containing functions and transitionality.

Psychoanalysis put to the institutional test: postulates, problems and findings

In my introduction I mentioned a peculiarly French way of tackling relations between psychoanalysis and institutions, which was prominent in the debate about criteria for the theory and practice of psychoanalysis in institutions, and tends to revolve around a critical and often ambivalent allegiance to the idea that the collective itself is caregiving. Before describing the ways in which relations between psychoanalysis and institutions are developing today, I would like to isolate a few general psychoanalytic premises that have been tested out in practice in psychiatric institutions.

Psychoanalytic postulates

It is important to recognise the uniqueness of its influence upon institutional thinking and practice, with which it has a conflictual relationship. Psychoanalysis is based on the hypothesis that there is an unconscious produced by psychosexual conflict and by defensive measures taken against it. Any reference to psychoanalysis in institutional or group practice comes up against this premise. It raises problematic issues about the unconscious psychic reality of, or in, institutions and its connection

---

[20] Cf. discussion of training institutions and training functions in caregiving institutions in work under the direction of Sapir (1992).

with particular individuals' unconscious psychic reality when considered in themselves.

Although aware of diagnostic categories, psychoanalysis addresses ailing individuals rather than illness itself. Psychoanalysis has influenced thinking and practice in institutions by relocating the boundaries between the normal and the pathological, and its conceptualisation of psychic suffering and mental pathology, especially in the understanding of psychotic disturbance, has given it credibility in the psychiatric sphere.

For psychoanalysts, a patient is a single individual, and therapeutic work is undertaken on an individual basis in acknowledgement of this singularity. As soon as their work needs to be done in an institution, questions are raised about the institution's ability either to facilitate or obstruct it. Psychoanalysts who credit the view that an institution as such can function therapeutically are obliged to define the conditions and obstacles in its way: testing out this idea, they tend to turn to Freud's work on what he called his 'social psychology'.[21] By accepting the institutional challenge and making progress with it, psychoanalysis is beginning to recognise the intersubjective and trans-subjective dimensions that are active in the formation of the psyche. On these premises, it will need to redefine its sphere of competence and metapsychological representations, leading to conflict within psychoanalytic doctrine. The methodological, clinical and theoretical developments made possible by a psychoanalytical approach to groups, the extension of the sphere of institutional practice beyond psychiatric care, and contributions by non-medical psychoanalysts to institutional practice in various ways (interventions, supervision and membership of caregiving teams) will lend substance and precision to the debate.

In demonstrating its competence within a setting very different from individual treatment, psychoanalysis has therefore faced, and not always been able to resolve, a number of problems which I will now examine as I describe a few directions in current research.

Institutional psychic reality

Psychoanalysis claims that psychic reality is made up of unconscious formations. How can these be described in institutional space?

The model of group psychic apparatus

Since I have devoted a great deal of my own research to this problem, I will begin with the model I have constructed to account for psychic reality in

---

[21] On this aspect of Freud, see Enriquez (1983), Kaës (1993).

groups. Other researchers have extended this model's competence to analyse psychic reality in families and institutions.

Group psychic apparatus is a concept whose object is to describe the formations and processes of psychic reality in human groups. It covers:

● The work of linking, transformation and differentiation amongst the parts of each individual's psychic apparatus that are mobilised in building the group's psychic apparatus. Seen from this perspective, formations that arise from intrapsychic group processes (notably internal groups) are unconscious organisers of group psychic reality. The main processes that contribute to the alignment of psyches within a group are identifications, diffraction and projection mechanisms, resonant phantasy phenomena, and a search for complementary objects.
● The psychic work of creating, maintaining and transforming the psychic processes, functions and formations that are shared by group members: this includes functions of repression and renunciation, ideals, identificatory reference points, shared representations and the group's self-representation, shared defence mechanisms, and the unconscious pacts, contracts and alliances that are functions of representation and delegation.
● Relations of mutual support in the reciprocal structuring both of individual and group psychic apparatus; imaginary fusion of individual psychic apparatuses with the group psychic apparatus (isomorphy); and differentiation of these two types of apparatus (homomorphy).

Psychic reality and institutional complexity

I have maintained (Kaës, 1987) that an institution is more than merely a social and cultural complex. It also performs a range of psychic functions for individual subjects in areas of their personal structure, dynamics and economy. It mobilises investments and representations that promote endopsychic regulation and strengthen the basis of individuals' identification with the social whole; they also form a backdrop for psychic life into which certain parts of the psyche that tend to escape psychic reality can be deposited and find containment. It generates psychic reality on the model of a group psychic apparatus, but in specific ways and with specific contents.

This is because institutions connect, assemble and deal with a heterogeneous range of formations and processes: social, political, cultural, economic and psychic. Different logics function in spaces that communicate and interfere with one another. This is why questions and solutions belonging to the *psychic* level and logic can intrude and prevail within the *social* logic of an institution. The psychic level encompasses both the relationships that individual subjects have with an institution and those that exist amongst the assemblage of subjects linked by and in the institution.

This is why every psychic event has a value *a priori* as a significant symptom for the institution as a whole. Political problems may therefore be expressed as a psychic symptom. It is, precisely, psychic work when heterogeneous groups sharing the same space reduce their heterogeneity in favour of homogeneity, support the principle of a single cause and the function of an ideal, reduce cognitive distance and dissonance, privilege metonymic functioning and gather heterotopic confusion into a uniform utopian space. To achieve such a task, all the processes that tend to produce non-differentiation and homogeneity come into play and an informed observer learns to recognise conglomerated or juxtaposed elements of disparate origin, resembling the situation in architecture when remnants of dismantled monuments are re-used in a new building.

Thus, in institutions a considerable share of psychic investment that goes into making different and complementary orders of logic coincide in an imaginary unity so as to be rid of their inherent conflictuality. Institutions encourage all the investments and formations that produce an illusion of coincidence and sustain isomorphic relations between individuals and their group to work in synergy, until such time as a violent irruption of the repressed or of negativity shatters the unconscious pacts that had sealed the consensus. By dismantling the grouping's paraphernalia such an event uncovers the distinct logics whose differences had been dissimulated in the shared formations that had been as necessary for single individuals as they were for the whole grouping to which they had belonged.

On the other hand, institutions' capacity to tolerate the functioning of relatively heterogeneous levels and to accept the interplay of different logics forms the basis of their metaphorical function. This capacity makes it possible to construct differentiated psychic space; it restores perspective and depth to histories whose actors are also of different orders, like palimpsest texts overwritten without totally erasing the traces of a succession of earlier writings.

The multiplicity of logical levels, economies and dynamics that develop in such an institution produces a range of different effects, such as management or transference effects between, for instance, individual subjects at their level and the whole ensemble, which might in its turn have enclaves of parallel form (groups, institutions) or parallel assemblages (families, institutions); the effects of conflicting or convergent means or objectives in the agencies that form the whole (institution, organisation, group of individuals, or individual subject); or the effects of forward or reversed synergy and fit between levels.

I have tried to analyse the way the jostling spaces that compose an institution fit together. My work has centred on the shared psychic formations and spaces that institutions produce and manage, starting with the contributions and investments they demand from their individual members. The interest and benefit the latter derive, and the pleasure and suffering they experience, must also in turn be assessed.

I have proposed conducting this analysis in terms of strategies for diverting psychic investments and institutional means for the benefit of certain of its members or the institution as a whole. In the process, we can observe the sideways shifts and reversals that tend to creep, rather perversely, into certain aspects of an institution's dynamics.

There are opposing forces at work in institutions: some pull towards unification, essentially due to the development of ideal functioning, representations of a single cause, and convergent libidinal investment; others serve to differentiate and integrate distinct elements within ever larger units; others, in contrast, are bent on a return to non-differentiation and on reducing tensions; while still others are dedicated to destruction and attack.

While an analysis such as this sheds light on fundamental aspects of psychic life in institutions, it risks passing over the tangled economy of psychic investments in institutional groupings that connect the interests of its parts with those of the whole that they are parts of and from which they draw their existence, or at least fundamental aspects of their existence.

Shared psychic spaces and intermediate formations

We must therefore attend to the intermediate formations between individuals' psychic space and that provided by their grouping within an institution. Such formations properly belong neither to the individual nor to the grouping, but to their relationship. A constant feature of these formations is their biface status: the reciprocity they induce between the elements they connect, and the community they cement through unconscious pacts, contracts and consensus. They thereby articulate connections between element and whole in various configurations: mutual fit, mutual inclusion, co-inherence or continuous reversal.

Some psychic functions seem to belong to only one element of the whole (for instance, the function of framework or container in a caregiving institution, attributed to the therapeutic team). These will appear as shared intermediate formations to whose development and maintenance all constituent elements will jointly contribute either directly or indirectly, depending upon the constraints and vagaries of their place within the institution's structure and their own psychic configuration.

The framework of a therapeutic group fits into and relates reciprocally to the institutional setting itself, as well as with the therapist's own internal (including theoretical) framework. Everyone in their own way – including nursing staff – participates in the maintenance and reciprocity of settings, engaging in antagonistic (institution's administration versus therapeutic framework) as well as complementary relationships. When the setting is attacked at whatever level, its effects have repercussions for all the different elements that hold the setting together. We are usually alert to the catastrophic effects of this process upon individuals, but we should also consider its consequences in terms of structural changes that affect the institution's psychic foundations and which face its constituent parts as a whole with a disintegrative comeback by undifferentiated and non-integrated parts that had been deposited in different places in the setting. This is why I support the view that certain psychic functions that have devolved statically upon a single element of an ensemble or upon the ensemble itself must be dealt with in terms of their reciprocal relationships.

Every crisis or failure in intermediate formations raises issues about the institution itself and each individual's relationship with it, and the extent to which its unconscious contracts, pacts, agreements and consensuses either liberate trapped energies or paralyse the merest hint of finding new relationships. The logic of crisis and breakdown therefore includes various different levels and needs a multifocal analysis.

Unconscious alliances, pacts and contracts

Unconscious alliances are formed by the psychic apparatus of individual members of an intersubjective ensemble: a couple, group, family or institution. They determine the mode of linkage between individuals, and the ensemble's psychic space as a whole. Shared psychic reality is cemented by such alliances.

More precisely, by unconscious alliance I mean an intersubjective psychic formation constructed by individual subjects out of the links between them in order to strengthen certain beneficial processes, functions or structures in each member to such an extent that their mutual ties assume a decisive value for their psychic life. An ensemble bound together in this way derives its psychic reality solely from the alliances, contracts and pacts made by its members and which their place within the ensemble obliges them to keep. The concept of unconscious alliance implies obligation and subjection.

Describing them as unconscious means associating such alliances automatically and fundamentally with the process of repression, probably in the formation of the unconscious itself. Unconscious alliances certainly serve the repressive function, but they are also measures of super-repression, applying not only to unconscious contents, but to alliances themselves, which become instruments for maintaining repression. In other words, such alliances are themselves unconscious, and produce and maintain unconsciousness.

They tend to remain unconscious, and shape the unconscious most efficiently if the deepest interests of each individual party to the bond must for their own reasons be repressed. Then, the bond, its object and its rules are preserved, as are the alliance as an instrument of repression and the unconscious position of every party to it.

Freud (1930), in 'Civilization and its discontents', wondered about a third source of suffering apart from what nature inflicts and what comes from within our own bodies, stemming from human beings' inability to regulate their relationships with one another within the family, the state and society. The fact that the institutions we create make us suffer and fail to protect us from suffering led him to suspect that we are architects of our own suffering. He proposed an explanation for this curious behaviour in terms of the renunciation of direct satisfaction of narcissistic and object instincts, leading to the possibility of a pact that would benefit members of a community which 'protects us from violence, imposes duty, and makes love possible' in so far as it is a community with laws. What Freud was describing in this text is a psychic biface: instinctual renunciation and the advent of a community with laws have functions and significance both in individual psychic space and in the psychic space of social and institutional groupings. Freud was simultaneously describing the psychic basis both of the juridical function of institutions and of the legitimate affiliation of its members to a social whole.

Castoriadis-Aulagnier (1975) introduced the concept of a narcissistic contract to emphasise that each individual enters the world of society and succeeding generations as bearer of a mission to ensure the continuity of their own generation and social ensemble. The individual has a place in an ensemble, and if it is to ensure its continuity, the ensemble must make a narcissistic investment in its new member. The narcissistic contract assigns each individual a particular place, one that is offered by the group and given meaning by all the voices that have joined before each individual in a particular discourse congruent with the group's foundation myth. This includes ideals and values and transmits that social grouping's culture and certainties. Each individual must in some fashion take this discourse up as his or her own, forging a link with the group's founding ancestor.

A third form of unconscious alliance is defined by what I have called a negatory pact. By this I mean dedication in a trans-subjective ensemble, by general and unconscious agreement, to a doom of repression or negation, denial, disavowal, rejection and encapsulation. The pact functions to structure and maintain the alliance through complementarity in its members' interests. It ensures continuity in the investments and benefits connected with the maintenance of ideal functioning and the narcissistic contract. The alliance's cost tends to go unquestioned by those it joins in mutual interest, thereby satisfying the requirements of the interwoven economics both of its individual subjects and of the multi-subjective network to which they belong. The negatory pact therefore seems to be the narcissistic contract's opposite face and complement.

i have stressed two poles of the negatory pact: one organises alliances and trans-subjective ensembles while the other is defensive. Thus, each particular ensemble shapes itself around the pact's dual valency: positively on the basis of mutual investments, shared identifications, a community of ideals and beliefs, a narcissistic contract, and bearable modes of realising wishes, and negatively on that of common renunciations and sacrifices, effacements, rejections and repressions, omissions, and remainders. The negatory pact contributes to this dual organisation. Within an ensemble it generates non-signifiable, non-transformable matter: silent areas, toxic pockets, dustbin-spaces (Roussillon, 1987) or escape routes that keep the subject a stranger to his or her own history. In couples, families, groups and institutions, unconscious alliances, contracts and pacts are important in promoting repression and repetition.

In institutions, the pact applies to gaps in unrepresentable aspects of its origins (precisely the things that myth does represent), to the institution's foundations, to power play, death, sexuality and knowledge.

These propositions sketch what could be described as a twofold institutional topology, in which psychic and institutional 'places' may, or may fail to, achieve anamorphic figuration, for instance as places where things are put or disposed of (the 'skeleton cupboard') or interstitial places where intermediate or transitional formations come into play, or places created to receive and manage attempts to represent psychic and/or institutional conflict in figurative terms.[22] It also hints at the concept of an institutional genealogy whose purpose would be to describe and make sense of the unconscious psychic transmissions that clutter the institution's crypts and cupboards, namely those aspects of its ancestors' psyche that remain unrepresented.[23]

---

[22] Duez (1996) gave an excellent example of such a place when describing group psychoanalytic psychodrama practised in an institution for antisocial people.

[23] On this question see Rouchy (1978), Baranes (1984a, b), Missenard (1986), Kaës (1995).

The effort to conceptualise psychic reality in or of institutions leads to an attempt to define them in terms that take this reality into account. Thinking about institutions with therapeutic projects, Tosquelles and Oury judiciously described them as social apparatuses that facilitate exchange, organising them on this basis and exploring their issues, dynamics and economy from that perspective.

The perspective I suggest implies a different approach, in which institutions are not merely places for the imaginary fulfilment of repressed wishes. They are also places that provide opportunities for defences against these wishes to be organised. What is more, they tend to produce specific defences against anything that threatens their existence or the relationship of their members to the primary task that unites them. Finally, they ensure defence against anxieties whose origin or source do not seem directly connected with the institution itself.

The methodological problem

The methodological requirements of psychoanalysis could be expressed as follows: to construct a setting that is apt to reveal the effects of the unconscious and its subjective repercussions, so that where unconscious formations had been, I and We can be thought about as subject to them.

In referring to psychoanalysis, organisations for psychiatric care have tended to place more emphasis on its psychopathology and its metapsychology's interpretative 'grid' than on its method, which, if transposed wholesale, can only lead to an impasse. Considerable difficulties had to be overcome not only to adapt psychoanalytic technique to institutional conditions, but to perfect new methods that would conform to the methodological requirements of psychoanalysis and also be congruent with the therapeutic aims implicit in institutional mechanisms.

The ongoing debate about psychotherapy has been conducted with constant reference to the model of the classical cure, above all in the psychoanalytic critique of possible ways of bending psychotherapy towards readaptive or corrective ends.

Turning to psychoanalysis in an effort to understand 'interactions' between patients and their environment meets some internal resistance because the dominant psychoanalytic representation of causality is in terms of endopsychic determination. As soon as institutional therapy, whatever its historical expression, adopts as its primary aim the treatment of patients' profoundly disturbed relationships with other people, its metapsychological representations cease to be congruent with a method of treatment through transference and interpretation on the model of the classic psychoanalytic cure. Psychotherapy by an institutional 'milieu' implies acceptance and recognition of the transference of patients' relations with their families: an implicit offer is made to experience a situation in the institution's more or less differentiated spaces, in which all of a patient's interpersonal (and social) relationships will be considered. What can psychoanalytic technique offer for the gathering, location, management or analysis of transference modalities and contents of which it has no knowledge from practice on the couch, and for which, *a fortiori*, it has no training? Moreover, the very notion of treating a patient's entire relational network tends to raise the spectre of therapeutic omnipotence whose effects psychoanalysis has specifically repudiated.

Original settings structured around the therapeutic potential of group and institutional phenomena

Psychoanalysis has been under pressure to devise original settings whose structure might provide a better match between mental pathology and the therapeutic potential of group and institutional phenomena. While it recognised the pathogenic and alienating effects of institutional ties, it also saw *their* value for containment, transformation and symbol generation.

The critiques of groups and therapeutic communities most often formulated *a priori* by some Lacanian psychoanalysts were certainly revealing of their ideological position. Therapeutic communities were seen as vectors of an imaginary conception of society, while groups were regarded exclusively as places for alienating idealisation. They disregarded the structure-giving value of group work, which could offer a profound experience of the Unconscious and where subjectivity could emerge. Other Lacanian psychoanalysts, by contrast, favoured group arrangements as therapeutic psychoanalytic settings and manifested an extremely sensitive understanding of the processes that individuals worked through in them. Thus, Michaud wrote,

> In a group, what we will describe as transference relationships are ones in which parental imagoes appear transferred to persons, groups of persons, or the entire group, relationships that allow avoidance of appropriate separations, and thus invest these persons, or the group, with a role that is difficult to own completely. [...] It is through transference that individuals will gain access to the symbolic order, provided that there is exchange between the group and individuals. *It is precisely to regulate exchange between individual subjects' demands and the group's response to them that an institution will come into existence.* (Michaud, 1977, pp. 108–109)

We can endorse this proposition, which accords with work on the psychoanalytic approach to groups: it emphasises the difficult issue of treating the relationship between individual, group and institution and poses the problem of the settings peculiar to each order of psychic reality and their interplay.[24] Widening the field of psychoanalytic inquiry into institutions and the practice of brief or long-term intervention in institutions has contributed greatly to a refinement of work on methodological problems. A position somewhat on the outside makes it possible to see more clearly which routes are being taken to attain the aims and objectives that institutions set themselves. More detailed work on groups conducted on strictly psychoanalytic lines has also contributed to critical reflection on the methodology of institutional practice.[25]

Setting, container function, institutional envelopes and figurability

Reflection on the frame, in Bleger's sense of the word, prompted a number of psychoanalysts to think about individual or group psychotherapy within the institutional setting (Cadoret, 1984; Bégoin-Guignard, 1992) on a different basis from that in the early days of institutional therapy. They addressed the function of the setting in institutional patient care (Pinel, 1989), the multiplicity and interconnectedness of settings within institutional space, and whether the latter produce intrusion, collusion or differentiation.

This led to a redefinition of the guiding principles for therapeutic work in institutions. Houzel (1987) formulated three rules, analogous to the fundamental rule of psychoanalysis and inspired by the rules for psychoanalytic groups, within which a therapeutic institutional space should be created: the rule of confidentiality ('everything said at an institutional meeting belongs to the institution and should never cross its boundaries'), the rule of congruence (a problem should be discussed at a corresponding level of responsibility), and the rule of commonality (joint work between several teams concerned with the same problem).

The idea that an institution may function as a container in which under certain conditions transformation can occur is due to greater familiarity with Bion's works. The concepts of container–contained (Bion) and container–function (Kaës) have reactivated thinking about the need to find a psychic place in institutional space-time in which intrapsychic and

---

[24] There has been considerable progress in understanding these relationships, inspired notably by Bléandonu (cf. Bléandonu, 1987, 1992). We will take account of it when reviewing research on the setting and psychic envelopes.

[25] On these developments, cf. the work of Anzieu on groups and the unconscious (1975), my own research on the group psychic apparatus (Kaës, 1976), the group and the subject in the group (Kaës, 1993), and more recently my research on associative processes in groups (Kaës, 1995). On the conditions for psychoanalytic intervention in institutions, cf. Pinel (1996).

intersubjective anxieties and conflicts can be actualised, heard and thought about. In a recent thesis, Mellier (1994) produced an analysis of the paradox of institutions' containing function for anxieties aroused inside them: starting with the observation that individuals in institutions tend to lose their own boundaries and alter in their capacity for containment, he showed that institutions do have potential for containment if a work setting is sufficiently well established. He did his research on crèches, where he studied the teams' capacity to contain babies' anxieties in relation to staff anxieties.

Building on the original ideas of Bick, Anzieu's work on the skin ego and psychic envelopes stimulated research into group and institutional envelopes. Houzel (1987) emphasised their properties of elasticity, resistance, containment, permeability and consistency, specifying that institutional envelopes must be able to integrate contrasting elements, as Tustin had stressed in connection with autistic children: educational with therapeutic, masculine with feminine, paternal with maternal, and parental with fraternal.

Similarly, Pinel (1996) has analysed interactions that occur in institutional space, relating the characteristics of patients' psychic functioning to that of the caregiving team. He suggests thinking of the counter-actions, the symmetrical effects, and the splitting identified in a clinic as the result of massive projective identification by its patients. The functionality of the setting as a potential container is seen as dependent upon the caregiving group's capacity to analyse the intertransferential formations that have been mobilised.

These matters connect with other questions about the conditions necessary for an institution to function in a caregiving and therapeutic capacity. This is partially dependent upon constant work to avoid, anticipate and treat pathogenic phenomena variously caused (effects of patients' pathology, return of an unthought past into the present, instinctual unbinding and reversals, the workings of death on an institution),[26] but preservation of patients' relationship with a psychotherapist who has no power to make decisions about them is also a key feature. Bégoin-Guignard (1992) showed how this relationship provides a meeting-place between two structured and heterogeneous worlds: between private space and social space in the encounter between the intimacy of the analytic relationship and the patient's (and psychotherapist's) family, group and institution. Other research, for instance by Cahn (1978), illustrates the conditions and effects of the therapeutic process in

---

[26] Cf. research by Enriquez (1988) on the workings of death and process of coming apart under pressure, and by Diet (1996) on thanatophoric functions in institutions.

institutions. In a day hospital for adolescents therapeutic work had been compromised by a long period during which extremely archaic manifestations of the repetition compulsion had been in evidence. Caregiving staff were able take up these displays in day-to-day activities, understand them and work on their contents in a group setting in which playing with the multiplicity of experience and thought made it possible to start giving them representational form.

All this research raises the recurrent issues of how and under what conditions institutions and the spaces they contain may be able to deal with matters that cannot be worked on in private space, and how they deal with what is latent in the institution itself.

On the suffering of institutional alliances

Contemporary research is raising more detailed questions about the ways in which institutional settings either permit or prevent figuration and symbolisation. Research in this area has arisen especially from work on specific aspects of the suffering and pathology of institutional alliances (Kaës, Pinel and Kernberg, 1996).

I have tried to show that what psychoanalysts repress or deny in themselves tends to be transmitted and represented in the groups they are in and is organised symmetrically: what is not analysed and remains repressed or denied becomes the object of an unconscious alliance to ensure that the parties to an alliance shall know nothing of their own desires. These alliances shore up each person's own defence mechanism, and the contracts they are based on become associated with the beliefs and shared ideals on which the team and the institution's unity of identity and representation are founded. These concepts may shed fresh light upon the genesis of pathologies of linking. Analysis of the defensive manoeuvres performed by caretaking staff permits us to follow the effects that alliances have upon vagaries of thought processes and transference manifestations. It is the unconscious agenda of these alliances that comes back on to the institutional stage in the actions of patients and caregivers, and sometimes it is actually patients who try to give them figurative shape. A silenced and traumatic past may return in enigmatic form on to the institutional scene, looking for meaning.

In innovatory institutions, shared commitment to a new ideal involves recasting identificatory reference points and revising representations of identity through membership in such a way as to prevent the gap between ideals and identifications resolving into an alienating alliance. Caregivers face an activation of archaic anxieties: they sense danger every time the ground that supports their unconscious alliances, their narcissistic contracts and their identification with the object of the primary task is shaken. In institutional innovations the fantasy of bringing another institution into being that will ultimately come close to the fulfilment of narcissistic projections and mobilise heroic identifications, can put heavy pressure upon the individuals involved in the project, and eventually uncover buried and partially anaesthetised doubts, failures and sufferings.

My own analyses have produced a hypothesis – that if psychic disorder in the relationships amongst members of an institution, or in their individual relationships with the whole institution and its representatives, cannot be signified, interpreted or symbolised, it will go back into the institution on a stage in which psychic reality and other orders of reality are bound together in a confused and anxiety-ridden way.

7 CONTRIBUTION FROM SOUTH AMERICA
From the Group-as-Jigsaw-Puzzle to the Incomplete Whole

JANINE PUGET

Since the discovery of the 'group' as a therapeutic instrument and psycho-analytic entity, theorisation has proceeded in stages in which sometimes reductionist attempts to apply psychoanalytic theory have alternated with the production of new hypotheses, some of them extensions of classical theory and others truly innovative. The discoveries made within this movement in the field of group dynamics have yielded some terminology that has found its way into psychoanalytic theory.

A number of researchers in 1940s Argentina, including in particular Enrique Pichon Rivière, Juan José Morgan, Raúl Usandivaras and, later, Salomón Resnik, independently began to use therapy groups in hospital units for severely disturbed patients (Pichon Rivière, 1946). The same happened in other Latin American countries, involving among others Carlos Whiting (1958), Ramón Ganzarain and Hernán Davanzo in Chile and Ciro Martins, David Zimmerman (1958) and Blay Neto in Brazil. This work involved both medical and ancillary staff.

The results, in terms of the mobilising potential of groups, initially proved fascinating and surprising, as is usually the case with a new instrument or approach that re-opens a path thought to have become blocked. Work commenced on the group effect, which became an entity in its own right. Argentina gradually came to be the focus of this new instrument, whose protagonists – Madeleine Baranger, José Bleger, Alberto Fontana, León Grinberg, Marie Langer, Jorge Mom, Juan José Morgan, José Luis Muratorio, Janine Puget, Francisco Pérez Morales, Emilio Rodrigué, Gilou García Reinoso, Salomón Resnik, Marcela Spira and Raúl Usandivaras – formed a study group. They subsequently established the Argentine Group Psychology and Psychotherapy Association (AAPPdeG), on which a substantial proportion of present-day group-psychoanalytic activity centres. The Association held the first Latin

American Group Psychotherapy Congress in 1957. It gave the region's psychotherapists an opportunity to meet and acquaint themselves with different hypotheses and their theoretical and clinical consequences. In the same year, the widely known psychoanalysts León Grinberg, Marie Langer and Emilio Rodrigué (1957) published an initial psychoanalytically oriented book, *Psicoterapia de Grupo* [Group Psychotherapy], which summarised the work of the wider study group. They here developed the idea of the group as a closed unit and as a metaphor of a dissociated psychical apparatus along the lines of Sturgeon's (1954) science-fiction stor. *More than Human*. The work was a standard textbook for a number of years. The influence of Melanie Klein, as well as of the concepts of Bion and Ezriel, was clearly evident, and so too was the application of Freud's structural model. Another model used at that time was of the group as a jigsaw puzzle, whose pieces had to be fitted together to yield a picture. The theoretical foundation of these two models was complementarity and the homogeneous articulation of differences, together with the search for the unconscious group fantasy. Unconscious fantasy and unconscious group fantasy were seen as overlapping.

Pichon Rivière (1965) saw the group as a bridge between the social and individual levels and proposed a notion of group development based on a continuous dialectical spiral. He coined the acronym ECRO – from the Spanish initials of Operative Conceptual Reference Schema – for the set of always modifiable concepts that made group working possible. A group allowed the creation of a common denominator without eliminating the differences that transformed it into something complementary. He invented the technique of operative groups, which gained acceptance in various kinds of institutions in this part of the world.

Bleger's (1972) work on psychosis and the questioning of ideology resulted in the discovery of archaic levels of mental functioning with the emphasis on primitive processes. Among his ideas was that the setting could be seen as a space to deposit the products of primitive forms of functioning that might be manifested in it. For this purpose he drew upon the research of Elliot Jaques on institutions and their rules of operation. This concept became fundamental both to individual analysis and to the understanding of archaic levels of functioning.

By virtue of his intense interest in the unconscious aspects of communication and language, David Liberman (1956, 1960) contributed ideas on the dynamics of groups and couples, in which he emphasised in particular the mechanisms of projective and introjective identification. Working with seriously ill patients and using LSD, others, such as Alberto Fontana, Luisa Álvarez de Toledo and Francisco Pérez Morales, created their own group technique. The work with LSD was subsequently broken off for political and public-health reasons, but yielded some interesting results on regressive states.

On the basis of ideas due to Foulkes, Usandivaras (1970) devised an original technique – the marbles test – for the methodical investigation of group functioning. Later, drawing on the work of Jung, he identified various phases in regressive states. He saw the Jason myth as a paradigm of group activity.

Many other models were conceived and put forward, most of which regarded the group as a unity made up of a number of parts. Hence such concepts as the leader, the scapegoat (Pichon Rivière), the spokesman or announcer (Berenstein, 1976) or the monopolist (Puget, 1992).

These authors, all active members of the Argentine Psychoanalytic Association (APA), each introduced a personal understanding of group dynamics. However, the many different approaches had in common the aim of discovering primitive levels of communication and of distinguishing between the group and individual settings.

Diversity of the conceptual field today

The psychoanalytic entities to which group theory is currently applied are couples, families and groups. Those active in this field today (apart from the workers already mentioned), using a setting of this kind with a psychoanalytic approach, have come from different backgrounds. Some, such as Ana María Fernández, Ana María Cueto and Armando Bauleo (who at present lives in Italy) are psychoanalytically oriented social psychologists of the Pichon Rivière school (Pichon Rivière et al., 1970). Others are psychiatrists working with psychotic patients, who have independently developed the ideas of Pichon Rivière, Juan José Morgan, Raúl Usandivaras and Salomón Resnik (for instance Resnik, 1985). Still others, such as Berenstein, took as their starting point the difficulties of treating psychotic patients in individual analysis, but then came to concentrate on family analysis. Berenstein (1976) put forward his own theory of family psychoanalysis, in which he laid the foundations for the understanding of the 'unconscious family structure'. Others again were originally child analysts who then turned to family analysis. A final group – Bernard, Romano, Puget, C. Paz, Rodrigué and Mom (Puget et al., 1980) – were no doubt inspired by the failures or limits of day-to-day practice with individual patients to develop a group theory including the concept of the 'group configuration', which is now enshrined in our culture.

In the field of couple and family psychoanalysis, important research has also been conducted by Janine Puget, Augusto Picolo, César Merea and Edmundo Zimmerman (Zimmerman et al., 1997). Berenstein and Puget set up a department for psychoanalytic research on couples (Puget, 1992) and families (Berenstein, 1976), in which a number of professionals are involved. These two authors train therapists in Uruguay, Brazil and Colombia, where institutions based on the so-called link-type configuration have been established.[27]

Psychoanalytic theory has also been applied to various theories of psychodrama, such as, in particular, those of Eduardo Pavlovsky, Hernán Kesselman, Olga Albizuri de García and Mónica Zuretti.

Each of these workers has set up either an institution of his or her own or a department of link-based psychoanalysis within an official psychoanalytic institution.

Institutions

I should now like to mention just a few of the institutions established since the beginnings of group psychotherapy in Latin America. First, there is the entire welfare-based official Institute of Neurosis in Argentina, comprising thirty therapy groups led by Luis Basombrío and Carlos Paz. Enrique Pichon Rivière formed the Argentine Social Studies Institute (IADES) and, in 1958, conducted an experiment at Rosario in which he applied his operative-group technique to students from different faculties, an approach that subsequently spread to all the country's universities. Dr Luchina's initial work with groups of heart patients as well as with groups of doctors eventually led to his adoption of the Balint group technique.

Mothers' and children's groups have also been established in various hospital units. The pioneers of these settings include Jorge Mom, Arminda Aberastury, Gilou García Reinoso and Clara Sapochnik.

---

[27] We use the concept of the link (*vínculo* in Spanish) in a precise sense that differs from that of Bion, Pichon Rivière and others. For us it denotes an unconscious structure that joins two or more subjects connected by two types of relationship in such a way as to generate an unconscious choice. The subjects find themselves determined by this relationship, which is original and transcends the individual wish. This implies a distinction between an object relationship and a relationship between subjects (a link). The members of the group maintain a mutual relationship of externality whereby the other is always alien, different and other (in the sense of 'otherness'), while at the same time similar. The mechanism of identification is thus displaced, so that an important place is occupied by everything that has to do with psychic work on difference and what the presence of a subject imposes on another. [Translator's note: The Spanish noun *vínculo* translates readily as 'link', but the adjectival form *vincular* and the abstract noun *vincularidad* present difficulties of translation. The former has usually been rendered here by a phrase such as 'link-type', while the word 'linkness' has been coined for the latter.]

Argentina, and indeed South America generally, seems to have lacked long-established institutions like the Tavistock Institute or Northfield. However, Pichon Rivière's early experience at the Buenos Aires Psychiatric Hospital may be deemed to have yielded the concept of the scapegoat, or the 'patient designed in the group structure', and also marked the appearance of the link as a concept with a life and theoretical status of its own. Work with community, family and group structures thus assumed particular importance.

Later, in 1958, Dr Mauricio Goldemberg established a psycho-pathology unit in the Dr Luis Alfaro General Hospital, involving psychoanalysts and others and working with both outpatients and inpatients, as well as within the community outside the hospital. The basis of his approach, as well as of the organisation of the hospital unit, was psychoanalytic theory and the concept of unconscious group structure. This work was interrupted by the dictatorship in 1976. A part of the organisation is now operational again, but without Dr Goldemberg, who has moved to Caracas, Venezuela. Today, work on psychoanalytic and link concepts centres on the AAPPdeG. This association remains the umbrella organisation for a large number of research workers and professionals. In a phenomenon that may be peculiar to Argentina, the country's official IPA-recognised institutions have for some years now included departments of group, family and couple psychoanalysis which operate as research units.

The many group psychotherapy institutions in Brazil include in particular those headed by David Zimmerman (1957) and Blay Neto. Saúl Peña in Peru has developed a system of his own in which he sees his groups four or five times a week, using an approach grounded in psychoanalytic theory. Family and couple psychoanalysis have progressed further than group analysis in Colombia, although some institutions in that country are conducting field work against the troubled background of social violence. In Chile, Davanzo has been working with groups since the 1950s. Note that all these approaches had their origins in the first Latin American Group Psychotherapy Congress, held in Buenos Aires in 1957.

Individual analysis and group analysis, an alliance with vicissitudes

There was both a negative and a positive aspect to the commencement of our analytic work with groups.

As to the former, the criterion for a group indication was at first economic: those who could not afford individual treatment could join a group. Alternatively, patients whose one-to-one analyses had failed could try group therapy. Groups were said to be superficial, and so on. Such ideas were handed down by tradition, and it is a legacy of this resistance that many still consider them valid.

The positive aspect is the fact that failures were used creatively. Hypotheses were extended, thereby conferring legal status on link-based psychoanalysis in the specific forms of family, couple and group analysis. Each of these settings is subsumed under the heading of the 'link-type configuration'. Janine Puget, Marcos Bernard, Esther Romano and Gladys Games Chaves (1980) first developed this idea in their book *El grupo y las configuraciones vinculares* [The group and link-type configurations].

Once again, failures, desertions and the ills afflicting patients who experienced the limits of a given setting were the main driving force behind our emphasis on this concept.

Link-type configurations

In Argentina, dissatisfaction with theory thus led to the creation of a concept combining space and time within a stable link-type structure. This system involves the unconscious representation of a link that differs from the classical conception of an unconscious representation.

The link-type configuration now extends to all settings involving more than two persons. In one-to-one analysis, only a small space is reserved for the link, which is the aspect of the analyst that cannot be reduced to fantasy, by virtue of which the analysis with this particular analyst is not exactly the same as it would be with another. Each analysis, or rather each analytic couple, has a particularity, which is conferred on it by the reality of each ego.

Theoretical and technical consequences of the proposed models

In all the models proposed, interpretative technique from the beginning comprised interpretations directed towards the group as a whole, understanding being based primarily on the mechanisms of introjective and projective identification, or on the fantasies constructed by the group as a whole. In addition, attempts of varying scientific validity have been made to explain the group phenomenon by such mechanisms as unconscious-to-unconscious communication, the primordial matrix or the unconscious structure. While seeking to confer a status on intersubjectivity, these approaches have at the same time made for limited understanding of an intersubjectivity involving such concepts as difference and otherness.

Foreign influences in Argentina

We in Argentina and in Latin America at large were at first strongly influenced by, on the one hand, Foulkes, Ezriel and Bion and, on the other, Slavson and Schilder. We later became familiar with the contributions of the 'French school', headed by Anzieu and Kaës, who established CEFFRAP,[28] an organisation that positively influenced a group of Latin American professionals and indeed continues to enrich their work today. The ideas of Elliott Jaques helped to facilitate developments in the field of institutional functioning. The social psychology of Kurt Lewin and others also opened up the field of observable phenomena and underlay aspects of the research of Pichon Rivière and his followers. George Mead, too, featured in the frame of reference of many of us. Hare, Borgatta, Bales and Homans (see Hare et al., 1961; Homans, 1950) helped us to understand group dynamics from a different point of view. The exchanges proceeded mainly in a single direction: from abroad – that is, from Europe or North America – to Latin America. A two-way flow arose only with the passage of time, although it has not yet become a steady stream owing to the traditional north–south geopolitical divide.

The main schools of psychoanalytic psychotherapy from which the various institutions derive their inspiration break down as follows. One group, headed by Raúl Usandivaras (1957) until his death, has developed Foulkes's ideas on the primordial matrix and profound regressive states within a Jungian frame of reference with the addition of shamanic techniques. Another group, led initially by Janine Puget and later by Marcos Bernard – a follower of Kaës – developed its own approach and established an important research unit within the AAPPdeG (Puget and Bernard, 1986). I shall concentrate on these ideas, because they exemplify their author's creativity in further developing a clear theoretical foundation. Others, among whom I would today count Berenstein and Puget, have been developing the concept of the link and the link-type configuration as a system involving different modes of contact between the subject and the outside world – the outside world being the subject's own body, other people or the group as a whole. This model establishes the status of the unconscious foundation of 'linkness' and recognises the unconscious effects arising in link-type settings. A great deal of intensive work with therapy groups is, of course, being conducted in other Latin American countries, and the relevant trends and theories all bear an individual stamp, but I believe that they all broadly conform to the model outlined above. The workers concerned include Dr Waldemar Fernandez (São Paulo), a former President of the Latin American Group Psychotherapy Federation, Dr Saúl Zimmerman and Dr Saúl Peña (Lima, Peru). Today Dr D.E. Zimmermann and Dr L.C. Osorio (1997) are pursuing their own research in this field (Zimmermann et al., 1997).

---

[28] Centre d'Etudes Français pour la Formation et la Recherche Active en Psychologie [French Study Centre for Training and Active Research in Psychology].

Others, too, not belonging to the AAPPdeG, have contributed to the field from a psychoanalytic standpoint within other institutions and university bodies. Group, family and couple therapy is taught at various universities.

Theoretical problems

In the introduction to this book, R.D. Hinshelwood and Marco Chiesa perspicaciously draw attention to the obstacles to conferring a status of its own on the group as an entity and to the various issues that thereby confront us. Considering the group as a psychoanalytic entity, two main orientations emerge. The first sees the constitution of a group as an extension and transformation of individuality (from the intrapsychic to the interpsychic or intersubjective); while the second regards the group as an entity in its own right having a link-type unconscious representation that brings the link into existence and distinguishes it from what is understood by the term 'object relationship'. I include Puget in the latter school, and recognise that this formulation demands a substantial rethinking of metapsychology and hence a revision of the fundamental hypotheses of psychoanalysis.

The first group, which sees 'groupness' as a transformation of early object relations, must also be subdivided. Here we find a long list of possibilities, which merely reflect the diversity of psychoanalytic frames of reference and the ways in which they are combined with group theory. However, the ideas of Kaës, as he himself presents them in the previous chapter, constitute an original theory of the group psychical apparatus.

Marcos Bernard has further developed the ideas of Kaës and proposes the following.[29]

The 'working unit' of group psychoanalysis is unconscious phantasy. This confers content and, *more importantly, structure*, not only on the psychical apparatus, to whose formation it contributes, but also on the links which the subject will forge throughout his life. One of these fantasies is that which establishes the *internal group* (which differs from the groups of Pichon Rivière and René Kaës) – a triangular structure constituting the basis of personal identity. Fantasy, and in particular what Freud called primal fantasy, is seen less as a repertoire of contents than as *structural forms established from birth* – experiential contents that construct structure. These forms allow the establishment of a series of categories – inside/outside, before/after, the same/other – which gradually delimit the *edges* of the psyche-to-be, 'closing' it off in a process that

---

[29] This summary of Bernard's ideas was supplied to me by the author.

culminates in the Oedipus complex. These categories constitute Freud's primal repression, which takes place during the course of a process. Even if the closure of the psychical apparatus is never wholly completed (so that primal repression, too, is never complete), the onset of the Oedipus complex marks the point where it becomes possible to perceive the other in his or her otherness and the predominance of neurotic structures in the psychical apparatus. Whereas the formation of structure in the earliest psychic life of the *infans* coincides with its experiences in the context of its significant links, subsequent experiences will meet with a protostructure that will condition them and tend to interpret them. This phenomenon lies at the root of the transference, in which a prior experience conditions a present-day one.

Groups (links) are the natural locus for the unfolding of fantasies, which takes place simultaneously on a number of levels or planes. The deepest primary fantasy level indicates the limits of each individual – or the lack of such limits – relative to the group as a whole. The level of the more elaborate fantasies gives rise to the 'transference neurosis', whose foundation is thus non-discrimination (what Bleger called 'syncretic sociability'), which is deposited in the group setting (whether the group is psychoanalytic or spontaneous). As postulated by Freud in 1905, the more elaborate levels come to hold sway over the simpler ones.

The concept of transference can be superimposed on that of the unconscious, as one of the characteristics of the latter is the loss, or relative lack, of limits of the self. It consists in the projective superimposition of an unconscious fantasy on a link-type structure. The transference is produced by a subject on to a link. It thus also affects the transferor.

In the countertransference, the 'other' of the link finds himself or herself forced to occupy the place assigned to him or her by the unfolding of the transference, or to confront the alternative of remaining outside the link. The link being a necessary instrument for underpinning the syncretic aspects of identity, remaining outside it places the subject in a situation of deidentification, which is all the more serious the more his or her primary narcissism remains unresolved. If, as Bleger put it, at this level the subject is the link, without this link there is no subject.

Two levels of the enactment produced by the unfolding of fantasy can be distinguished. If Eros predominates, there is at least a partial recognition of the otherness of the other (a phenomenon I call *drama*): the *as if* is preserved and a context of play or trial exists. The main purpose of repetition is then working through. If Thanatos has the upper hand, however, we have what Freud called the repetition compulsion. What is then dominant is something that is exhausted in drive discharge. Recognition of the other's otherness is minimal and an *in itself* substitutes for the *as if*. This constitutes a psychotic moment in the group situation or session.

This model does not call into question the essence of Freudian metapsychology, although consideration would need to be given to the metapsychological status of drama, since it has features of both the primary process (thing presentations) and the secondary process (recognition of the object and a certain internal logic). It probably has to do with what André Green calls tertiary processes. At any rate, the logical level of abstraction of fantasy, like that of the transference, is lower than that of the drive of metapsychology.

Belonging and identity

In Puget's frame of reference, which she shares with Berenstein, the construction of belonging differs from that of identity and takes on a status of its own. In this connection, the research of these authors has yielded insights into the vicissitudes of the psychic system. They regard the unconscious representation of the occupation of respective places as a structure, because it determines the feeling of belonging to a certain context – a couple, family or socio-cultural group – just as one's belonging to one's own body, as a link-type space, is delimited by an edge. The system is made up of different representations, which we call, respectively, intersubjective (that constructed between two or more subjects); trans-subjective (that of subjects permeated by culture and living within society); and intrasubjective (that of the subject with his drive and fantasy world). Each representational group can be thought of as situated in a virtual space, and a gap is deemed to exist between each. Only certain contents pass from one space to another, so that the concept of transference has called for revision. The mechanisms involved in the definition of places and the way in which they are occupied are correlation and interrelationship. One defines a subject in relation to another. There cannot be a father or mother without a child, or a sibling without another, and so on. Interrelationship defines what circulates between two or more subjects. For these mechanisms to assume their link-related meaning, sharing of a context of space and time is essential, for this is the only way to construct the network within which the link-type representation is and will be forged. This takes the form of the acquisition of a code and a history. I regard these mechanisms as possessing the same status as those described by Freud for the primary process, complementing those of displacement, condensation and symbolisation. The link-based representation excludes all meanings that inherently oppose the formation of a given link. These come to occupy the place of negativity that forms the link-based unconscious. The link also includes a representation for what permanently identifies the external and the surprising, establishing a specific temporality that differs from the temporality of intersubjectivity.

The sense of belonging is established by a mechanism, similar in some respects to identification, that we have called *attribution*, which defines the place occupied by a subject in a context.

The mechanism of attribution is made up of two movements that always conflict – a passive one, whereby the subject receives from society as a whole or another group, certain characteristics and values; and an active one through which he adopts the attributions assigned to him by that society or group. Although it is impossible not to belong, one can impress an individual stamp on belonging in so far as one can choose how to belong. This capacity to choose (Puget, 1992) is conceived as primal and based on the faculty of judgement that underlies the birth of thought (Freud, 1895).

If we regard belonging as different from the acquisition of identity, we can explain the conflicts of transculturation, the mental concessions involved in the demand to belong without questioning the relevant values, and the strength of certain psychic breakdowns in situations of social or natural upheaval. We can then also more readily understand the mechanisms underlying institutional conflicts, where the subjects involved appear to be behaving irrationally and emotionally, for these are forms of functioning inherent in the 'social subject'. Ultimately, we need not think systematically in terms of dissociation when a subject displays conflicts in one link and not in another.

On the empirical level, living – or simply being – with another, thinking and sharing experiences activates an unconscious mechanism which has two implications. The subject on the one hand tends to confuse sharing with being the same, and on the other rejects having anything to do with another when the experience is felt to be an invasion of his or her own boundaries. The proximity of the subjects gives rise to the illusion of the disappearance of the space between them, so that we may come to believe that the strange, or alien, has been eliminated. The strange can, of course, readily be associated with the sinister in the various senses of the word. Understandably, what is most difficult to accept in a link is the unattainability and ungraspability of the other, although becoming a subject is conditional upon this acceptance.

I also see the link in terms of the construction of subjectivities on which the creation of an area of meeting depends. The other's subjectivity as a necessary condition gives rise to problems absolutely different from those occurring when the psyche reconstructs a past scene with another who is now absent. Speaking about another who is absent is not the same as speaking in the presence of this other, who imposes an inescapable externality on the subject concerned. This introduces various connotations of the concept of representation, such as mourning and loss, or model-related aspects.

Subjectivity is constructed during the course of a process that makes the link a unity necessary for a subject to exist. The presence of the other, while essential, is also a source of suffering which could illusorily be avoided if there were an object relationship only. The space within which a link is constructed possesses an anxiety-transforming potential which makes the toleration of anxiety feasible.

Inherent in object relationship is the idea of unidirectionality, a flow from the demand towards the object, whereas the link contains the idea of bidirectionality: the fact of being at one and the same time the subject of one's own demand and the object of the other's demand constitutes the basis of the link and of its limits.

Object relationship and the link oppose each other in that, the more 'linkness' is invaded by the (intrapsychic) object relationship, the less potential the link space has for development, and vice versa. This leads to the conclusion that, in order for there to be a link, the object relationship must be repressed – in particular, those object relations that make the original links incompatible with a certain type of 'linkness'.

These notions help us to understand why patients may long for individual sessions when in a link-type setting and for the presence of the other when in an individual setting.

The ongoing debate concerns the constitution of a link-based unconscious as an extension of the unconscious defined by Freud. Without this concept, it is impossible to think of a primary 'groupness' or to discuss whether the concepts of parricide and the primitive horde as an application of the Oedipal theory are valid explanations of the capacity to forge links. However, given that many authors refer to a group unconscious, a group matrix and so on, very clear and detailed descriptions are necessary for the purpose of distinguishing between frames of reference.

My position may be summarised as follows. The human subject *is condemned to belong and to cathect the other*. This sets in train an unconscious representation in the form of a 'zero structure', which is a representation of virtual places and of functions, to be subsequently occupied by persons (subjects).

The group as an open, incomplete system

In view of the theoretical transformations arrived at above, I would now define a link and its capacity for transformation as a whole that is always incomplete, which lacks a piece and tends to become dislocated. To an external observer, it appears as an incomplete landscape, which the mind defensively completes in the illusory belief in the existence of completeness. It is characteristic of link-type configurations that the image is ephemeral and not repeated.

In order for a 'group effect' to come about, a connection, a space or a meaning must be lacking. This is what gives rise to sense. The other(s), being always alien for structural reasons, is/are defined as including an unknowable element, which becomes the engine of 'linkness', fuelled by the wish to know.

The paradigm of linkness is the misunderstanding – equivalent to a parapraxis in an individual patient. I define misunderstanding as a form of language overlain by a clearly understood assumption. In it, different meanings are confused with similar meanings, thus reducing the difference between the originators of acts of communication. This abolishes the beneficial capacity of distance to give rise to rich communication.

Extrapolation of hypotheses

Psychoanalysis customarily uses hypotheses applicable to, and devised for the understanding of, the functioning of a single mind, and hence a certain type of relationship that concentrates on the object relationship, unconscious fantasy and how these unfold in the transference/counter-transference in an individual analytic setting. The same hypotheses can be applied to the constitution of a link.

This carries certain risks. The underlying assumption in this case is that only a single-patient setting can be deemed to be analysis and that anything else is a mere application of psychoanalysis or 'psychotherapy', which is regarded as inferior to the prestige discipline of psychoanalysis.

Who is the patient?

The work of Berenstein and Puget on the metapsychology of the link and of the object relationship has led them to rethink the concept of the patient. They now consider that the 'patient' or 'analysand' may be an individual subject, a couple, a family or a group, each of these being an analysable psychoanalytic entity.

It is therefore our work in other settings that has confirmed the validity of our instrument, namely, analytic understanding with certain necessary additions. Let me stress the importance of the presence or absence of an interlocutor. A single mind carries on a dialogue with its internalised interlocutor, whereas two or more do so with persons of irreducible externality. There is therefore a difference between an analyst as the recipient of the intrasubjective transference, which is thus included in the different identificatory models proffered to him or her by the analysand, and an analyst occupying one of the poles of the link between two subjects involved in a link-type transference with its particular features. A distinction must also be drawn between an analyst included in an intersubjective configuration and one who forms part of a scene in which an intense link-type transference is unfolding.

The transferences arising in groups may be said to differ from those mobilised in individual psychoanalysis. This implies that not every object, not every setting and not every situation is appropriate for arousing transferences. This notion therefore also includes the idea of a reality not susceptible to modification by fantasy. This takes us back to Freud's idea that every delusion rests on a foundation of reality, which it seeks to obliterate. If a component of the real other presents itself as a resistance to the wish to turn the other into an extension of the subject, the theory of projective identification may only support the resistance and be insufficient for working with groups. On the other hand, better results will accrue from a theory in which the other/the alien/the unknown confronts the ego with the need to deploy mechanisms for avoiding the painful contact with the unknown or, conversely, to connect that which belongs to the subject to that which is alien to it. This has to do with the capacity of the psychical apparatus to use partial analogies for the creation of models whereby it can apprehend the different and produce something new.

I have discussed this model at some length because quite a number of analysts are now investigating the relevant problems in depth.

Social violence and groups

A special place ought perhaps to be assigned in Argentina to the workers who have researched social violence and its metapsychological status (Puget and Kaës, 1989). These concerns have led to an emphasis on the ideological and ethical components of the theory. The many psychoanalysts who have investigated these matters include Julia Braun, María Lucila Pelento, Marcelo Vignar and Maren Ulriksen de Vignar – the last two Uruguayan – as well as Vicente Galli, Lia Ricón, Diana Kordon, Lucila Edelman and Janine Puget. Some Argentinian analysts living outside the country should be included in this list, namely Silvia Amati, of Geneva, who has concentrated on ethical issues connected with torture, and Yolanda Gampell, in Israel, who is studying various situations of social violence and with whom we maintain important contacts. We have also had valuable exchanges with René Kaës, who has stimulated our research from his own viewpoint. The topic of family violence, too, is the particular concern of a number of workers headed by Diana Golberg. This research has afforded an understanding of the torturer–victim relationship, the state of threat, impunity, the status of external reality as different from that potentially resulting from projections of the subject's ego, and problems of transmission to the second and third generations. At the same time, however, precisely because of the social violence that prevailed under the various dictatorships, therapy groups in institutions and, on occasion, privately organised ones too, disappeared or were at least reduced in number. Periods of great social upheaval in the Latin American countries have constituted a direct attack on the life of therapy groups. The message from the dictatorial systems was that groups were dangerous hotbeds of subversion. As a result, groups declined or were attended by fewer people, and those who continued to attend did so with a greater or lesser degree of rationalisation. This situation was also observed in Brazil. Group activity has resumed only in recent years. At present there are more psychoanalytically oriented therapy groups within institutions in Brazil, Peru and, perhaps, to some extent also in Chile, than in Argentina. An evaluation of this situation would call for statistics, which I do not for the time being have at my disposal. However, it is important to take note of the phenomenon, as the compilation of data is at least a beginning pending the availability of a valid theory.

The socio-political context has penetrated into our science and consulting rooms and compelled us to gain a rapid understanding of our contemporary situations. This may be contrasted with the fact that it took Europe 40 years to come to terms with Nazism and its consequences. We succeeded fairly quickly in producing some ideas based on our particular experiences, thus enabling us to make the best of a sorry situation.

One consequence has been a series of interdisciplinary exchanges with epistemologists (Gregorio Klimovsky, Juan Indart, Eduardo Rabossi and Guillermo Maci), historians, anthropologists and semiologists. Interdisciplinary study groups have frequently been formed over a period of many years. In Argentina, unlike other countries, prominent personalities are relatively accessible. Elsewhere such people usually belong to universities and official institutions and have no time, or need, to lead private study groups. Once again, we may conclude that, although Argentinian political society customarily ill-treats its research workers by denying them an appropriate economic status, the scientific community has been enriched by the exchanges that have thereby proved possible.

Alternation of enthusiasm and disappointment

The life of our science has been characterised by a constant alternation of so-called individual, two-person or one-person psychoanalysis with psychoanalysis based on other settings, resulting in reciprocal flows of theory and idealisation.

Idealisation is a necessary condition for the establishment of a link and the creation of a project. We are accustomed to see idealisation as a disturbance, and so it is when it leads to the paralysis of certain linking movements or to excessive distortions. As stated earlier, work with groups began in an atmosphere of enormous enthusiasm due to the discovery of a method and setting which answered some of the questions that our day-to-day practice had left unresolved. It is a matter of observation that this phenomenon is not peculiar to our community. Many of us have been more enthusiastic about one setting than another, and perhaps the same thing happens to us during the course of a single day. Why should this be? It is because we assess the quality of our instrument by the criterion of clinical findings or the new ideas that have arisen, and then believe that we can solve all our problems. However, another reason is the perpetual conflict between individuality and sociability, self and others, internal world and external world. These waves of enthusiasm, falling-in-love and excitement have a creative element, but the other side of this coin is the disparagement, discontent or anxiety that ensue when a setting does not yield the hoped-for solutions.

An analyst who is aware that his or her working life involves these distinct phases will probably adopt a calmer attitude to them and use the periods of enthusiasm to develop novel hypotheses.

On the one hand, then, these reflections constitute a retrospective look at what we have achieved, at the various phases through which we have passed On the other, however, they represent in particular a perhaps illusory attempt to predict the possible fate of our therapies. It is for this reason that history is sometimes made.

Scientific vs social context

A possible approach to the foregoing is that of the relationship between the socio-cultural context, the scientific context in which theories are developed, and the personal context of the subjects responsible for them. Our basic data will be the language of scientific discourse, which, as we observe, is replete with words, terms and ideas used in day-to-day communication. The oscillations that sometimes become harmful to the growth of science and theories are manifest. The social context, the theories and the theorists constitute a whole, whose rules of transformation must be known. The social context exercises alternately a negative and a positive influence, depending on the more or less chaotic vicissitudes affecting each of these situations. As everyone knows, the bourgeois ideology of the beginning of the twentieth century impressed a particular stamp on Freud's theoretical findings. Equally, the interpretations of patients' sexuality that were revolutionary at the time have now ceased to be so, whereas today, if we interpret our patients' ideologies, we may well be told that we are ideologising them or – even worse for a psychoanalyst – that we are concentrating solely on the manifest content at the expense of the unconscious. Ideologies nowadays occupy the place formerly assumed by sexuality. Analysing the ideology of a group's members is tantamount to reaching the limits of compatibility necessary for the creation of the area of meeting.

The work of forging connections between individual (singular) and group (plural) is, as a rule, strongly coloured by the need to obtain the consensus of the scientific community of one's own country or institution. Hence the need to recognise the role of such factors as an individual country's culture, the therapist's training background and so on.

Questions

A number of questions are posed by the history of group psychotherapy in Argentina and certain other countries, such as, for example, Brazil, Uruguay, Chile and Peru. Here are some of them.

- Does a group have specific defence mechanisms, alternating between compaction and dispersion, or is the main anxiety phobic, with the group's members swinging between claustrophobia and agoraphobia? Or is it a matter of basic assumptions as formulated by Bion? Alternatively, are projective and introjective identification the main mechanisms underlying the life of a group? Does the struggle between individual and group elements permit interventions directed both to individuals and to the group, or should interpretations be made to the group only? Given the impossibility of not communicating, do the defences deployed have the purpose of avoiding the information overload resulting from the fact of belonging to a group? Are difference and externality the main factors of resistance, or do they, on the other hand, perform a dynamising function?
- The group being a structure, a system governed in closed or open form, a dissociated mental body, and the theatre of an unconscious fantasy, can one speak of a group unconscious, and if so, what is its status? Is the unconscious singular only, and is the group unconscious preconscious?

● Is group psychotherapy an application of psychoanalysis or an extension of it? In the latter case, we should need to revise and extend the basic psychoanalytic hypotheses, such as the theory of the unconscious, the theory of narcissism, object relations and the transference, the theory of identification and the theory of meaning, to postulate specific group defence mechanisms, and to distinguish the specific anxieties pertaining to groups.

● What is the locus of the drama and of the language of action?

● Should we use free association and allow freedom to act as well as to speak? Should interpretation be directed to the group or to each member? Should interpretation be of the group unconscious, of an unconscious fantasy constructed jointly by the members, of the object constituted by the group, of the group configuration, or of the role structure?

● Should we work with patients, with students, or within institutions – whether hospitals, commercial and industrial undertakings, educational establishments, etc.?

My provisional conclusion, based on a consideration of the above questions, is that groups focus attention on a number of factors – in particular, the failures of the individual setting, patients' requirements, the importance of the socio-cultural and political context, the influence of British, American and French workers in our field, and a particular anxiety on the part of the Argentinians about psychoanalysis, coupled with a permeability to it and a curiosity that impels us to delve further into these matters. For the same reason, a large number of professionals from different backgrounds have seized upon the group phenomenon and turned it to account.

Groups, of course, are now acknowledged to have a huge potential for transformation, and are used in a wide range of disciplines, where they as a rule yield favourable results. This is an observable phenomenon, as is also the difficulty of forming ongoing, satisfactory groups in the present social context. Could it be that groups formed for specific purposes are now tending to become collective entities intended to offset the increasing trend towards isolation?

A final point

The above account throws light on certain trends that I regard as promising in that they make us aware of new problems. However, like any story, it is not necessarily what actually happened, but it is nevertheless the story that can be constructed.

Part Two
British Contributions

As in Part One, there is an introductory chapter by the editors (Chapter 8) to give a general overview of ideas that have developed in Britain in the last 50 years. This is followed by three chapters (9–11) from authors who describe different aspects of this development.

Group analysis is not accorded the status of a chapter on its own, but is dealt with quite thoroughly in the introductory Chapter 8. This is partly to do with the uncertainty whether group analysis recognises itself as sufficiently within the psychoanalytic arena, or whether it is now a divergent tradition which has broken from its origins. This growing independence is perhaps to be recognised in the difficulty the editors found in finding a group analyst who was experienced in organisational work, and who would contribute a chapter to our book.

8 Introduction to the Span of the British Tradition

R.D. HINSHELWOOD AND MARCO CHIESA

Early roots of a psychoanalytic social psychology in Britain were emerging, as elsewhere, contemporaneously with the development of social psychology as an experimental science in the early part of this century (Jones, 1923; Sofer, 1972). But the most remarkable single locus of development in Britain occurred in wartime in Northfield Military Hospital in the early 1940s (Rees, 1945). Partly inspired by Northfield were parallel developments in the war effort (Harrison, 2000): the War Office Selection Boards (WOSBs) (Bion, 1946; Vinden, 1977) and the Civil Resettlement Units (Curle, 1947).

Northfield

Rickman (1950) had set out a typology of groups – one-person, two-person or multi-person; and he had influenced his one-time analysand Wilfred Bion to draw up a memorandum on the 'group' life of a mental hospital where they were both at the time working. This so-called Wharncliffe memorandum is now lost (Trist, 1985). The experiment did not take place at the Wharncliffe Hospital in Sheffield, but something of it did gain a brief life at Northfield Military Hospital where Bion established a novel regime in the rehabilitation wing (Bion and Rickman, 1943; Bléandonu, 1984). Bion designed the wing with a military rather than a hospital culture. His men in the rehabilitation wing were slovenly, and had little zest for rehabilitation, so he withdrew his medical presence (Main, 1983). When some of the men began to present themselves for his help he demanded they dress and conduct themselves in proper military manner. He announced that, if they wished for his help, the men should consider for themselves how to tackle the problem of their wing. He conceived the problem as a neurosis of the group, and that should be designated the enemy which, with him, they should fight. He designated himself as the

145

leader of this 'scallywag battalion' (Bion and Rickman, 1943). This the so-called 'first Northfield experiment' succeeded in establishing a fighting morale amongst the men, as a group.

The Northfield 'experiments' (Bridger, 1946, 1990; Main, 1978; de Maré, 1983; Harrison, 2000) were various, and gave rise following World War II to developments that fan out in a number of directions. The new way of looking at the organisation as a field of dynamics in its own right was brought into being and forged in the heat of the clash with a military approach to organisation. Some of the experiments were quickly terminated; other commanding officers took a more conciliatory and compromising approach (Main, 1983).

What was novel was the attempt to substitute a non-judgemental observational method into an institution which was, by tradition, administered with military discipline (Hinshelwood, 1999). At the same time, the focus on the group and organisational level of behaviour confounded the medical mind, focused as it is on the individual. What happened at Northfield was inevitably short-lived, limited by the duration of the war, and no persisting institution survived. As a result the particular psychoanalysts took their ideas elsewhere for more permanent development, and in order to provide a supportive context for themselves.

Many of the participants had been psychiatrists at the Tavistock Clinic before the war; and it was there they returned to create a context congenial for developing these new ideas.

The Tavistock Institute

Before World War II, the Tavistock Clinic did not see psychoanalysis as having very much application to group therapy. Those psychiatrists were recruited into the army psychiatric service, and there, came under the influence of Rickman, from whom they learned a more specifically psychoanalytic approach. Rickman, a psychoanalyst, worked particularly closely with Bion whose analyst he had been in the 1930s, and through Bion others were strongly influenced. During World War II, this group of military psychiatrists and psychologists also came in contact, via Eric Trist, with the work of Kurt Lewin in the USA (Lewin, 1951). Returning to the Tavistock Clinic after the war, Lewin's ideas, 'group dynamics' and 'field theory' were exploited together with psychoanalytic ideas.

Basic assumptions

The self-reflective quality of the Northfield experiments prompted a view of organisational development (and indeed of personal development) as a learning process. It had grown up in parallel with the WOSBs (Bridger,

1946; Bion, 1946), and began to be employed within the paradigm of the sensitivity groups as used by Lewin (Bradford, Gibb and Benne, 1964). This gave rise to a model called the Tavistock group.

Bion, still with Rickman's influence in mind, conducted research on the behaviour of small groups in the late 1940s (Bion, 1961). He developed the notion of the 'group as-a-whole', derived from Lewin's field theory (and from German Gestalt psychology), and from Trigant Burrow (1927) who had influenced Rickman after World War I. This reduced the individuality of the individual members.

In Bion's well-known theories of the basic assumption group, individuals are endowed with a specific valency to form a sense of a social entity with each other. There are three valencies, each one taking the form of unspoken or unconscious assumptions which the members of the group collectively adopt.

- First, the members may support a *dependent* basic assumption. The individuals then cluster around one person elected to a leadership role that involves constant supply of good resources to the members – comfort, wisdom, correct decisions, etc.
- Second, the assumption may be that there is a common enemy, either within the group or without. This is the *fight/flight* basic assumption group, where there is an expectation that a leader will emerge to mobilise and to represent hatred within the group.
- The third alternative is an assumption that suffuses the group with a hope that it is this group and its activities which will produce some as yet unborn idea or messiah which will have the properties of saving the world, or at the least the individuals of the group. This is the *pairing* group, which is characterised by the seeming exclusive occupation of two members with each other, to the excitement of the rest of the group.

These basic assumption groups are characterised by a timelessness, by being oblivious to reality and the real task of the group, and by an irritability towards anything which seems to go against the assumption active at the time. Clearly this lack of realism is not the case in all groups, and groups can achieve a very different level of functioning in which realistic tasks can be addressed, and a proper differentiation of the group and its members can take place to achieve the task. That, Bion called the 'work group', which, though opposed to the 'basic assumption group' in description, was usually suffused with basic assumption feelings – the army for instance, a group with work to do, is suffused with *fight/flight* group aspects.

This notion that a social entity can exist in a 'mature' reality-oriented form (the work group), or in a more primitive basic assumption state, has been crucial to the further development of most of the contributions subsequently made in Britain (excepting perhaps the group-analytic tradition). These ideas have proved very productive in thinking about phenomena in organisations which appear to be irrational or unrealistic.

The difference between the basic assumption group and the work group relates, partially, to Freud's differentiation between primary and secondary process. Later, however, Bion was at pains to relate these processes to Melanie Klein's theory of projective identification (Bion, 1952). The coming of individuals together (or valency) is based on non-verbal communicative intrusions into each other known as 'projective identification'. Projective identification describes an *interpersonal* process but from an *intrapsychic* point of view. It is a conceptual bridge to link the personal and the organisational.

Bion's research on basic assumptions became for a long time the basis for a specific Tavistock form of group psychotherapy, which has since lapsed. It owes its fate perhaps to the tendency for individuals within the group to fall out of the perspective as attention is focused on the collective assumptions. Such marginalising of the individual self conflicts with the wish of neurotic individuals to come for personal therapy for themselves!

Group relations training

The Tavistock group was developed not merely for therapy but also for group learning which came to be a specific method. And in fact, more successfully, it has produced the successful Group Relations programme, centred around the Leicester Conference, set up as an annual collaboration between the Tavistock Institute and the University of Leicester, and still running in little-changed form (Rice, 1965). These are 'conferences' in which the task of the conference members is to learn about group processes through studying the group processes of the conference itself. The conference set up in various group formations becomes a surprisingly powerful *personal* experience, in which individual members are confronted with their learning as a struggle to be a group member as well as an individual (Turquet, 1975).

The psychosocial process

At the time that Bion was experimenting with Rickman's ideas on groups, in the 1940s, attempts were also underway to develop a bridging theory between psychoanalysis and social psychology, and Trist produced his founding 'manifesto' declaring his search for a concept that was able, externally, to make comprehensive reference to the structure of social systems or, internally, to reach down to emotional phenomena at the deeper levels of personality (Trist, 1950[1990], p. 540).[30]

He needed a bridge between the individual and social forms, and he called this bridge the 'psychosocial process'. The concept he hit upon to be that process was the 'culture' of the social grouping. 'Culture' he believed had two aspects, in which he could find both individual purposes and the functioning of the social system. It embraces the active techniques, or instrument, for the goals of the institution – this is not the functioning of the individual, not a psychological person, but a person placed within the task, roles, values and belief system of the social entity. He cites rituals as an example of cultural functioning. It is not the individual, but the individual, nevertheless, has both a role *within* the ritual, and also enfolds it in himself. He is not determining *of* the ritual, but has his own objectives (conscious and unconscious) for taking part in it. The individual in a social role has private and unconscious values and belief systems, in this role, which are nevertheless related to others in the forming of a social system.

The individual aims do not comprise the objective of the ritual itself, though at the same time, the ritual has an impact on the individual. It promotes behaviours, identifications and aims for the individual who in turn invests them in the ritual. We might consider the function of a church service. This is the functioning of a social structure – the church. Its ritual has the function to call people to worship and instil religious awe and devotion – in short, corralling the individuals into the aims of the church. At the same time individual people find personal expression of their devotion and explanation of their awesome religious experience in the rituals of the church.

Trist's thinking gave rise to many projects involving action research methods to study a nursing service (Menzies, 1959), families (Bott [Spilius], 1957; Rapaport and Rapaport, 1990), the mental hospital (Bott [Spillius], 1976) and with industrial and commercial organisations (see Trist and Murray, 1990b). Shortly after the war, the Tavistock Institute of Human Relations (Trist and Murray, 1990a) was formed separately from the Tavistock Clinic. The outcome there of Trist's thinking was the sense 'that a new paradigm of work might be emerging' (Trist and Murray, 1990a, p. 9). Many institutions worldwide were inspired by the Tavistock research, and took it up themselves.

---

[30] This text, written in 1950, was published only in 1990, and in a revised form. Nevertheless it retains sufficient of the original flavour to regard it, in our view, as a key document in the founding of the Tavistock tradition.

In 1948 the Tavistock Clinic was about to enter the National Health Service, and could not contain within it a commercial enterprise. The Institute was funded by commercial contracts with businesses, as well as academic, government and charitable grants. It therefore held together a disp u ate culture; those involved in a commercial 'fix-it' results-focused set of projects, and 'purer' research projects that aimed at ontological, 'what is' questions rather than 'how-to' demands. Much of its heady excitement seems to have stemmed from that tension, although it took its enthusiasm too from the atmosphere of post-war reconstruction in Britain which was fed by ideals of social justice, and sheer survival.

Later, in the late 1950s, after key figures (notably Eric Trist) had left, this tension subsided and the commercial ethos supervened. The result, according to Spillius, was the difficulty of taking into account the environment of the units studied:

> I think the difficulty here, and it affects paid consultancy studies particularly, is what Trist used to call 'wrong level'. You can't get a handle on the environment if you're paid to keep your nose in the institution. So for example, I think the matron of Isabel's [Menzies] hospital really wanted to change the training and culture of her nurses but couldn't because she didn't have the requisite authority, and Isabel didn't have sanction from the higher next levels up to study the potential for change; that was not the way the study was set up. (Bott [Spillius], 2000, personal communication)

Social defence systems

One outcome of Trist's thinking at this stage was the idea developed by Elliott Jaques (1955) that unconsciously people can come together in collective support of each others' defensiveness. He formalised the idea as the 'social defence system' of the organisation which can operate to quell members' anxieties, if these threaten to be intolerable.

Isabel Menzies (1959) conducted an exemplary case study in which the way the work is done by nurses in a hospital has grown up so that the individual nurses are supported in splitting off experiences and feelings arising from the work which otherwise would distress them. In particular, the authority structure is so laid out that responsibility can always be projected elsewhere for someone else to deal with; thus the individual nurse can be relieved, when she so wishes, from the life-and-death anxiety of the work she has to face for the full time of her shift. In addition the nurse–patient relationship is split up so that nurses do not have to be unduly close emotionally to the suffering of patients who are in pain, mutilated or dying. These implicit aims, unspoken in the culture, appear to exist for the purpose of protecting the nurse against the stress of being with patients who suffer, and against feeling responsible for their life.

These unconscious principles take the form of leaving others to make decisions – passing the buck, up, down and sideways, till a confusion of responsibility reigns. Another form is the depersonalisation of patients and of staff. Such practices involve the uniform of the nurse which allows individuality only in terms of rank, or the nursing of a part of the body of the patient – the bed-pan round. The practices which make the aims manifest were called 'defensive techniques' of nursing by Menzies.

Parallel with this social defence system is the problem that the operation of an organisation can be distorted by these implicit aims. An understanding of these implicit, hidden and unconscious aims can lead to a grasp of certain problems in organisations. In particular, the frustrating observation so easily made, that maladaptive practices persist as if with a life of their own, becomes understandable if they exist to relieve members of unconscious suffering. If these unconscious aspects of the culture are unspoken they will of course be impossible to manage effectively. Change in these collective practices cannot be addressed because their nature is unconscious and therefore unspoken. In addition change threatens (also unconsciously) to release once again the anxiety which has been locked away from conscious experience by the members.

The classic early work was conducted by Jaques (1951) in a company making boxes, and by Trist and Bamforth (1951) in a coal mine. Because the specific work involves quite specific technical operations upon the raw materials, the social system adapts within limits imposed by the technical alternatives. The system adapts as a whole to both the emotional and technical requirements and has come to be known as the socio-technical system (see Perrow, 1972; Trist and Murray, 1990a).

Psychodynamic and systems theories

The formalisation of the ideas of the socio-technical system was contributed to by many people, but notably Rice and Miller (Miller and Rice, 1967; Miller, 1976) who began to combine the approach with system theory as it emerged in the 1960s and 1970s. The 'discovery' of systems theory by the Tavistock tradition rejuvenated the consultancy work. Emphasis on the system, and how systems behave, was particularly suitable to research that relied upon commissions from industrial and business managers.

The subsequent emphasis has diverted slightly from Trist's original attempt at a 'new paradigm'. Managers require a means of handling the system, not necessarily understanding where the problems come from. Increasingly a stress has been laid on system maintenance (Miller, 1993): the features and problems of role, boundary, task and aspects of leadership and authority (Rice, 1965). Though the change has not been a striking one, there is more of an interest in a 'doing mode' that relates to management as opposed to an 'understanding mode' that might be more in key with a psychoanalytic approach.

The development of this approach to contemporary issues is described by Barry Palmer (Chapter 9), while Trist's original focus on 'culture' has remained more important for other workers.

The Tavistock Clinic

Meanwhile, the work of the Tavistock Clinic has included a return to working with organisations – particularly the non-commercial sector of healthcare. The idea of the social defence system has remained more central to the thinking of Stokes (1994a) and Obholzer and Roberts (1994).

The notion of personal anxiety as a root determinant of distorted organisation is strongly applicable within healthcare where anxiety is very prevalent, and many studies have derived directly from the original case study by Menzies in a nursing service. Although this paradigm persists it has been modified by a particular focus of interest on the distortions of the system management – task, authority and leadership – which have been borrowed from the adjacent Institute. This kind of work on organisations has also been influenced by the development at the Clinic of infant observation in the 1940s, and this method has used the psychoanalytic idea of counter-transference by assigning a research status to the feelings of the participants and observer. This has been adapted for 'work study' learning projects and for the observation of organisations (Hinshelwood and Skogstad, 2000). The Tavistock Clinic has been influential in some understanding of the general management of psychiatry in the NHS in Britain, for instance Foster and Roberts (1998) on the emotional vicissitudes of 'community care'.

Group-analytic approaches

A very different approach to groups also started at Northfield, but has remained focused on therapeutic groups. Foulkes trained as a psychoanalyst in Vienna, and while remaining loyal to Freud, he became interested in experimental psychology as it had developed in Germany (Gestalt psychology). As a doctor, he worked for some time with the neurologist, Kurt Goldstein, who was applying Gestalt psychology ideas to neuroscience. Foulkes equated the neural net to a social network and was influenced by the sociologist, Norbert Elias (Mennell, 1989; Dalal, 1998).[31] Both became exiles in England, and it would seem that Elias became the

---

[31] Elias in fact later trained as a group analyst in London, though his written work is entirely as an academic sociologist.

strongest influence on Foulkes apart from Freud (Pines, 1983). Elias (1970) critiques sociology which acquiesces,

> in a tradition which restricts the scope of sociological theories to 'society' alone, which puts ideas about society under the magnifying glass, critically examines them and seeks to reconcile them with other available knowledge – yet does not do the same for ideas about the individual (Elias, 1970, p. 129).

He attacked the 'reification' of 'I' or ego, and developed his 'pronoun model': 'I' does not exist except in the constellation of you, we, it, etc. (p. 123). There is a 'figuration' of individuals, and each in the group has his own perspective – the 'you' to a particular person is 'I' to himself – he gave the example of the person who has lost a loved one – and thus a part of himself – pp. 135–136.

After World War II, Foulkes developed his views on how to apply psychoanalysis to therapy in a group, more or less on his own, and restricted himself entirely to group psychotherapy. Even in his work at Northfield Military Hospital (Harrison, 2000), he seemed to treat the whole hospital as a collection of small groups (de Maré, 1983). Foulkes invented group therapy by applying the practice of psychoanalysis, rather than its theory. And he modified the practice for the setting of a group; in particular he took the notion of 'free association' from psychoanalysis proper, and described what he called 'free-floating discussion' as the corresponding process in group therapy. The practical aim remained the same – free expression of the individual. As in his psychoanalytic training in Vienna, development of free association was the task of the patient and analyst, so in Foulkes's group analysis, free-floating discussion is the aim of the group.

The key psychoanalytic concepts – unconscious, psychological defence mechanisms and transference – do occur in Foulkes's writing, but do not have central importance. Instead he evolved a new set of concepts; those which have proved most significant are the 'matrix' and 'mirroring'.

The matrix and free communication

The matrix is a blend of the Gestalt idea as Foulkes experienced it with Goldstein, and the notion of 'figuration' that Elias later developed As in the neural network the nerve cells are nodal points between which communication flows, so the individual in the group is a nodal point between which communication (free-floating discussion) flows. Elias asserted that the individual is always indissolubly part of a social context, and that context is incontrovertably composed of its individual members.

The matrix is the medium in which the focal principle of free-floating discussion takes place. Foulkes created group analysis as a practical discipline, aimed at creating optimal conditions within a group. That condition is the free communication of all members with each other. Within an organisation his followers have applied a similar practical principle. The 'sensitivity group' has become, in the hands of group analysts, a practical tool (especially in healthcare organisations) to create a matrix for the free expression of emotional and personal reactions to each other at work.

There is a surprisingly optimistic quality about this approach which regards the obstacles to free communication as eliminable, a view strongly expressed by de Maré, Piper and Thompson (1991). Foulkes and group analysis may tend to idealise the group and its possibilities (Nitsun, 1996), but others (Roberts, 1980; Zinkin, 1983) have offered a balancing view; most forceful is Nitsun's (1991, 1996) notion of the 'anti-group'.

Such a practical aim for the group depends on a belief in the possibilities of group change, and the development of the desired free-floating discussion. However, it differs from other orientations, notably the Bion/Tavistock tradition where the task is seen as a learning one – to learn about the obstacles to a group functioning – including the obstacles to learning within the group (Rice, 1965). The aim is not directly to change those group conditions, but for members to learn about them.

Because of this practical focus on free communication there has inevitably been a restriction to those settings where face-to-face communication is realisable. De Maré has for many years attempted to apply group analytic principles of free-floating discussion to larger groups (de Maré and Kreeger, 1974). However, the possibilities of achieving even the physical arrangements for such a setting have modified de Maré's research to the 'median group' – around 20 members (de Maré, Piper and Thompson, 1991). And that same focus – free-floating discussion – has inevitably limited work in large organisations where many people never come face to face with each other, let alone communicate freely.

Mirroring

The application of group analytic ideas has arrived late (Blackwell, 1998). The implication of group analytic ideas at the level of organisations is that the amount of communication increases exponentially with the numbers of individuals. The purpose of the organisation is not best served by everyone having a place in a completely freed-up communication matrix. Limits to free communication begin to become important at levels of not much more than a dozen. Some, though not all, group analysts exercise caution in transposing the practice of therapy groups to the groups of a working organisation (Whitaker, 1992). The freeing of communication, *per se*, as an organisational aim contrasts with the early Tavistock work – for instance, Jaques's box factory (Jaques, 1951) and his prescription of communication on a need-to-know basis.

The problem of the limitations on communication in organisations has been addressed by adding to the core concepts of free-floating discussion and the matrix, the further idea of mirroring (Pines, 1982).[32] Originally, in Foulkes's definition (Foulkes and Anthony, 1957, p. 150), it was the opportunity for an individual to see aspects of himself in others. However, latter generations of group analysts have found it useful in going beyond Foulkes's limitation of the small therapeutic group. Like the Tavistock Institute, group analysis some time during the 1970s acquired an understanding of, and then an integration with, systems theory as applied to social systems (Durkin, 1981; Pines, 1983). Whereas the relations between the two levels, individual and organisational (or group), are held by the notion of identification from Freud (1921), in systems theory these levels are interacting systems which refine their own patterns in correspondence to each other.

Initially it was a way of understanding the discrete system of the individual in the context of the system of the group. Mirroring can now refer to the occurrence of similar patterns of communication (or culture) at different systemic levels (Nitsun, 1998). About working as a consultant in a social service setting, Mhlongo comments: 'Patients' conflicts are frequently mirrored by staff or replayed among them' (Mhlongo, 1983, p. 196). So, an organisation can be studied in terms of the replication of cultural and social forms between its various levels of complexity – 'isomorphism'. From a group analytic point of view the interest is in the quality and 'freeness' of communication at different levels, or more specifically the repeat of characteristic patterns and difficulties in freed-up communication at the various levels. However, at this point it may be hard to expose the psychoanalytic roots – the unconscious, anxiety and defence – of the group-analytic application.

The key characteristic of both the Tavistock approach and the group-analytic ones is that they have been rooted in working with groups and organisations in a tradition which is particularly British (or 'Anglo-Saxon').

Contributions beyond the Tavistock tradition

Most work in Britain owes some influence, greater or lesser, to the Tavistock Clinic and Institute. But some of it is sufficiently distinct to demand specific attention.

---

[32] Foulkes identified a number of 'group specific factors' to complement the psychological factors in a psychoanalytic setting: mirroring, condenser, chain and resonance, of which the mirror phenomenon is now a much enhanced concept (Pines, 1982).

Culture and the psychosocial process again

Other researchers deriving from the Tavistock tradition have retained an emphasis on the culture of the organisation as Trist originally suggested – see, for instance, Stapley's (1996) discussion of a psychoanalytic approach to culture, 'one which is independent from clinical psychoanalysis, but independent and parallel to it' (p. 11).

Tom Main (1946), another psychiatrist from Northfield, returned to clinical work after the war to concentrate on mental health institutions. He regenerated the Cassel Hospital using his idea of a therapeutic community. Main's work existed in parallel to another wartime development, Maxwell Jones's experiments with democratisation of the hospital or ward settings (Jones, 1952). Jones employed Jacob Moreno's psychodrama techniques at a ward level, and he also had links with Eric Trist at the Maudsley Hospital during the war period. He, like Main, contemplated psychoanalytic training after the war and even had some analysis with Melanie Klein, but eventually took a different career path. This interlacing of Main's and Jones's ideas has resulted in a particularly vigorous tradition of therapeutic communities (Kennard, 1983). Despite this lively interest in the cultural features of a therapeutic environment, it has been a somewhat secondary theme to the consultancy and group relations work at the Tavistock.

The practical results of this work, together with that of others who have made contributions to the vagaries and vicissitudes of culture from a psychoanalytic point of view, are reviewed in Chapter 11. Those studies tend to cohere around unconscious aspects of the development of cultural attitudes that arise collectively within organisations and in society, and they look at the effects that an unconscious yet collective allegiance to certain cultural attitudes might have, and whether there is unconscious motivation to achieve those effects.

Freedom and repression

A further development has come more recently to Britain, though it owes much of its character to having grown up in the context of the Tavistock approach to social issues. This more political interest corresponds to those on the continent and in South America. The revolutionary movements in Europe espoused, in a cautious way, certain aspects of psychoanalysis. Marcuse (1955, 1964) was read avidly in the May 1968 revolution in Paris. This gave rise to a developing interest in France, partly gathering around Lacan. It has also provoked a number of academic disciplines to address psychoanalysis anew: history, literary studies, women's studies, etc. In Britain these interests have often taken on the character of the British object relations and Kleinian schools of psychoanalysis. Suspicious of the commercial base of the Tavistock Institute, these trends have gathered especially around the group of psychologists and academics who founded the journal *Free Associations*, and also in the academic departments of psychology and sociology of the University of East London (previously the Polytechnic of East London).

This FA/UEL group has attempted to adapt the Tavistock tradition to non-commercial projects, to academic interests and to political debate (Richards, 1984b, 1989; Rustin, 1991). This is the field of cultural studies – the attempt to analyse cultural artefacts, like the media, pop music, films, etc. – which has taken hold, especially in British universities. It is reviewed by Barry Richards and Karl Figlio in Chapter 10.

Recent attempts have been made to apply some psychoanalytic ideas to the goals and practice of politics. If politics has the goal of providing citizens with a 'good life', Kraemer and Roberts (1996) have provided a discussion of a society offering 'security' in terms of Bowlby's attachment theory (Holmes, 1993). Rustin (1991) also published a series of articles attempting to define 'the good society' in Kleinian terms. Bollas (1996) examined the strategies of the 1996 US presidential election as intuitive attempts to use psychoanalytic concepts.

9 THE TAVISTOCK PARADIGM: Inside, Outside and Beyond

BARRY PALMER

My task in this chapter is to construct an account of the psychoanalytic understanding of organisations which has evolved from the work of the Tavistock Institute and Clinic over the last fifty years and more. I have found myself approaching this task with a mixture of awe, anticipation and dismay. I am awed by the magnificence of my object which is for me, as the poet George Barker (1962) said of his mother:

> . . . a procession no one can follow after
> But be like a little dog following a brass band.

My sense of anticipation arises from the importance, to me, of this endeavour to see this body of work whole, although that is impossible, and to achieve the kind of distance which is necessary to produce a map of a large territory (Barker's mother is 'as huge as Asia'). It is important because of the degree to which I have become identified with this frame of reference: writing this chapter provides me with an opportunity to look critically at my own practices and concepts, and in so doing to raise questions about the limits of what I shall call the Tavistock paradigm.

My dismay may be readily understood. The relevant body of work is large, with a growing literature in many countries and languages; there are already several accounts available (to which I shall refer); and it is impossible to characterise the generic elements of the Tavistock approach in an uncontroversial way. Furthermore, I am not an impartial observer: I have worked closely with many practitioners in this tradition, but know of others only through what they have written or by hearsay. So this may be what Vega Roberts has called a 'self-assigned impossible task' (Obholzer and Roberts, 1994, p. 110).

Accepting the ambiguities of the undertaking, I shall approach it in this way:

- I shall seek to characterise what I take to be the Tavistock *paradigm*, focusing upon the socio-psychological development within that paradigm; I shall not attempt to describe every ramification of Tavistock-inspired theory and practice.
- I shall restrict my attention almost entirely to the *British literature*.
- I shall *not expound the basic theory* in detail, assuming the reader has access to the several excellent accounts.
- I shall suggest lines of approach to a *critical* account of this work, as I go along and through three case studies.

The Tavistock tradition as a paradigm

Within the Tavistock literature and oral tradition a number of early, definitive ventures have become exemplars for subsequent practice and theorising. They can be seen as elements in a Tavistock paradigm, using the term 'paradigm' in the sense defined by Kuhn (1970): a body of 'recognised achievements', which 'provide model problems and solutions to a community of practitioners'. A paradigm defines the terms in which assertions about reality are framed, and legitimates the practices which are accepted as means of exploring that reality. Much present-day psychoanalytic work with organisations in Britain and beyond is rooted in this Tavistock paradigm.

The 'recognised achievements' of this paradigm include the experimental regimes at the Northfield military psychiatric hospital, Wilfred Bion's studies of group dynamics, the Glacier Metal project, the study of longwall coal mining by Eric Trist and his colleagues, Kenneth Rice's work with the Ahmedabad company in India, Isabel Menzies Lyth's study of nursing, and Harold Bridger's working conferences on group relations (e.g. Bion, 1948–1951; Jaques, 1951; Trist and Bamforth, 1951; Rice, 1958; Menzies, 1959; Rice, 1965; Bridger, 1990a). The list could be extended; Menzies Lyth, for example, frequently refers to the more recent Baric experiment of Alistair Bain (which was written up in 1982). This list privileges what Trist (Trist and Murray, 1990a) has called the socio-psychological emphasis within the Tavistock tradition, with which I am most familiar; his own anthology of definitive Tavistock papers, which was still incomplete when he died, includes volumes on work with sociotechnical (Trist and Murray, 1993) and socio-ecological emphases.

I want to use the term 'discursive formation' to refer to the constellation of terms through which descriptions and interpretations are constructed within this or any paradigm. A discursive formation provides the content of a corresponding 'discursive *practice*', by which objects and concepts are generated, assembled in statements and authorised. The terms are derived from Michel Foucault (1972). By 'discursive formation' he means what might more loosely be called the specialised *language* of the paradigm or the practitioners' distinctive 'way of talking' (Babington-Smith and Farrell, 1979).[33] The corresponding term 'non-discursive practice' refers to the context of institutional arrangements and practical know-how within which descriptions and interpretations are articulated (see also Dreyfus and Rabinow, 1982; Palmer, 1996).

The Tavistock paradigm is an action research paradigm, drawing upon several social science disciplines. Its purpose was defined retrospectively by Emery (1976) as 'the mutual enrichment of social science and practical affairs'. It thus incorporates other discursive formations besides that of psychoanalysis. This paper focuses upon the psychoanalytic dimension, but must necessarily take this eclecticism into account. It must also consider not only how Tavistock writers conceptualise behaviour in organisations, but also how they conceptualise their own practice.

Core concepts of the Tavistock paradigm

Several writers in this tradition summarise the conceptual framework within which they work (e.g. Miller and Rice, 1967; Richardson, 1973; Grubb Institute, 1984; Klein and Eason, 1991; Obholzer and Roberts, 1994). I suggest that the following concepts are constitutive of the Tavistock paradigm:

- A predominantly Kleinian account (e.g. Klein, 1959) of *the individual, and the mechanisms of defence*, in particular splitting, projection and projective identification, introjection, denial, the interplay of the paranoid-schizoid and depressive positions, and Bion's (1970) concept of the container and the contained. We should probably also include Winnicott's (1965, 1971) concepts of the holding or facilitating environment and of transitional spaces and objects.
- A concept of *role* distinct from that which is dominant in psychology and sociology (cf. Edward Klein, 1979, p. 99). Reed and Armstrong (1988) write:

---

[33] A discursive practice creates the objects which constitute the 'furniture' of any paradigm or discipline, as well as the concepts which characterise them and describe their relations. So for example there is now an extensive literature about stress. This can be seen as a discursive practice which creates stress as its object. (The word 'object' is not used here in a psychoanalytic sense.)

> To take a role implies being able to formulate or discover, however intuitively, a regulating principle inside oneself which enables one, as a person, to manage what one does in relation to the requirements of the situation one is in, as a member of this organisation or group.

- Reed (1972, p. 166f) distinguishes between work roles, understood in this way, and roles like that of scapegoat or magic leader assigned to individuals under the sway of basic assumption mentality.

- Bion's account of *group processes*, and in particular his distinction, in *Experiences in Groups* (1961), between work group and basic assumption group mentality. Work group activity is similar to that which Freud (1911) attributed to the ego, and is seen as oriented towards reality. The concept of the work group is not developed in *Experiences in Groups*. It has been elaborated by Armstrong (1992), drawing upon Bion's later writing, and in the institutional sphere by Hoggett (1992). Several writers have described additional basic assumptions, including Turquet (1974), Hopper (1989), and most recently Lawrence, Bain and Gould (1996). Reed (1972, 1995) has used Bion's concept of the *specialised work group* to develop a theory of the function of churches in society.

- A theory of the *use of social systems as defences against persecutory and depressive anxiety*, developed by Jaques (1955), who draws upon Freud's (1921) theory of identification as applied to institutions. The theory provided a means of articulating the observations of early Tavistock practitioners in several key projects, including the Glacier Metal, coal-mining and nursing studies already mentioned; it makes it possible to articulate the dilemma,[34] inherent in organisational life, between adherence to professed definitions of purpose, and recognition of 'unthought' purposes (Bollas, 1987) concerned with providing the subject with an identity – purposes which, when threatened, arouse primitive anxiety.

- The concept of *boundary*. Elizabeth Richardson (1973), for example, asserts that the concept is central to the theoretical framework of her study of a British secondary school:

> Whether we are looking at the person, who can live as a human being only in so far as he is able to relate his own inner world to its outer environment, at the group, which exists by virtue of some kind of membrane that separates it out from other groups, or at the institution, which exists in the community. . . . by virtue of what it has been created and set apart to do we must be concerned with defining boundaries. (p. 16)

---

[34] This is one of three fundamental dilemmas described by Boxer (1994) as inherent in the processes by which organisations are constituted as objects of experience.

- The concept is linked to that of the depressive position, at and beyond which the ego 'can define the boundary between what is inside and what is outside, and can control the transactions between the one and the other' (Rice, 1965).

- A *systemic* or holistic view of groups, organisations and larger collectives, going back to the work of Kurt Lewin (e.g. 1951) who insisted on 'the importance of studying the "gestalt" properties of groups as wholes' (Miller, 1990, p. 170).[35]

- The organisation as an *open system*: that is, as a system of activities which is open to transactions with an environment and which survives by successfully regulating these transactions. As an open system an organisation has a fundamental *raison d'être* or *primary task* defined as the task it must perform in order to survive. An optimum organisational structure is a structure which most effectively supports the performance of the primary task (e.g. Miller and Rice, 1967). This concept of a system is derived from von Bertalanffy's (1950) theory of physical and biological systems. It was developed by Trist, Rice, Miller and their colleagues in response, I imagine, to the practical necessity of finding a way of constructing models of the institutions they studied and advised.

- The open systems model proved to be a powerful conceptual tool. From this model Trist, Emery, Rice and their colleagues developed the concept of the *socio-technical system*. This represents a working unit with a technological component, such as a coal mine (Trist and Bamforth, 1951) or an operating theatre (Klein and Eason, 1991, pp. 25ff), as comprising a social and a technical system each with its own internal logic. The aim of organisational design is to achieve a best fit between the conditions for optimal functioning of the two systems.

- The concept of the *'organisation in the mind'* (e.g. Lawrence, 1979, p. 228; Stokes, 1994b; Hutton, 1995). This and related terms were introduced by Pierre Turquet in unpublished briefing notes for a group relations conference, as a way of conceptualising the images and fantasies of the organisational context which determined relations between the individuals and groups within it. The concept thus invites the exploration of unconscious images of an organisational context.

---

[35] The first issue of *Human Relations* contained two posthumous papers by Lewin (1947). His influence on the formation of the Tavistock paradigm was considerable. It seems likely that Bion's focus upon the group-as-a-whole goes back to Lewin, and also his use of the term 'valency', which appears in Lewin (1935), p. 51.

Its importance lies in its potentiality for relativising all descriptions of organisations, since all descriptions, including those of Tavistock consultants, are products of the minds of individuals with particular interests, positioning themselves within a particular discursive practice. It has been illuminatingly examined by David Armstrong (1995), who concludes that the term denotes:

> . . . not the client's mental construct of the organisation, but rather the emotional reality of the organisation that is registered in him or her, that is infecting him or her, that can be owned or disowned, displaced or projected, denied, scotomised: that can also be known but unthought (p. 9).

● Concepts of *authority and power*. These two terms stand for a cluster of related notions. Some time after the publication of his account of the Leicester group relations conferences, Rice (1965) concluded that they were fundamentally concerned with questions of authority. As I remember it he was concerned with the authority attributed to an interpretation. Ideally, as he saw it the speaker takes authority for the validity of his or her interpretation, and the listener takes authority for assessing and either accepting or rejecting it. The paradigm also includes a distinction between authority as an attribute of role, and power as an attribute of persons, which is central to the work of the Grubb Institute (e.g. Reed and Armstrong, 1988) and has also been elaborated in Jaques' concept of requisite organisation (e.g. 1989).

Core practice

There seem to be few systematic accounts of Tavistock practice (but see for example Menzies Lyth, 1988; Gould, 1991; Klein and Eason, 1991, pp. 161f). This gap is partly filled by the many published extended case studies, which provide illuminating glimpses of practitioners at work. I see these elements as constitutive of Tavistock practice.

● *Working with groups* as a preferred method of diagnosis and intervention. This has its roots in the paradigmatic projects already referred to, in particular the studies of group behaviour published by Bion and developed in the Leicester and Bridger working conferences. It involves a distinctive form of process consultancy, in which the consultant works interpretatively with the 'material' presented by the client group.

- Availability as a *temporary holding environment and container for client anxieties* (individuals, teams, management groups). It is assumed that if they can use the consultant to contain and give meaning to their persecutors and depressive anxieties, they will retain their wits, and be released to use their resources to address their own difficulties. Thus Lionel Stapley (1996) writes:

> In any extensive change process the culture and the holding environment can be severely disrupted. The consultant can assist the client by providing a substitute for that holding environment until it and the culture have reintegrated. (p. 178)

- *Working with or in the transference.* This entails mobilising and recognising a transferential relationship with the client system, and working through it to a collaborative relationship which acknowledges the autonomy and capabilities of consultant and clients. The term 'transference' is not widely used in Tavistock writings. My impression is that transference is thought of as a process which may arise within a consultancy assignment, rather than as the precondition of there being a consultancy relationship at all. [36]
- Working with the *countertransference*; that is, interpreting and using one's own feelings, fantasies, impulses and behaviour as indicators of having become not only *in* but *of* the client system. For example, Lisl Klein (Klein and Eason, 1991) describes an assignment in which she spent a weekend preparing a report for a client organisation, and 'was filled with a growing sense of pressure and anxiety':

> Eventually, the consultant stepped back from the situation to ask some questions: what are they doing to you, that you are spending Sunday, your so-called free time, trying to deal with this impossible task? Knowing that you have taken on more than can possibly be handled in the time? Eating margarine sandwiches because you haven't allowed time to buy and cook food? The answer came, They have turned you into a mini-version of the company! This is what they do'. (p. 20)

This is one example of how practitioners *work interpretatively* with their experience of the client system. Practitioners differ about whether and how they work, privately or publicly, with their interpretations.

---

[36] Cf. Evans (1996), p. 214: 'Thus it is contradictory to claim that the transference can be dissolved by means of an interpretation, when it is the transference itself which cor c itions the analysand's acceptance of that intervention: "the emergence of the subject from the transference is thus postponed *ad infinitum* (Lacan, *Ecrits* [1996], p. 231)"'.

- *Working through*: as we have seen, there is a core assumption that individuals use organisational forms to create an identity for themselves (as a defence against anxiety), so that moves to change these forms arouse persecutory anxiety manifesting itself in resistance to change. Jaques (1951) describes the practice of enabling client groups to recognise and work through these resistances:

  > The method used was to draw attention to the nature of the resistance on the basis of facts known to those concerned. Opportunities were taken to illuminate in the specific situation the meaning of the feelings (whether of fear, guilt or suspicion) that constituted the unpalatable background to anxieties that were present about undergoing changes that were necessary. (p. 306)

- Defining and clarifying *boundaries*. It is assumed that articulating and enacting a coherent array of roles and task systems is functional for organisational work. (For an elegant worked example in which the boundaries of systems serving overseas students in the United Kingdom are defined, see Reed, Hutton and Bazalgette, 1978.)
- Designing and installing new forms of organisation, based on the open system model, in relation to new or clarified definitions of primary task. (For a diverse series of worked examples, see Miller and Rice, 1967.)
- *Designing experiential learning events*; most characteristically, training in group relations. Historically, several large-scale interventions in institutions based on group relations eventually activated their immune systems and were rejected. On the other hand the Menninger Clinic ran an influential programme (Menninger, 1985), and some universities in the UK are currently incorporating group relations training in degree courses.

The bounded organism, with an inside and an outside, as a root metaphor within the Tavistock paradigm

This whole, discursive practice generates a 'reality' which is internally (fairly) self-consistent but which inevitably leaves things out – or rather, does not constitute some aspects of 'what-is-going-on' as things, or relations between things, at all. What I earlier referred to as the 'furniture' of this discursive practice – the objects which the rest of the language is about – are individuals, groups and institutions, conceived of as bodies or organisms, with an inside and an outside and a skin or membrane between the two. The idea of this bounded object is, as I see it, a root metaphor within this paradigm: it structures the perceptions and interpretations of those who work within it.[37] It is also a dead metaphor, like the metaphor of a container and its contents in the statement 'Bion was in the army': we don't hear a statement like this as metaphorical, even though it is impossible to point to containers called armies which people are literally in. And it is a pre-psychoanalytic metaphor, adopted by Freud and Klein from the metaphor-pool of their day, which shapes the conceptual scheme at every level – the individual person, the (individual) group, the (individual) organisation.

With respect to the person, this has the effect of collapsing the distinction between the individual as a physical organism and the person as a social being, and of locating the subject within a boundary. Similarly, in the domain of groups and institutions, Blackwell (1994) has pointed out that the term 'boundary' is used in a way which makes no distinction between physical skins or membranes on the one hand, and limits defined in language by rules and conventions on the other. (See also the discussion of 'Internal reality' in Hinshelwood, 1989, p. 330f.)

Once social reality has been divided into an inner world and an outer world, psychoanalysis becomes the analysis of the inner world, and of its traffic with the outer world through projective and introjective processes. This has the effect of privileging the inner world relative to the outer world. This is evident in the neglect of the outer world in Melanie Klein and the lack of development of the concept of the work group in Bion, and of the environment of the institution in Rice (e.g. 1963). It is also evident in the emergence of the concept of the group or organisation 'in the mind': if the organisation is not out there, there is nowhere else to put it but in here.

We can distinguish several processes here:

- That of creating distinctions between me and not-me, us and not-us, without which it is difficult to imagine how human life could go on.
- That of forgetting that these distinctions (or boundaries, in that sense) are conventional and intentional.[38] The metaphor becomes a dead metaphor.

---

[37] It is an example of what Lakoff (1987) calls the 'container' schema. This is 'a schema consisting of a boundary distinguishing an interior from an exterior . . . We understand our own bodies as containers – perhaps the most basic things we do are ingest and excrete, take air into our lungs and breathe it out. But our understanding of our own bodies as containers seems small compared with the daily experiences we understand in container terms' (p. 271)

[38] Or, in Lacan's terms, constructed in the domain of the Imaginary (the domain of the ego and its images): People are separate, atomistic individuals only on the Imaginary level, which is the level of the ego. On the Real and Symbolic levels there is no boundary that can be drawn between them (Wilden, 1972, p. 277).

- That of valuing what is included in the boundary so drawn, and devaluing what is excluded by it – a manifestation of an individualism characteristic of much western thought (see for example Wolfenstein, 1990; also Wilden, 1972, pp. 217ff).

Intimations of alternative paradigms

No discursive practice is watertight. Within the literature there are glimpses of alternative ways of describing and interpreting social life. For example:

- Joan Rivière (1955) speaks of the inner world as an unconscious phantasy. She also refers to it as a psychoanalytic concept implying a recognition that the inner/outer distinction exists only in the language (or discursive formation) which the analyst brings to her understanding of the patient.
- Bion speaks of the gathering of a group of people in one place as having 'no significance whatsoever' for the observation of group phenomena (1961, p. 132), and of belief in the existence of a group as a sign of regression (1961, p. 142). However, neither he nor Rivière maintains a consistently critical distance from these constructions.
- In the 1960s Emery and Trist (1965, 1975) developed a typology of the environments of institutions, making good the neglect of the environment in earlier Tavistock work. They sought to conceptualise the turbulence which is now a 'given' in organisation theory. This thinking was not, however, incorporated into the theory of organisations of Rice and Miller. Philip Boxer and I have revisited this typology in a recent account of a consultancy assignment (Boxer and Palmer, 1997).
- S.H. Foulkes introduces the concept of the group matrix, which is like a neuronal network within which 'the individual is conceived as a nodal point' (1964, p.118). He is in effect proposing an alternative root metaphor.
- Grubb Institute (1984) writers distinguish between the biological individual which 'is born, matures, grows old and dies', and the person, as an 'information system', which 'extends through a network of social relations' (p. 55).
- There is an interpretative move which reframes the reported experiences of individuals as the voice of a larger system; in other words, the line between inner and outer is recognised as imaginary, and redrawn. This could be restated in terms of Foulkes's metaphor. Thus David Armstrong (1996), describing an intervention with a group of university staff, writes:

> What had begun as an expression of one individual's disease with his own relation to the University could, now, be reframed and given new meaning as a representation or registration within the individual of a more pervasive experience of dis-ease within, the whole institution.

- The metaphor of the Möbius strip has now entered organisation theory (Sabel, 1991). Möbius-strip organisations are those for which, 'as with a looped ribbon twisted once, it is impossible to distinguish their insides from their outsides' (p. 25).

One of the inherent dilemmas of consultancy work is that between working within an established paradigm and trusting the method, and working across and beyond the limits of the paradigm with the risk of losing one's way entirely. Unwillingness to risk transcending these limits leads to a Procrustean approach in which new problems are chopped or stretched to fit old theories. The challenge to those of us who work within the Tavistock paradigm is I believe to welcome and develop lines of thought like those above, without insisting that they are incorporated into one coherent scheme. This creates the possibility for what David Armstrong calls 'co-evolution' of the paradigm and contemporary context.[40]

Case study 1: Disturbances of rationality in groups

It would be possible to amplify and comment on this complex apparatus of theory and practice, and these glimpses of alternative paradigms, from many points of view. Following Emily Dickinson's (1929) injunction to 'Tell all the truth but tell it slant', my own comment will take the tangential form of three case studies, two from the work of the early practitioners and one from my own. Several other case studies have been left on the cutting-room floor. They would have suited my purpose equally well, which is to show the edge and the beyond of the Tavistock paradigm as they can be discerned in these pieces of work. (They are also illustrations of the paradigm in use, but I shall not draw attention to this.) This edge is what Kuhn (1970) describes as

> the growing sense that an existing paradigm has ceased to function adequately in the exploration of an aspect of nature to which that paradigm itself had previously led the way (p. 92).

---

[40] In conversation: I am grateful to David Armstrong for a large number of illuminating comments on an earlier draft of this chapter.

My first case study is an episode in a group therapy session described by Bion, involving six patients and himself (1961, pp. 143–146). A member suggests that 'it would be a good idea if members agreed to call each other by their Christian names'. Her suggestion is initially received with approval but 'within a few minutes', he says,

> the discussion has languished, and its place has been taken by furtive glances, an increasing number of which are directed towards me. . . . The mood is now a compound of anxiety and increasing frustration. Long before I am mentioned it is clear that my name has become a preoccupation of the group. (p. 144)

The proposition that Bion is setting out to explain is that this session shows evidence of mental activity which he calls work group activity – activity which in this case is soon disturbed by what he calls basic assumption activity. So he is seeking to elucidate the *patterning* of the behaviour he is describing: not just *what* happened but a way of reading the *form* of what happened. He is developing a language, a system of distinctions, for making sense of what happens in groups. In what groups? Well, it is most likely to be useful in his groups, but his later invitation to readers (p. 146) to think about a committee or other gathering they have attended indicates that he believes this is pertinent to a wider range of gatherings.

While Bion's group-as-a-whole perspective is expected to be new to us, we are expected to recognise the shape of the theory. Of the work group he says: 'Its characteristics are similar to those attributed by Freud (1911) to the ego'. So when he comes later to the basic assumption group he can expect readers to think: This must be analogous to the id. This homology with the Freudian psyche suggests a model in which the activity of the ego–work-group function is disturbed by 'powerful emotional drives' which erupt or insinuate themselves from an id-like group unconscious. Trist (1985) describes the origin of this idea:

> At one of these pub discussions he began to talk of a new concept he was developing, tentatively called 'the group mentality'. Disowned and disavowed responses the patients which were hostile to the purposes of treatment were split off from what they would consciously acknowledge in the group and collected anonymously into a pool which constituted a negative unacknowledged system – the group mentality.

Analysis

The disturbance of the work group can thus be seen as a symptom of what is accumulating in this sump of negativity to which all the group members contribute. It is a symptom (or sumptom!) of something attributable to processes within its imagined boundary. This way of framing the description does not initiate the reader to wonder how this disturbance might be attributable to processes beyond where this imaginary line has been drawn – outside the physical boundary of the room, as it were.

It is possible to construct another reading of this episode. (I am not suggesting that this reading is 'right', but simply indicating the kind of story which is excluded by the line which Bion draws round his field of enquiry.) For this meeting does not take place in a vacuum. It is a meeting, probably in a clinic, between someone designated as the doctor and six other people designated as patients. Whatever Bion has so far done to probe this assumption, the meeting is taking place in a context in which, as Tom Main (1989, p. 129) says of the Northfield hospital, there is 'the usual hospital convention of regarding all the staff as being totally healthy . . .; and all the patients as being totally ill'. We can imagine that this ambience is underlined by the way appointments are administered, where patients wait, the old copies of *Punch* and *Country Life* which they read while they are waiting, how they are addressed, and so on.

The fate of the proposal to use first names can therefore be attributed, not just to archaic images accumulating in a group sump, but to contemporary experiences, and to the culture of the medical milieu within which those designated as patients meet. Perhaps the discussion languishes because the patients are taking on the dominant societal code around medicine, but have no way of saying this. As soon as the wish for a more friendly, first-name atmosphere finds a voice, they begin to despair. There is no way Bion is going to say, 'Call me Wilfred'. Probably they think and speak of Bion as 'Dr Bion'. Every time they say his name they are reminded that he is the doctor. Is it his name or his title that they are concerned about? Whatever 'therapeutic need' dictates one member's suggestion of pseudonyms, he or she may also be speaking ironically, sending the whole situation up. Another member withdraws, Bion says: Dr Bion will never hear what they are inarticulately seeking after, so what's the point?

Bion is not unaware of the institutional context of his groups, but his references to it have an ironical quality which it is possible to misread; for example he says: 'It was disconcerting to find that the Committee seemed to believe that patients could be cured in groups such as these' (p. 29). The impression remains, for me, that he ignores the power of the symbolic universe within which he acts, even while he is questioning it.

Main (1989, p. 131) describes how, in his view, Bion's inward perspective led to the end of his tenure at the Northfield Military Hospital:

The unpublished secret is that Bion was sacked from Northfield. Neither the commanding officer nor his staff were able to tolerate the early weeks of chaos, and both were condemning and rancorous about Bion's refusal to own responsibility for the disorder of others. . . . Bion had been therapeutic for his ward but anti-therapeutic for the military staff, successful in his ward, a lower-order system, but highly disturbing to the hospital, the higher-order system.

Bridger (1990b) believes that Main overlooks the fact that Bion was confronting the unit with radical contradictions in its view of its work but nevertheless concludes:

Bion, in my view, was not at ease with the group as an open system. He was not at ease with the implications of ecological change in groups, institutions and communities.

It is arguable that this limitation in Bion's way of constructing his reality has had a pervasive influence within the tradition of which he is a founding father. If that case were more carefully argued, we might for example conclude that the focus on behaviour in the 'here and now' in group relations working conferences perpetuates this tendency, by adopting a literalistic notion of what is *here*. So there is a pervasive slippage between what is physically 'here' and what is psychically 'here', corresponding to the confusion between physical limits and psychological boundaries which we have already noted. In other words, practice tends to focus not only upon behaviour which is here and now, but upon explanations constructed in terms of conscious and unconscious processes imagined to be contained within a physical space.

Case study 2: Innovation and conflict in a coal mine

This is an episode in an eight-year action research project, carried out by Eric Trist and colleagues at the Tavistock Institute, in the British coal mining industry in the 1950s (Trist and Bamforth, 1951; Trist et al., 1963). It can be seen as an expression of the intention of the Institute at that time to bring to bear the resources of the social sciences upon the economic problems of post-war Britain. It is a paradigmatic study in the development of the concept of socio-technical systems.

The Tavistock team was engaged as researchers, and not primarily as consultants to individual collieries. It is not clear to what extent they influenced decisions in the collieries they studied. Their task was to conceptualise what was being learned about work organisation as new technology was introduced into the mines, and to make their findings available to the industry as a whole. It is interesting, therefore, in view of my previous comments on Trist's work, that the intervention is aimed at developing the knowledge environment of all the production units in the industry, rather than at helping individual collieries.

The incident concerned the introduction, in an unnamed village colliery, of a new form of work organisation known as 'composite working' in which, Trist says, teams working at the coal-face

> are multi-skilled . . . they can thus exchange shifts and practice task continuity (denying themselves as necessary to carry on with succeeding tasks); they share equally in a common pay note. Teams are self-regulating and practice what we called 'responsible autonomy'. (Trist et al., 1990, p. 478)

Previously coal-face teams had worked under the instructions of managers, and had been allocated single-shift roles. The innovation 'occurred spontaneously in three different coalfields and heralded what Emery has called a 'new work paradigm' (p. 476). Although composite working had been introduced at a neighbouring colliery with 'phenomenal success', the innovation ran into serious difficulties in the colliery in question, and did not reach an acceptable level of production for about a year. Trist's paper sets out and analyses this 'chronicle of how things went wrong' (p. 486).

Interestingly, this case study has been published at least four times: in an extended form in *Organizational Choice* (1963), and subsequently as a paper in various journals and anthologies in 1989, 1990 and 1993. We may wonder why it has proved so popular. One reason may be that it provides a clear worked example of how dysfunctional behaviour in an organisation can be explained in terms of Bion's theory of basic assumptions. If so, why was it necessary to go back to material from the 1950s to find such an example? But the re-publication of the case study turns out to be illuminating in another way, in that it gives us an opportunity to see how, through small amendments, Trist reassesses the episode after years.

History

The new production unit at the village colliery was opened under singularly unpromising circumstances. The geological conditions were extremely difficult. The team was drafted rather than self-selected, and had no previous experience of the technology or of composite working. The local community was totally dependent on the colliery. Trist infers that there was a pervasive fear that the new 'drift' (horizontal shaft) would fail, and that this would lead to the death of the colliery and hence of the village.[40]

The new drift was in difficulty from the first day. Progress was slower than expected, so the manager assumed direct control of the work. After

---

[40] The word 'death' was not used in the 1963 version.

six days twenty yards of the tunnel collapsed and a fortnight was lost digging the face out again. This should have given 'a big enough shock to cause a radical reappraisal of the whole undertaking' (1990, p. 489). Instead, the manager took firmer control, overruling the time-honoured convention by which the men allocated tasks amongst themselve;. The men perceived this as an attack and began to oppose management decisions, bringing the management and the lodge (trade union) into increasing conflict, with the threat of a dispute. At best the team had been meeting 50% of its production target; in the eleventh week it was down to 30%.

In week 12 the Area Labour Relations Officer was called in, the mood changed, and a settlement was reached by invoking a higher authority in the person of the Area General Manager who was a 'good object' to everyone in the pit. From this point on, productivity began to improve, although it was eleven months before the production target was being consistently reached. Even after eighteen months the managers and the Tavistock researchers reckoned that the team had not attained the level of responsible autonomy of the successful neighbouring team.

Analysis (Trist et al., 1963)

The researchers' original reading of what took place was this:

● From the start, and even in face of major setbacks, the management, the lodge and the members of the team assumed and acted as though the drift was an ordinary production unit, to be run in the ordinary way. When things went wrong, the unit

> was treated throughout as a production unit under difficulties, rather than perceived for what it was – a training and development unit working under the stress of a demand for full production (1990, p. 486).[41]

● The researchers interpret this 'assumption of ordinariness' as a collusive defence, suppressing the intense anxieties aroused by the demand to make radical changes in working practices, in circumstances where failure to achieve production targets was believed to threaten the future of the colliery and of the community which depended on it.
● When, in about the ninth week, the project had reached an impasse, basic assumption fight/flight took over and suffused the behaviour of managers and workers. 'Management and workers fought each other in common flight from the problems that had to be solved in the real

---

[41] References are to the 1990 text of the 1963 account.

task situation' (p. 490). By this time a quarter of the team had left, so the tendency to flight had emerged earlier. In week 12 the intention of the Area Labour Relations Officer triggers a transition to basic assumption dependence, in which the 'good' Area General Manager can reach a settlement with the men.[42] The residual problem in the colliery appears to have been that, having mobilised basic assumption dependence by invoking familiar outside authorities, managers and workers were then unable to establish the culture of responsible autonomy which was essential to the composite working method – a culture which can be seen as entailing the mobilisation of fight/flight in a sophisticated way, against the day-to-day challenges of mining the face.

- It is not clear from the 1963 account at what point the researchers arrived at the interpretation of what was going on which they subsequently published. This account concludes with the observation that the prevailing work norms permitted the crisis to be resolved, but did not provide

> any precedent, or 'tool kit' for analysing factors in the socio-psychological system in a way that would have broken down the assumption of ordinariness in the starting situation and avoided the consequent tensions and loss of production (p. 492).

Analysis (1989–1993)

The versions of the chapter published from 1989 onwards include this further observation:

> The Institute had begun its studies of group dynamics in industrial settings by feeding in appropriately timed interventions as the work proceeded. This followed the psychoanalytic tradition and had been successful in projects such as the Glacier Project (Jaques, 1951). This, however, had not been concerned with an order of change that constituted a paradigm shift as did the change from conventional to composite working in longwall coal-mining (1990, p. 492).

---

[42] Trist may also have in mind Bion's notion of emotional oscillation in a group (1961, pp. 124ff). Bion proposed that the members of a group may find themselves torn between the belief that their leader is dependable and the belief that he is mad (or, in this case, that composite working under present conditions was both necessary and impossible). They damp down the resulting emotional oscillation by bringing in outside authorities as 'inert material', so that 'the new and much larger group ceases to vibrate' (p. 125).

The 1993 American version of this chapter concludes with a summary of Bion's theory of the sophisticated and basic assumption groups, and the statement that:

> The function of a consultant is to help the group become aware of its ba [basic assumption] activity, so releasing the learning process (p. 175).

The 1990 version of the chapter concludes differently:

> The present project points to one set of conditions under which the psychoanalytic model of intervention has to be transcended in action research in organisational settings (1990, p. 493).

Trist is proposing that it is necessary to transcend the Tavistock paradigm, in order to be able to support members of an organisation in making what he calls a paradigm shift. When the organisation of the client system is not in question, the practice of interpreting defensive strategies and working through may be successful in enabling people to extricate themselves from repetitive, dysfunctional patterns of behaviour and to learn from their experience. But when they are confronted with a demand to develop a new organisation, there is 'a cognitive as well an emotional problem in making the shift'(p. 492). This 'double difficulty' creates confusion and requires a different kind of intervention through which:

> they can clearly envisage the alternative as an articulated systematic whole and find that it is suitable for them (p. 492).

The purpose of the whole research programme was to develop and disseminate this 'articulated systematic whole'.

On the basis of this case study we can formulate a number of propositions:

- The theories of Jaques (1955a) and Bion (1961) provide ways of understanding dysfunctional behaviour in the workplace, but such understanding of unconscious processes is not always a sufficient condition for an intervention which enables the client system to develop from a stuck situation. The proposition is affirmed most forcibly by Jaques himself (1995b, and see response by Gilles Amado, 1995 and Jaques' further riposte, 1995c, pp. 351–357, pp. 359–365.), in his later repudiation of a psychoanalytic approach to organisations:

  > The reason we have bad or dysfunctional organisations is not a reflection of pathological forces to be understood and resolved by the application of psychoanalytical concepts and methods. Far from it. The reason is that there has never been an adequate foundation for understanding of organisations

per se. We have simply not yet learned how to construct adequate organisations. That job is only just beginning. (1995b, p. 343) [43]

Practice within the Tavistock paradigm may not meet the challenge of
the client situation, when – for whatever reason – that situation requires
what Trist calls a paradigm shift in organisation. This is because members
of the client system may be unable to conceptualise the change required,
particularly when they are defensively identified with the existing
structure. (This is not the whole story, since the first collieries developed
the composite method of working without outside assistance, and it was
only later that the new model was conceptualised by the Tavistock team.)

Trist speaks of transcending the psychoanalytic mode of intervention,
Jaques of rejecting it. My present view is that what they wish to transcend
or reject is *one particular psychoanalytic discursive practice and the
non-discursive practice which supports it*, that is, the Tavistock paradigm.
They are right in asserting that practitioners frequently require knowledge
and skill in addressing the design of the social and technical systems of the
organisation in their own right. They are mistaken if they mean to imply
that the forms in which these systems are constructed and explained are
outside the domain of psychoanalytic enquiry. Autonomous work groups
and requisite employment hierarchies are expressions of strong ethical
and political commitments on the part of those who design and sanction
them. From a psychoanalytic position we cannot foreclose on the question
of the unconscious desire which animates these ideals and necessarily
goes beyond every attempt to articulate them.[44]

Case study 3: Professional identity in a healthcare setting

My third case study is a reading of an assignment of my own. It is shaped
by the supposition that I was unable, from within the Tavistock paradigm,
to articulate the challenge the client system was facing with sufficient
clarity. The case study is thus an attempt to illustrate how some of the
problematics explored in this chapter were experienced from the inside.

The client was a group of senior psychologists responsible for the
psychology, psychotherapy and counselling services provided by a Trust
within the National Health Service. They approached OPUS for help in

---

[43] Jaques does not comment on the value of psychoanalytic understanding in the
process of installing new and more adequate forms of organisation, when 'pathological forces' are likely to be aroused.

[44] Cf. Lacan (1973), Chapter 20, 'In you more than you'.

meeting a requirement of their senior manager that they should identify objectives for the unit for the next two to five years.

The first meeting with the head of the unit and his four colleagues presented me with a more complex array of concerns. These included anxiety about the possibility of becoming a 'limping service', if they were unable to secure the posts they needed and recruit and retain staff for them. In particular they were concerned about their continuing ability to attract psychologists in a competitive market. They were ill at ease at their limited discretion within a Trust wishing to set stringent business targets. Some wanted to explore the possibility of becoming part of an autonomous directorate, which would stand or fall by whether purchasers wanted to buy their services. In a note which I wrote afterwards I summarised the concerns they had expressed. I also commented on an ambiguity in the way they used the word 'we' in various statements they had made: were they speaking as the managers of a unit or as senior members of the psychology profession within the Trust?

In response to my report I was engaged for a total of about four days' work. The task of establishing objectives remained on the agenda, but I understood that what I was being asked to do was to enable them to engage with the questions which surfaced in the first meeting. Over a sixteen-month period I participated in five meetings with the group of five, and although I also had conversations with the head of the unit and interviewed the four section heads, attending their senior psychologist meetings and responding to what arose in them became the dominant method of intervention.

When the funding initially agreed ran out, we had not achieved a breakthrough in understanding their circumstances. We parted on good terms, but they did not renew the contract. In response to an earlier draft of this case study, the head of the unit said that he thought I underestimated the value of my intervention. Whatever that value may have been, I believe that, as Winnicott (1965, p. 193) put it, I did not succeed in 'meeting the challenge of the case'.

Analysis

As I now see it, the department was confronting the kind of transition which Trist refers to as a paradigm shift, in this case from a modus operandi based on professional assumptions to one based on managerial assumptions. The objective-setting process they had been asked to undertake was symptomatic of this shift. As it turned out, they were requiring their consultant to make the same order of shift himself. If I had recognised this, I would have been better placed to collaborate with them in articulating what they were up against.

One way of reading this story is to say that the 'challenge of the case' was to work with the group to *identify and conceptualise their emergent strategy* – that is, the strategy they were already adopting in response to changes in the demands of the Trust, their purchasers, government and the community of their catchment area. It meant assuming that they were already learning, in response to these pressures, acknowledging the anxieties that this was generating and finding ways of sustaining them. If we could arrive at an interpretative description of what they were already doing, and articulate the assumptions implicit in this, we might then be able to look critically at these assumptions and so establish a position from which they might work out a strategy for their future activity.

If we look at the situation in this way, this is what we find:

- They were already in the process of reconstituting themselves as a multi-professional service, which included psychotherapists and counsellors as well as clinical psychologists. This was calling into question their distinctive competence – not necessarily to undermine it, but to require them to articulate it in public debate. This meant being able to dis-identify with being psychologists. This can be seen both as a challenge to the *individual*, and also as a challenge to problematise clinical psychology as a *system* of discursive and non-discursive practices. This meant living with a lot of anxiety: 'people fear extinction', the head of the unit said.
- The department had already been renamed: it was no longer the Clinical Psychology Service, but the Psychology, Psychotherapy and Counselling Service.
- This reorganisation went beyond reconstituting themselves as a multi-disciplinary team. They were adopting a form of organisation in which all these disciplines would be integrated within a department with an explicit and negotiated aim, objectives and performance criteria – in Tavistock terms, under an explicit definition of the primary task of the department.
- There was evidence of the pain of these changes, and the resistance of the team to them, in the way they continued to refer to themselves as a senior psychologists' meeting, rather than a management meeting, and did not involve other disciplines in their strategic thinking (at least with me), and in the head of the unit's talk of taking early retirement.
- Without living on margarine sandwiches like Lisl Klein, the consultant was uncomfortably aware of a countertransferential process, by which he also felt himself being overwhelmed by feelings of helplessness and incompetence. However, a working note to the team in November

1994 shows that at that time he already saw the unit as in a transitional state, between a form of organisation based on professional and on managerial values, and attributed his anxiety to that:

> Threats to the quality and to the viability of the service, and the possibility of being impaled on one or the other horn of this dilemma, provoke considerable anxiety, which has made it difficult to think straight, and has at times certainly got to me. In particular it is difficult to pursue an objective-setting process looking two to five years ahead, when the enemy are already at the gates, or inside: the merger with other therapy disciplines has already happened, staff are already leaving, proposals for three per cent cuts had to be ready by Friday.

- As this note indicates, I was aware that the department was receiving contradictory injunctions: on the one hand, to think up to five years ahead (as though the rate of change in the environment of the Trust was negligible or predictable), but on the other hand to prepare for absorbing substantial budget cuts to come into effect within a few months (implying a turbulent environment in which it was impossible to look even one year ahead).

Critique

Why, then, was I unable to construct and implement some such strategy? Looking back, it is possible to see several limitations in my mode of intervention, including the ways in which I fell in with the clients' budget and in which I let go of the original objective-setting task. In the terms developed in this chapter, however, I would pick out four ways in which I was both constrained by, and seeking to transcend, the Tavistock paradigm.

- Although I felt constrained by it, I was unable to extricate myself from the role of consultant to meetings of the client group. In consequence I hooked into the paradigmatic method of working with groups (cf. p. 163), and became over-preoccupied with the internal dynamics of these meetings. The head of the unit was himself a group analyst, so that he also may have had a bias towards this approach. After the first of these meetings I did in fact recognise that I needed to take the initiative in gaining a greater understanding of the work of the department and arranged to interview the heads of the four sections about the services they provided. Significantly, however, I never recycled the picture built up back into the whole group, so this work was not as fruitful as it might have been.
- My preoccupation with the internal affairs of the senior psychologist group was reinforced by the emptiness of the concept of the

environment within the Tavistock paradigm. I had no conceptual tools for describing the complexities of the department's environment within the Trust and beyond. Modifying Jaques' position, I did not have an adequate foundation for the understanding of organisations *and their environments*, or more precisely of organisation-environments as fields of enquiry which can be cut into inside and outside at many points.

- I was unable to conceptualise the transition the department was going through as a radical change in discursive and non-discursive practices. Nor was I sufficiently clear at that time about the *inadequacy of the containment and interpretation consultancy strategy* (footnote p. 164) in the kind of circumstances Trist had recognised (p. 175). The situation can be seen as requiring an intervention, similar to that identified by Trist through which *'they [could] clearly envisage the alternative as an articulated systematic whole and find that it [was] suitable for them'* (p. 175). (I was in fact already familiar with Boxer's series of organisational transitions, which bring successive levels of organisational assumptions within the arena of explicit examination and debate (e.g. Boxer and Palmer, 1997). I was however unable or unwilling to take the risk of trying to make this theory work for me with the client group.).

- In particular I was unable to conceptualise the transition the department was going through, in a way which related the managerial performance criteria they were adopting to their assumed professional and personal commitment towards promoting the good of their clients. They experienced the transition from professional to managerial values predominantly as a loss. A practice which focuses upon defences against anxiety (p. 16) is sharp in articulating ways in which people in organisations resist change, but *weak in articulating the unconscious desire* which animates their work and which they may be tempted to give up on when the landscape of their work changes. Boxer (1994) identifies what he calls a 'relational strategy', which is the strategy necessary to be responsive to a turbulent environment, and to needs and demands of clients which can never be fully specified in advance. It thus goes beyond concepts of organisation based on primary task, and requires a corporate openness to the needs of clients analogous to that of the professional mental health worker at the individual level.[45]

---

[45] Thus it appears that the shift towards a relational mode of control can reconnect practitioners with a client-centred ethos which is lost in a positional mode – although they can no longer think in terms of 'my client'. There is an analogous process in the coal mining study, in which, according to Trist et al. (1963), miners drew upon the ethos of the pre-mechanisation era in evolving the composite method of working.

For the department to work towards a relational strategy would have entailed conversations with others involved in mental health services about what members of the community wanted from them. Such conversations would have had to take into account the desires which focus upon mental health services, including – to paraphrase Anton Obholzer – the wish for a 'keep-madness-out-of-sight' service.[46] In an early note to the team I in fact proposed that they should set out to:

> . . . articulate an aim (which wasn't just a motherhood statement) for mental health in [the locality] – one which all services could identify with – an answer to the question 'What are we trying to do?', in which the 'we' is all those broadly concerned with mental health services. . . . If the overall vision is clear, concern about professional identity may fall into perspective.

We eventually attempted to do this, and it did produce motherhood statements, because the intervention was not based on an understanding of the significance of this move. Moreover, the whole point of such an activity would be that it made possible a shift of attention from the concerns of the unit to the needs of the community – what might be called a decentring of the unit as a subject. This could only be achieved if new voices were brought into the conversation.

Inconclusive postscript

To attempt to summarise the conclusions of this chapter would be to succumb to the very wish for completeness which it has sought to question. It must speak to the reader through its gaps and prevarications and what it takes for granted, as well as through what is clear and coherent. For the writer it has crystallised a number of propositions:

- It is possible to characterise the Tavistock approach to organisational behaviour as a paradigm which includes certain identifiable model examples of practice and theorising, key theoretical concepts, and core practices – in spite of the fact that this characterisation cannot do justice either to the depth and diversity of the work which has been done within this paradigm or to the significance of the dissensions and divergences from it.
- It is possible to adopt a critical position in relation to this paradigm by viewing it as rooted in a discursive formation of which the basic building blocks (objects) are persons, groups and institutions

---

[46] Obholzer suggests that the National Health Service is unconsciously expected to be a 'keep-death-at-bay' service (Obholzer and Roberts, 1994, p. 171).

conceived as bounded entities with an inside and an outside; in which the inner 'reality' so constituted is regarded as the domain of psychoanalytic enquiry and is elaborated in detail while the excluded 'outer reality' is left to other disciplines.

- It is possible to begin to delineate a new paradigm for psychoanalytic understanding and practice in organisations, which reframes key elements in the Tavistock paradigm – a new paradigm which acknowledges the necessity of drawing boundaries in order to think and act but in which the consultant (manager, practitioner) does not identify with these boundaries, regarding the whole field of inner/outer and individual/environment as accessible to psychoanalytic enquiry.

10 PSYCHOANALYSIS IN THE PUBLIC SPHERE: Some Recent British Developments in Psychoanalytic Social Psychology

KARL FIGLIO AND BARRY RICHARDS

The idea of a psychoanalytic social psychology generates resistance both inside and outside the psychoanalytic world. Inside, there is a tension between the reclusiveness that is intrinsic to analytic work (see Rustin, 1991; Richards, 1984a) and the wish to look outwards and contribute directly to the wider society. Everyday exigencies of clinical work, and probably some degree of inertia, keep the analytic world focused on itself, and maintain the tension at a low level. But the idea of a psychoanalytic social psychology is likely to heighten it by reminding psychoanalysis of its wider ambition – the kind that Freud had for it – of throwing light on the nature of human communities and their problems. Outside psycho-analysis, there is a tension between the materialist and rationalist orientation of social sciences, and the importance to a psychoanalytic social psychology of the *individual*, of the emotions and of the irrational in social processes. The project of a psychoanalytic social psychology may also be seen as an attempt to subvert the knowledge and authority of other disciplines in the social sciences, or as an attack upon common sense generally.

Despite such criticisms, psychoanalysis is a source of profound insight into human behaviour, and the project of developing and disseminating a psychoanalytic social psychology is very important. While there has not been such a field in Britain, there has been an informal project. Perhaps it would be more accurate to speak of a grouping of psychoanalytic clini-cians and people grounded in other ways of understanding society, each having a commitment to learning from the other, and to approaching political issues and cultural life on the basis of a psychoanalytically informed understanding.

Loose as it has been, this grouping has certain defining features. On the psychoanalytic side, it has drawn largely upon the 'British object relations' tradition, which includes a particular British form of Jungian depth psychology as well. On the political and social side, it has derived largely from a tradition of British 'ethical socialism', with a strong cultural leaning, as opposed to a strictly economistic 'scientific marxism' (Thompson, 1978).

It would be misleading to name this grouping. There are a number and a variety of people and activities that could be included, and the boundaries could be drawn in several places. But there has been a sense of a project based on an informal alliance between the journal *Free Associations* and the associated publishing house, on the one hand, and the University (previously the Polytechnic) of East London, on the other. We will call this project FAEL. Our account of it is more impressionistic than systematic, though we will seek to identify some of its crucial features.

Roots

We can delineate the grouping that supported the project by pinpointing where gatherings of like-minded people might have been found; in particular, we can point out at least two levels, each with key organisations, events and publications. At the basic level, we might mention, firstly, a range of groups that sprang up in the 1970s, concerned with the health and well-being of individuals and society, within or linked to an ethical socialist tradition (we will deal with the second, psychoanalytic level later in the article). The Society for Social Responsibility in Science published *Science for People*, and other groups, made up mainly of people working in related fields, published journals such as *Radical Statistics*, *Radical Science*, *Radical Philosophy*, *History Workshop Journal*. Many of the members of these groups were professionals who sought to narrow the gap between popular culture and the authority of experts, and to enhance democracy and a sense of collective responsibility through the dispersal of expertise throughout the political body.

One should also note the influence of academic fields and their institutions. Social history, the sociology and social history of medicine, and the history and philosophy of science and medicine were changing. No longer satisfied with antiquarian documentation of interesting people or historical situations, they moved towards a more systematic understanding of social life and the place of a professional middle class in it. They included scientific naturalism and the production of scientific theory in their understanding of the lived experience of social life, along with customs, rituals, craft and art.

As we cast a wider and wider net, we can trawl the influences from fields as diverse as cultural anthropology, which compared belief in 'traditional' cultures with science in western culture (e.g. Horton, 1971), the sociology of knowledge, which analysed the idea of truth and opened it to a more sociological understanding (e.g. Barnes, 1974; Bloor, 1976), and literature, which explored the relationship between culture and the material conditions of life (e.g. Williams, 1958). In general, they brought to the surface for criticism the implicit assumption that western middle-class culture possessed an inherently more rational, more objective, more effective knowledge of the natural world than either western popular culture or non-western culture; and that experts earned their status and authority through their mastery of this knowledge. They showed that these assumptions were integral to western middle-class self-consciousness to such an extent that their basis in class and race dynamics was hidden, and that revealing these dynamics added force to the democratising of expertise.

If we tried to write a collective biography of the people involved in the FAEL project, we would find these fields well represented. If there was a common aim, albeit not espoused as a project, it was to understand the full range of social life as social – as lived experience rather than as determined from the outside – and to use that rediscovered liveliness to mobilise a belief in change, a sense of responsibility for change and an agency to realise it.

At the time of the crystallisation of the project in the late 1970s, marxism was still a predominant body of ideas amongst significant sections of the British intelligentsia. For FAEL, the core ideas were Marx's concepts of living and dead labour, use- and exchange-value, labour and labour-power. These ideas encapsulated the feeling that under capitalism, human creativity was thwarted, and the capacity for it was often lost from personal experience, being projected into external forces. Human capacities and activities could be recovered as lived experience through a thorough analysis of the way they were lost and through changing the social organisation of labour – the relationships of production – and, in particular, the organisation of labour that was formed by the expertise held by a small stratum of the workforce.

In Marx's formulation, the capacity to work included the capacity to plan, the skills needed to execute the plan, the control over production and the integration of labouring into life. This labour process was lost as an experience, as it was increasingly incorporated into machines and into an organisation of labour that was owned – outside the experience and capacities of workers – by capitalists and, more abstractly, by capitalism. Living labour and the sense of agency and existential integrity were estranged.

Many people involved in the broad networks and trends which we have listed might have recognised the concept of estrangement. They would have argued for the need to recover a sense of connectedness with work, and between work and everyday life, as well as for the capacity to affect the organisation of labour. But few of them would have turned to psychoanalysis to understand what Marx was trying to describe: the loss of self; the feeling of estrangement or depersonalisation; the possession by dead objects and alien powers; the secret admiration for relentless forces; the yearning for a good, protective other, who was also attacked and denigrated; the containing as well as the oppressive function of social structure and processes.[47]

When some of them did turn to psychoanalysis, they turned to those psychoanalytic orientations – Kleinian and object relations theory, or the 'British' traditions – that concentrated most intensively upon just these aspects of experience that they had found in Marx. There seemed to be a kinship waiting to be found between 'ethical' or 'cultural' marxism and psychoanalysis. The themes mentioned above delineated an area of common interest, called estrangement in marxism and projective identification in psychoanalysis.

We think that there was another, less easily defined kinship. On the marxist side, the authors whose works were most admired were probably Christopher Hill, Eric Hobsbawm, E.P. Thompson and Raymond Williams, who influenced the *History Workshop Journal*, and numerous authors and groupings who studied everyday life as a dynamic interplay of conf'icting forces. In general, they eschewed any notion of a predetermined social reality on the one hand, or a free individual agency on the other. Culture was the territory created out of these forces, as what could not be wholly possessed by anyone: it contained, in Raymond Williams' words (1989), 'resources of hope' as well as enforcement of authority. Whether it was the British pub, grain laws, the form of the landscape, enclosure, poaching, direct action or elections: all was culture, all was politics, all was economics; all was, in marxist terminology, both (economic) base and (social) superstructure.

It was an easy and inviting move from this cultural marxism to Winnicott's notion of transitional space (Winnicott, 1967), that indefinable unpossessable mediator between self and other, held in being by mother and child, and materialised in the transitional object. It was equally easy to see in the dynamically maintained social order the loops of

---

[47] The idea of a 'labour process' in which intellectual and cultural, as well as material, production occurred became a guiding mode of analysis. For a collection of FAEL essays, written within such an analytical framework, see Levidow and Young (1985).

projection and introjection and the containing function that, in Klein's and Bion's thinking, respectively, stabilise the psyche. And in all cases, there was a striking analogy between the loss of self into dead labour, as Marx described it, and into the object by projective identification, as Klein described it.

Thus in the intellectual context of the late 1970s and early 1980s there was a broad possibility, seen by some, for closing the gap between primitive emotional states and social/political processes. The emergence of the project we are discussing was an attempt to grasp this possibility, to insert a psychoanalytic model into cultural marxism and its less ideological 'fellow-travelling' currents in left thought.

The groups we have mentioned were not necessarily sympathetic to psychoanalysis, but most of the people who later would find their way to psychoanalysis as the most profound understanding of human experience and social forces were members of them. One cannot speak about a British psychoanalytic social psychology without mentioning them as the milieu from which it grew.

Organisations and activities

At the next, more strictly psychoanalytic level, there were very few institutional locations for this project. They were principally the journal *Free Associations* and the Sociology Department (particularly that part of it which is now the Department of Human Relations) of the University of East London. In later years, one would also have to take into account the growing number of academic centres for psychoanalytic studies, which aim to introduce psychoanalytic thinking into British universities, and groups of socially concerned psychotherapists, such as Psychotherapists and Counsellors for Social Responsibility, who seek more immediate practical opportunities to make use of psychoanalytic understanding in social situations. We would also include OPUS, 'An Organisation for Promoting Understanding in Society', which had applied psychodynamic and group relations thinking to social issues; Psychoanalysts Against Nuclear War; and The Higher Education Research and Information Network in Psychoanalysis (THERIP), within which there was a strong Lacanian presence. But at the outset and in the more strictly British psychoanalytic orientation, FAEL was the main gathering point.

The work of FAEL has taken three main forms:

● the publication, from 1984 to the present, of the journal *Free Associations*

● the organisation of conferences at UEL, from 1987 to the present, under the general heading of 'Psychoanalysis and the Public Sphere', and the publication of work presented and developed at those conferences
● the publication of books and articles by various members of the FAEL group.

As we have said, to refer to the existence of a 'group' is perhaps presumptuous, since a wide range of work is represented here, and there are some important differences of approach among key individuals. Also, while, for some people, FAEL provided their main intellectual orientation during this time, for others whose contribution was no less significant it was one of a number of contexts in which they worked. Nonetheless, some kind of grouping can be identified, as a collection of people with a broadly common project.

A brief outline of the institutional contexts in which this work has been produced will help to situate the intellectual agenda which we will describe shortly in the socio-political circumstances of its emergence. This will point towards one of the main themes of this chapter: whether psychoanalysis can give rise to an effective *applied* social psychology, one which is widely understood and respected, and which has a significant influence upon the wider society.

The journal *Free Associations* first appeared in 1984, as issue Number 15 of the *Radical Science Journal* and simultaneously as the pilot issue of the new journal. *Radical Science Journal* had been published since 1974 by a London-based collective of academics, journalists and others seeking to apply a libertarian marxism to the critique of science as a key institution of capitalist society through its role in 'naturalising' and legitimating all kinds of social inequality and oppression. Through some chance connections in recruitment to the collective, a number of its members, by the late 1970s, were, or were becoming, primarily interested in psychoanalysis.[48] The new journal was given a decisive lift-off by the formation around the same time of Free Association Books, which provided a professional publishing infrastructure.

---

[48] The first fruit of this informal subgroup was an essay which appeared in 1978 in *Radical Science Journal* No. 6/7 – Waddell et al., (1978). Written jointly by four of the collective, it was a review of Juliet Mitchell's *Psychoanalysis and Feminism*, one of the founding texts of psychoanalytic studies. Later, a 'Marx/Freud' reading group was formed, with the aim of exploring the literature on the psychoanalytic understanding of society and politics. This group, which met regularly for several years, self-consciously identified itself with the ethical and cultural Marxist tradition referred to earlier.

One of the hallmarks of Free Association Books was a markedly high standard of design. The attention to design, which included everything to do with the book as a physical object, was integral to the publishing ideology. It aimed to bring together 'head' and 'hand', intellectual and physical production, the ideas conveyed by the book and the material product. It aimed to exemplify the intellectual work as a kind of production, and material production as the realisation of an idea. It was itself a form of cultural marxism (*Head and Hand* was also the name of a broadsheet journal, consisting mainly of review articles, published by the Conference of Socialist Economists, to which FAEL members contributed).

Free Association Books was founded by Robert Young, who had been a prominent figure in the *Radical Science Journal* Collective.[49] Under his direction it published *Free Associations*, as well as continuing with *Radical Science Journal*. (In 1987 *Radical Science Journal* was replaced by a second new journal, *Science as Culture*.) It went on to establish itself as a leading publisher of psychoanalytic books, with many eminent authors on its list. It combined this with a pioneering role in publishing books in the then unrecognised field of psychoanalytic studies. During the second half of the 1980s the existence of Free Association Books as a resource, support and focal point for the writing and intellectual work of many people was a valuable and important factor in the development of a psychoanalytic presence in British cultural and political discourse, and of a psychoanalytic influence in social thought.[50]

In 1987 the University (then the Polytechnic) of East London collaborated with Free Association Books in staging a conference entitled 'Psychoanalysis and the Public Sphere'. The journal was by then well established and there was clearly a growing constituency for the kind of

---

[49] As a sign of the times, unlike its predecessor (*Radical Science Journal*), the new journal did not conceive of itself as produced by a 'collective'. From its inception to the present, Robert Young has been editor, and has worked with a series of managing editors and book reviews editors. Until 1990 (with issue 19) there was also an editorial committee, a small group with various degrees of active involvement in producing the journal, though some members of the wider advisory editorial board, which continued to meet for several years, also played active parts in the planning of future issues.

[50] The publishing house reflected Young's wide intellectual interests by mixing its psychoanalytic output with a smaller number of titles in the fields of science and technology studies, social theory and Left politics. By 1995 Free Association Books had changed hands, and *Free Associations* was being published by the American publisher Guilford Press in association with Young at his new company, Process Press. It is now published by Karnac Books, though editorial responsibility has been retained by Process Press.

intellectual work and political agenda it represented, and for exploring the further potential for exchange between clinicians and academics. It was thought that a conference would extend the reach of the journal, the British readership of which was based quite heavily in the therapeutic professions. The scale of participation in this event and the quality of work produced was such that it was repeated for the following ten years. Additional people external to both UEL and *Free Associations* were drawn in as organisers over the years, and a very wide range of work, some of it falling intellectually quite outside the FAEL project, was presented at the conferences.

There has been a significant overlap between FAEL and the work of various people at the Tavistock Clinic. Two Tavistock staff members have been active in the journal editorial group. In the 1990s, the University of East London validated a number of Tavistock training courses, and some joint postgraduate teaching was developed, thus institutionalising and extending a productive collaboration. Tavistock staff have been occasional contributors to *Free Associations* and frequent speakers at the Public Sphere conferences. As one of the major institutional homes of object-relational and Kleinian work, and moreover as a part of the British National Health Service with a 'missionary' tradition of seeking to extend the influence of psychodynamic ways of thinking to the public welfare sector (Rustin, 1991), the Tavistock could be seen as a major influence on the work we are considering here.[51]

In addition to the activities sketched above, individual members participated in the work of other organisations, such as the British Society for Social Responsibility in Science and the Conference of Socialist Economists, which were seen as kindred, albeit without the psychoanalytic dimension that was at the core of FAEL.

Politics and the primitive

The Tavistock link points to a distinctly British quality of the FAEL project (notwithstanding some strongly American colouring in the origins of some individuals involved). It also had a high level of political concern, and the Britishness can be seen in the political traditions which were involved as well as in the kinds of psychoanalytic work which have been drawn upon.

---

[51] Of course there are major differences. The Tavistock is a major international institution for clinical work, training and consultancy, not an intellectual grouping. Also, it is an important base for the development and application of ideas derived from systems thinking and from group therapies, as well as from individual psychoanalytic work. Although *Free Associations* has always proclaimed a primary interest in 'groups', it has run only a small number of major articles on group processes in culture (e.g. Berke, 1996; Wolfenstein, 1990), along with a few on therapeutic work in groups (e.g. Ellwood and Oke, 1987; Karterud, 1989).

A prominent theme has been the wish to breathe new life into socialism, as a way of understanding social problems, of imagining social change, and of engaging in practical matters of policy and politics. The insights that psychoanalysis can bring to the human condition in a general sense, and to particular human responses to particular social conditions, have been examined for their potential to revise and revive traditions of socialism which have (despite their limited appearance in government) been a dominant influence in British society, especially its intellectual life, during this century. These are basically traditions of *ethical* socialism, and – as described above – of cultural marxism, as distinct from the scientific marxism that enjoyed wide influence in the 1960s and 1970s.[52]

The present interest amongst some in the British Labour Party in its long history of ethical socialism, and in refashioning that tradition for the new millennium, may then be an appropriate context in which to review this body of work in psychoanalytic studies. A large ambition moves within this work: to transform the socialist tradition, and render it more powerful and effective for the present, by placing within it an understanding of human nature derived from clinical psychoanalysis. In all the spheres of politics – the analysis of problems, policy-making, cultivation of the democratic process within and outside political parties, and so on – a psychoanalytically informed input can add depth, clarity and effectiveness. Moreover, the basic values that all politics do or should pursue can of themselves be enriched by an understanding of unconscious mental life.

Of course such an ambition carries well beyond the British cultural context and beyond the concerns of self-conscious socialism. The work of this grouping has always had a strongly international dimension, and in identifying it as having a specifically British nature we are characterising its contribution to what are now global debates rather than limiting its relevance to the British context. It is distinct from adjacent bodies of work – for example, from the large body of work in cultural studies and gender studies – which draw mainly on French psychoanalytic theories and tend to be highly theoretical. By contrast, FAEL is grounded in object relations, and is persistently concerned with social justice, social policy and welfare, that is, with the traditional agendas of socialism. There has been, for example, a particular focus on the fate of the British welfare state. But,

---

[52] There was a brief ascendancy of a 'scientific marxism', which considered the 'super-structure' of culture to be only 'relatively autonomous' from the economic base, and therefore tended to think of culture more as an aspect of economic determinism. This orientation was a strong influence in the political formation of some of the members of the group, and part of a response in the 1980s to the triumph of the 'new', neo-liberal Conservatism; the leading intellectual figure for this orientation was the French philosopher, Louis Althusser.

more generally, this work can be seen as relevant to any attempt to understand the anxieties and defences that are mobilised at a social level (i.e.
within the group, organisation, society or culture), and therefore to a
psychoanalytic social psychology in the broadest sense.

The sources of the most distinctive FAEL output have been primarily in
British psychoanalytic explorations of the individual mind and its developmental roots. In the works of, for example, Figlio, Hinshelwood, Hoggett,
Richards, Rustin, Samuels and Young, the central themes are frequently those
of a psyche beset by terror at its own destructive possibilities and at the possibility of not finding a responsive other, but developing towards some capacity
to process and contain its fears and its impulses by the internalisation of a
nurturant and protective other. The exploration of how this dynamic process
takes shape within, and gives shape to, the politics and culture of contemporary Britain has constituted a considerable part of their work, in studies of
politics (Richards, 1986; Rustin, 1991; Hoggett, 1992; Samuels, 1993), drama
(Rustin, 1991), children's literature (Rustin and Rustin, 1987), popular
culture (Young, 1989, 1994; Richards, 1994), social policy (Hoggett, 1992),
and healthcare (Hinshelwood, 1987; Figlio, 1989). This work tends not to
emphasise organised political institutions and the implementation of policy,
but the underlying dynamics of a 'politics of everyday life': the forms of
coercion, compliance, cohesion, conflict and agency that make up ordinary
life. What makes it political is also what makes it psychoanalytic: the aim of
rejoining the fragmented and estranged parts of the self, individual and
social, and the sense of possibility and agency that follows from it.

These themes cluster around the work of psychoanalysts such as Klein,
Bion, Winnicott and others, with which the Tavistock has been particularly
associated. The common interests testify to the strong overall influence of
the Tavistock on FAEL, both as a powerful presence in the professional and
intellectual culture, as well as through more contingent individual links.
An example of the closeness of some long-standing 'Tavistock' concerns to
the agenda of the FAEL grouping is indicated by a volume of essays, *The
Politics of Attachment*, which is a wide-ranging collection based on a 1995
conference at the Tavistock. This event aimed to demonstrate the importance to politics of an understanding of basic emotional needs, specifically
the understanding developed in Bowlby's attachment theory.[53]

---

[53] Attachment theory has not been much present in FAEL, though Bowlby himself was
interviewed for *Free Associations* (Bowlby, Figlio and Young, 1986), and there has
been other sympathetic commentary, e.g. Bacciagaluppi (1989). This is probably
because of the tangential relationship of attachment theory to the conception of
unconscious phantasy, which – in the wish to have psychoanalysis take us to the very
core of experience – has been regarded within FAEL as a touchstone of theoretical
strength, echoing the way in which Juliet Mitchell (1975) 'rediscovered' Freud in the
concept of the unconscious.

The attachment theory of this volume sits closely alongside a Winnicottian understanding of emotional development, and, despite the tendency to import a de-subjectified biological tone to the discourse, asserts that the quality of attachments depends upon personal histories. In gathering together politicians and others in public life with social scientists and welfare professionals, and in trying to place emotional need on mainstream political agendas, this conference gave a very effective expression to a major aim of FAEL, albeit in the form of what turned out to be a quite eclectic conversation.

FAEL typically sought to sustain a more theoretically intense position. Though the journal has carried a wide range of material, the writings of its main producers, though very different in many respects, have, as noted above, characteristically drawn deeply and consistently on the theoretical language of Kleinian and object-relational psychoanalysis.

It is important to note that both *Free Associations* and the 'Psychoanalysis and the Public Sphere' conferences were open forums. Contributors were usually not self-consciously signing up to a 'project', but expressed their sense of common purpose in deciding that these forums might provide a congenial environment for their ideas. What we are doing in writing this chapter is trying, mainly from our own experience, to discern and describe the sense of a project and the themes around which it took shape.

Expertise and the everyday

From the point of view of a politics based on an understanding of emotional needs, the cultural marxism we have described above did seem to need completion by a psychoanalytic understanding. We put it this way around – the completion of cultural marxism by psychoanalysis – because that was the way it actually happened, not because psychoanalysis set the standard by which cultural marxism was to be assessed. So what was new about the project, in which psychoanalysis complemented the radical impulse of many of the participants?

We have already referred to the idea of estrangement in Marx and to projection and projective identification in psychoanalysis, and to their concern with the way in which the sense of self apparently comes under the sway of external forces. In a liberal democratic society with highly developed processes of organising consent and managing dissidence, and with production based on technology, authority operates more through everyday life and work than through the direct application of power or status. For people with a professional background, including, therefore, most contributors to the project, the 'organisation of consent', as opposed to the enforcement of authority, would have been the dominant root of a radical impulse. For them, the 'dead labour' that faced them as an alien force would not have been the machines that faced the working class of Marx's time, but the coalescence and hardening of knowledge, experience and expertise into a notion of nature – second nature – interpreted by experts: a new mandarinate whose authority rested on knowing the truth that was then the basis of the regulation of society.

The analyses that could loosely be included within this heading covered a range of specific topics concerned with the critique of scientific expertise, scientism and scientific reductionism. In general, psychoanalytic understanding was used to explore the loss of authority and self-sufficiency and the drift into passivity, not born of a conscious experience of futility but of the 'rightness' of deference to authority or to the seeming nature of things.

A related area might be called the 'estrangement of everyday life'. What we have in mind here is an experience of everyday life, in which the infrastructure maintained by human mutual dependence is repressed. Things are experienced as being the way they are, not on the basis of the 'living labour' of social life, but because of a lawfulness, whether social or natural. The revelation of the living human fabric of life can be as startling as the revelation in consciousness of repressed unconscious material. Articles such as those by Hoggett (1992) analysed this social repression and the ordinary incidents through which repression is suddenly lifted. Modena's (1991) discussion of labour relations in an Italian factory showed the unconscious dynamics at work in the organised area of labour management based on economic and production criteria.

Tensions and contradictions

But while this work has contributed significantly to the widening currency of that language, it has not achieved the breadth of impact on other disciplines, and in public debate, that it has aspired to. For one thing, the depth of affinity between cultural marxism and psychoanalysis did not override a tension between them. Although the connections between psychic primitivity and the social and political domains (e.g. Frosh, 1991; Rustin, 1991; Hoggett, 1992) produced an understanding of the complexity and paradoxical nature of many things, it also re-presented some old problems in a deeper form; in particular, the tension between the activism of marxism and the reflectiveness of psychoanalysis.

There has always been a tendency to oppose psychoanalysis to a radical impulse towards activism, and to see in it a dilution of a sense of social and political injustice, even its collapse into a preoccupation with individual and individualised misery. One might see the development of

FAEL as a wrestling with the traditional opposition between the collective and the individual. Also, though, it was poised between the sense of clear purpose that drives activism on the one hand, and the tentative open-endedness of psychoanalysis on the other. Thus, a number of contributors to the journal sought to institute a psychoanalytic critique of radical politics, intending to deepen or sophisticate its radical aims, or the means by which they were pursued, but the outcome was to dissolve the radical impulse of the critique.

There is a similar contradictory relationship, one of affinity and tension, between the psychoanalytic roots of the FAEL project and the political roots of feminism, its other major political source. In the pilot issue of the journal, the psychoanalyst Jane Temperley (1984) argued that women may have an unconscious investment in their disadvantage. Her argument deepened the feminist agenda, using an approach analogous to the understanding of 'secondary gain' in psychological disorder. She concluded, however, by asserting the need to accept complementarity between the sexes as part of the developmentally necessary task of accepting the creativity of the parental couple. Such a view, which stood prior to any political cause, at least moderated or revised a predominant form of feminism, if not actually regrounding its aims.

For most readers of this first issue, the papers that focused most sharply the tension between psychoanalysis and radical politics were by well-established leaders of the psychological Left in Britain and the USA respectively: the psychologist David Ingleby and the psychoanalyst Joel Kovel. Ingleby (1984) warned of the 'ambivalence' of psychoanalysis. While it had the potential to contribute to an emancipatory critique of society, it was also vulnerable to incorporation into the individualist and conservative practices of the 'psy complex' (the array of expertise and practices through which individuals are regulated and social order maintained). For Ingleby, the task of a radical psychoanalysis was to show the pathology of normalcy. This task became the basic agenda for two collections of essays, *Capitalism and Infancy* (1984) and its sequel *Crises of the Self* (1989), edited by Barry Richards and published by Free Association Books, which included work by a number of the people involved in the FAEL project and some papers from the first 'Psychoanalysis and the Public Sphere' conference.

Kovel offered some uncomfortable reflections on the practice of psychoanalysis, which, for the most part, he saw to be of little value beyond its benefits to the individuals concerned, and which therefore (in a manner conventional in Left thinking of the time, though now more easily questioned) he damned with faint praise: it 'is a not inconsiderable good – but it is predicated on an already bourgeoisified existence . . . is a bourgeois practice', linked with socio-economic privilege (Kovel, 1984, p. 152). For Kovel as for Ingleby, the hope for psychoanalysis lay in its potential as a critical tool in theory, not as an 'adaptationist' practice.

This view of psychoanalysis as a deeply compromised practice – ambivalent in theory as well, yet able as theory to transcend its bourgeois origins and contribute to the socialist project – was a dominant one at the outset of the FAEL project. We may see it as constituting an unspoken orthodoxy, a core to the project. But the more positive contribution of psychoanalysis, signalled in the pilot issue by Temperley and Richards, was to reappear. In *Free Associations* 3, Paul Parin, a leading figure in a group of radical psychoanalysts based in Zurich, contributed an article on 'The psychoanalysis of political commitment'.[54] He described the experiences and reactions of four patients during the invasion of Czechoslovakia in 1968, and argued that their concern for the fate of the Czech people stemmed from their psychic health, from their having arrived on the whole at good resolutions of internalised conflicts with parents. Far from diluting political consciousness, individual psychic health sharpened it.

But Parin's broader point was that political health and psychic health go together. Political commitment of any sort must involve the mobilisation of personal conflicts and identifications, and he acknowledged (p. 78) that 'in no way will only those people who have realised these ideals [of freedom and independence] in their individual development in fact pursue them' in the political domain. It was nonsensical, he claimed, to see political commitment as nothing other than an attempt to solve an internal conflict, but equally, he insisted that no commitment should escape analysis of the internal needs it meets. He did not intend to pathologise political consciousness, nor to remove it from individual conflict and needs. On the contrary, he aimed to make its links with health clear.

From another, more philosophical angle, Ian Craib (1986) brought socialist values into a critical space where they may be subject to amendment by confrontation with the forces of human nature as understood by psychoanalysis.

> Socialists need to think seriously about the forms of authority and social control which must circumscribe democratic control, as well as the forms of democratic control which encourage the development of our more rational capacities (p. 77).

---

[54] Parin and a number of other psychoanalysts formed the Psychoanalytisches Seminar Zürich, a psychoanalytic society with a training and a commitment to the radical political potential of psychoanalysis. Members of FAEL took part in PSZ meetings over several years, and it was this contact that led to the submission of articles from PSZ members to *Free Associations* (see also Modena, 1986).

Craib was invoking, as independent variable, what Joel Kovel had earlier called the 'transhistorical', and what more commonly might be referred to as 'human nature', but acknowledged its influence more than Kovel did. While 'socialism' has remained a point of reference, in a number of other contributions to the journal at this time and later, it now has a status closer to that of dependent variable rather than moral absolute.

Along with the exploration of the everyday, to which we referred above, studies of this sort began to undermine the orthodox opposition between the radical impulse and psychoanalysis, between the collective reaction to social injustice and the individual reaction to internal misery and conflict. From a psychoanalytic point of view, the distinction is not between individual and social, but between internal and external worlds; in particular, between actions that are driven by, and enact, unconscious fantasies, and actions that modify them and thereby lead to a healthier psychic and social condition.

Thus the defence against an internal threat could be transformed into a defence against an external threat. As Richards argued in another article in the pilot issue, an internal, psychic defence (against phantasies of massive destruction) could take shape in the external world as an advocacy of civil defence (against imagined nuclear attack). To understand the impulse towards civil defence, one needed to understand the way it became the vehicle for psychic defence. On the other side, for the anti-nuclear campaigners, the absoluteness of the phantasied destruction prevented any engagement with the possibly less than absolute reality. In refusing to countenance the possible value of any form of civil defence, they were as driven by phantasy as those who imagined that fallout could be avoided by crawling under a table.

This kind of psychoanalytic understanding of political issues is quite consistent with a radical impulse and a particular course of action, and indeed sought to strengthen the anti-nuclear cause by rendering it more self-aware. What it also does, however, is withdraw the automatic sense of rightness from radical politics, since neither the external problem nor the inner meaning of the response to it is as clear or as free from contradiction as it previously seemed to be.

So in one respect the claim that psychoanalysis is at odds with the radical impulse does hold, but not around the issue of individualism versus socialism. From a psychoanalytic point of view, engagement in the external world is healthy; individualised retreat is unhealthy. The difficulty in the way of the radical impulse is rather the sense of contradiction that psychoanalysis finds in both the psyche and in society, next to which the sense of clear purpose often expresses a manic defence: a flight from reality, instead of an engagement with it. Political conflict inevitably mobilises psychic conflict, as well as being driven by the need to externalise the internal world with its phantasies. Thus the problem of how best to resolve or manage conflict seems to sink into another stratum.

Thus a position emerged, which tended to be at odds with the 'orthodoxy'. It tended to distrust all ideology and rhetoric, and to deconstruct the radical ideal as thoroughly as the oppressive tradition. In *Free Associations*, the effort to breathe new life into socialism re-awoke another body of thought, and revived that as well: the encounter with ultra-Leftism and the turn to psychoanalysis refreshed the liberal critique of dogma in all its forms.

Other elements within the FAEL project may also have contributed to this effect. It was basic to the credo of the parent journal, the *Radical Science Journal*, that a libertarian critique of science was the key to social transformation, and this preoccupation with science and its values was carried over into *Free Associations*. A critique of the alleged 'scientism' of American ego-psychology could thus be smoothly absorbed into the journal's agenda, alongside the Marcusan attack on the conformist nature of most American psychoanalysis. (The 1984 pilot issue had opened with a piece about, and a piece by, Russell Jacoby, the American author of some of the most influential of such attacks.) Notably, as already described, the 'scientific' extension of British psychoanalysis in the development of attachment theory was given minor but respectful attention; its concern with relationships and nurture, and its close links with British state welfare practices, marked it as a topic for sympathetic treatment.

As a historian of the human sciences, Robert Young brought to FAEL his concern with combating scientism and reclaiming psychoanalysis as a form of humanistic understanding, in opposition to influential writers such as Sulloway (1979), for whom Freud was a biologist, and in sympathy with the assertion of Bettelheim and others that psychoanalysis was a hermeneutics of the soul (see *Free Associations* 6; also, see Figlio, 1984). For there to be a common project of politics and psychoanalysis, it was important that psychoanalysis was not seen as another form of scientism with its associated experts.

Again, however, this aim may have tended to subvert itself. The shift from scientific socialism to cultural marxism did not yield a coherent political agenda, and so the dissolution of the 'project' began. The inclusion of psychoanalysis in the intellectual engine room added a further dimension to the understanding of cultural life, but that made it even less likely that an identifiably distinct body of work would develop. As a humanistic discipline, even when oriented mainly towards the ethically grounded work of the British schools, psychoanalysis is too polyvalent for a recognisable programme of work to emerge spontaneously from its simple insertion into the political and cultural domains. There are no limits to the topics that might be addressed, and no rules about how the interface with other disciplines is to be ordered. Thus the pages of *Free Associations* came increasingly to be filled by a great diversity of isolated essays, making a variety of connections with other fields, and presenting illuminating forays into a host of territories, predominantly cultural and professional.

Outcomes

While other journals of its time may have imploded within the esoteric spaces of their defined projects, *Free Associations* sought to keep the boundaries of its project fluid, and to enrich itself by absorbing a range of experiences. In a cultural firmament already crowded with distinct constellations of activity, it was therefore at risk of being unnoticed. Those who have tracked its progress admire, and are grateful for, its richness and originality, as are those whose particular interests have been addressed by a specific essay. But like a minor comet, its trajectory and fire have gone largely unobserved by many potential readerships: sales remain limited, citation rates are probably low, and the journal, like the wider project of which it is a part, has not established a firm and well-recognised presence which – difficult though that may be in the context of massive intellectual over-production and of a fragmented intellectual community – has been achieved to some degree by other innovative UK journals of similar longevity, such as *Theory, Culture and Society*.[55]

Perhaps this fate, though it is by no means unique among the many intellectual journals founded in the last few decades, is inevitable for a journal that tries to create a space that is strongly psychoanalytic, but is not the journal of a profession; not tied to therapeutics, and therefore not grounded in the technical concerns and organisational structures of professional therapy. Unlike, say, the *British Journal of Psychotherapy*, which was established around the same time, *Free Associations* has no pre-existing constituency. The FAEL grouping became aware of itself in

---

[55] Recent years have also seen the founding of an academic field of psychoanalytic studies in British universities, with journals to go with it. And just as *Radical Science Journal* became *Free Associations* and *Science as Culture*, in a climate in which radical projects either disappeared or found entrées into the academic world, so psychoanalytic studies has absorbed the interest in the philosophical, cultural, historical and political dimensions of psychoanalysis. In Britain, new journals include *Psychoanalytic Studies*; in the United States, the *Journal for the Psychoanalysis of Society and Culture*.

finding a way through psychoanalysis to articulate a concern within cultural marxism. The FAEL project offered an opportunity for a psychoanalytically informed political consciousness. This consciousness may – or may not – be part of future developments on the 'Left' or in the new political spaces 'beyond Left and Right' (Giddens, 1994).

Perhaps, also, the qualities and limitations of the FAEL project illustrate something of the general possibilities for psychoanalytic social psychology. Psychoanalytic investigation in the clinical sense does not proceed from well-defined starting-points and move towards predefined objectives. It is a multi-levelled, continually negotiated undertaking, which must remain ready to attend to and absorb new concerns, and to consider anything relevant. FAEL, while it had ambitions to wed the psychoanalytic agenda to existing academic and political ones, has also (for whatever reasons, whether due to the primary commitments of its editors, or of its subscribers and contributors), remained attached primarily to a clinically defined agenda. It has, as a result, developed as a unique, creative, decentred body of writing. It is permeable to many concerns, but lacks a structured and stable strategy of its own. It has provided a space for a range of work, including many subtle and surprising essays, which do not lend themselves to generalisation. A psychoanalytic social psychology, unless constrained by some other parameters (offering more constraint and definition than that provided by 'cultural marxism'), is likely to offer such a space, but not a programme; to encourage a permissive spirit of enquiry, but lack an authoritative body of evidence.

Two reflections on the achievements of the FAEL project have been published in the journal in recent years. Cooper and Treacher (1995) noted that psychoanalysis brings a deep sense of complexity to the understanding of politics, and enables us as political actors to recognise and come to terms with the burdens of ambivalence, and particularly of guilt, which participation in the conflictual history of many societies will inevitably produce. Their example is the dramatic one of South Africa, but the point has universal relevance. They also comment, however, that, notwithstanding these gains in our understanding, and in contrast to the growing preoccupation with internal and private lives, an adequate mode of political and public life has still to be identified and lived. Indeed, the very category of the 'political' remains problematic.

They attribute this to the condition of western societies as a whole. Yet whatever the strength of this general critique, they also observe that there has been a specific failure of psychoanalytic work to insert itself into political and social debate.(Their example is another one related to race: the controversies in the field of adoption.)

In a later issue in the same year, Gordon (1995) suggested that a psychoanalytic politics may be possible in only limited ways. He noted the continued absence of political engagement by the psychoanalytic community, and doubted whether psychoanalysis had much to contribute to theorising the most urgent and global problems (again, racism is an example).

It may be true that progress has been slow in many fields of policy and practice, given the reluctance to espouse univocal positions in establishing the sensitivity to emotional life which psychoanalysis can impart. But there are reasons to take issue with Gordon's pessimism. British psychoanalytic work on racism and nationalism, for example, continues to build on the classical European and American studies, and to open possibilities for deeper, more sophisticated and more practical approaches to such issues (e.g. Rustin, 1992; Young, 1994; Davids, 1996; Dalal, 1997).

Conclusion

It might seem that we are ending on a pessimistic note. In one respect, that would be so: FAEL drew together currents of thinking from a period of optimism, in which the role of the intellectual and, more broadly, the professional, in promoting social change seemed important. The forces that pushed people into more individualistic preoccupations in the 1980s and 1990s no doubt also pushed members of FAEL into their personal concerns, including individual psychic health. But at the same time, given the character of the cultural marxism and the psychoanalysis which this grouping sought to integrate, it was certain to be called into question whether an overtly activist stance could continue to be espoused by a group; indeed, whether it could be an enduring source of its cohering as a group. After all, the idea of a coherent group is itself the object of psychoanalytic interest, and in that light, often seems to act as a defensive shield against conflicted feelings.

Many of the contributions to *Free Associations* have explored precisely the problem that group solidarity can be at odds with the individual yearnings that political activism aims to fulfil. The same unease would exist inside FAEL itself, as it tried both better to define its position in the Left and not to be able to do so. If we compare this situation with, say, that described by Parin (to which we referred above), one difference was the force with which the Soviet invasion of Czechoslovakia provoked a response. Perhaps, in the less explosive environment of Britain, we need better to appreciate the more individual contributions, say, to the NHS or to psychoanalytic studies, by psychoanalytically minded people.

One of the traditional definitions of social psychology has been the study of those areas where individual experience may be seen to be directly shaped by societal processes, as in the study of, for example, social attitudes. This distinguishes one area or type of social psychology from others in which the focus is more on the interpersonal or small-group determinants of experience. It also indicates the kind of psychoanalytic social psychology which FAEL represents. In its preoccupation with psychoanalytic accounts of individual development (especially, in the post-Kleinian tradition, accounts of psychic 'primitivity') and with linking them to accounts of human community (at an equally primitive level), the FAEL project was closer to the study of individual/society relations than to the social psychology of groups and interpersonal behaviour. Indeed, it challenges the very idea of conflict between two reified entities, society and the individual. Instead, it suggests (just as Winnicott said there is no such thing as a baby; only a baby with its mother) that there is no individual without society and no society without the individual; and that the matrix in which they cooperate processes primitive anxieties and thinking.

Its concerns with metapsychology, and with the sociological and historical resonance of metapsychological concepts, mark out its intellectual richness while also perhaps suggesting one reason why, in the aggregate, it has had limited practical application (notwithstanding the very applied work of some individuals as clinicians or consultants).

But perhaps a more effective constraint on the development of the FAEL project towards a consistent and focused impact has been the inner tensions as we have described them above, compounded by the libertarian tendency within it which has resisted the imposition of any kind of focus. In this weakness lies also its characteristic strength. The richest contribution of psychoanalysis to the social sciences, and to intellectual life generally, is more likely to be in its unsettling effects, in its characteristic perpetual search for the tensions between the outer and inner, and those within the person, which it has a unique and powerful language to describe. At the same time as being concerned with the extent to which defence, illusion and madness permeate all human activity, psychoanalysis is a source of hope, and a basis for the appreciation of the resilience and creativity of ordinary personhood.

We can remind ourselves at the conclusion of this chapter that the critique of expertise, especially of scientific expertise, was an enduring theme in the founding impulse of FAEL. From that point of view, the idea of an applied psychoanalysis – certainly a group of experts in applied psychoanalysis – or of a psychoanalytic social psychology runs against the grain. So too would an assessment of its achievements, which rested upon a notion of testability imported from outside. It is in the nature of the radical spirit and of the psychoanalysis which informed the FAEL 'project' that though there may be criteria of maturation in both political and psychic processes, there is no solution to their contradictory natures.[56]

---

[56] The inherently contradictory nature of psychological and political processes affects the nature and assessment of evidence and the extent to which psychoanalysis can be assessed as a sub-discipline of psychological or social science. We have not discussed, nor have the contributors to *Free Associations* or the conferences, the technical issues that arise from the extension of psychoanalytic method from its clinical 'laboratory' to the social domain that has informed the 'project'. Some members would no doubt see the posing of the problem in this form already to have introduced a scientistic bias, ceding the right to speak about a psychoanalytic social psychology to a small group of experts; others would concentrate on the epistemological aspect itself. The critique of objectivity and realism with respect to scientific knowledge, including the relationship between expertise and the nature and force of evidence, has been important from the 1960s onwards. Thomas Kuhn's *The Structure of Scientific Revolutions*, first published in 1962, was ground-breaking in connecting the progress of science with the stability, dissolution and replacement of scientific theories in terms of the stability, dissolution and replacement of social groups of scientists.

Psychoanalytic methodology should be included in these studies. The interest in the conditions, legitimacy and domain of scientific explanation, and of psychoanalytic explanation, has tended to remain inside the academy, and has not figured to any great extent in FAEL. Robert Hinshelwood, a long-standing contributor to FAEL, has developed a course on this problem, as part of an MA in Psychoanalytic Studies at the University of Essex.

11 The Psychosocial Process

R.D. HINSHELWOOD

The Tavistock Clinic and Institute have dominated the application of psychoanalysis to social science in Britain, and also, in many respects, abroad. They have given rise to innumerable practical projects, and many ideas have been generated. There is a mainstream, as described in the introduction to this part of the book. That mainstream developed on the attempt to blend psychoanalytic concepts with systems theory. Although its origins are very much wider (Lewin's social psychology, elements of marxist, anthropological and sociological stances in the 1940s) psycho-analysis and systems theory are the surviving partners. And perhaps more recently there have been increasing influences from the dominant schools of rational management.

There are several projects which are not central to that line of thinking and which move more towards the more current topic of 'cultural studies'. They deserve mention, not just for this contemporary relevance but because of their tendency to remain focused on a psychoanalytic approach to cultural influences. In this chapter, I survey some studies which rest more heavily on that emphasis on culture, which Trist originally spotted; his hunch being that unconscious aspects of culture would be a fruitful approach to the application of psychoanalytic ideas. And to that extent these studies move away from the use of systems theory. In Chapter 9, Palmer recognised a number of alternative paradigms that might incipi-ently diverge or be incorporated into the present trend. The innovations I refer to here do not form an obviously coherent group. If anything unites the contributions I have in mind, it is that they emphasise 'cultural systems'.[57] We shouldn't stress too much the differences from the Tavistock tradition, on the other hand. Generally speaking, they have not

---

[57] It may be that these contributions cohere for no other reason than that they have been of profound importance in my own thinking about organisations I have worked in (as a member of staff).

embraced the strand towards systems theory that has been the direction engineered by Rice (1963, and Miller and Rice, 1967) particularly and subsequently by Miller (1993).

The work included in this chapter has tended to be conducted in healthcare institutions. As Palmer hints, the forces confronted by a consultant to such institutions are difficult to progress. His own work failed and he treated that failure as an opportunity to learn the limits to the Tavistock paradigm. In particular the problems were a compound of the difficulty in taking the environment into account (i.e. the environment of the organisation); the difficulty in the Tavistock approach to encompass serious change (paradigm shift types of change); and the emphasis given to the interpretations of defence imported from psychoanalysis and the relative neglect of the more positive urge towards work achievements and the overall vision of the work.

Being largely rooted in healthcare institutions, the contributions tend to be less hampered by the commercial demand for results and interested in the nature of the object of study itself. However, it may be that special factors exist in working organisations where the 'raw material' of the work is human beings. In addition, the methods did not always involve a consultant invited *in* to an institution. With the increasing awareness of the effectiveness of thinking about institutions, there is already an increasing presence of this knowledge within certain healthcare organisations. Some of the projects in this chapter raise questions about operating with these ideas from within the institution – i.e. not as a consultant, but as a member of staff. There is a degree of 'blindness' in trying to look out from the burial chamber of the social role itself. However, this factor can be overrated, since the practice of psychoanalysis requires the analyst to exist within his role in the workplace, while also considering the nature of those high-intensity interactions of which he is a human part. Thus thinking from within entails a particularly psychoanalytic stance, in practice.

Whatever the quarrels with the criteria for inclusion here, I would claim that there is as much emphasis on the culture as on forms of practice which are themselves closely linked. The socio-technical system is the idea that the actual technical operations performed on the raw material determine the pressures, as well as the opportunities and limits for the variety of ways of doing the work. The technical system has an impact on those who do the work – coal mining is dangerous, and miners have to work with a general emotional background of apprehension for their safety; nurses witness disease and death and have to withstand a variety of emotions from disgust, to fear, to pity. Then psychological reactions set in on a collective basis – miners cling to the view that the work is ordinary, for instance, and the managing of the actual work is hampered by this assumption (Trist et al., 1963); nurses work in such a way as to keep an emotional distance from their patients, which can harm the quality of nursing work required. In the case of healthcare in general, the work and therefore the technology operates upon people rather than upon the qualities and behaviour of material things (see Hinshelwood and Skogstad, 2000). The interaction between care workers of the institution (people with particular sets of attitudes about their kind of work) and the 'raw material' (also people with attitudes towards the work) is likely to be vastly different from the cultural attitudes of an industrial enterprise with inanimate raw material. The scope for mutual impact between one set of attitudes and the other is obviously great – and is totally missing from work with inanimate raw material.

These studies do not particularly stress this difference but it is implicit in many of them. It is a pressure, I would claim, that steers thinking towards an emphasis on what would be called cultural – as opposed to the merely psychological.[58]

Originally, Trist's (1990)[59] formulation at the Tavistock Institute was that 'culture' was a bridging concept that could act 'as a medium through which I could bring together the sociological and psychological phenomena' (p. 539). It is a psychosocial term that suggests an internal personal culture. In psychoanalytic terms, Trist's use of 'culture' is that internal world of the person in some dynamic interchange with the culture outside. This idea conveys a psychosocial process, he says. Roles and relationships are engaged in by the individuals but within the social structure in which they are embedded. It is clearly a founding idea used by Jaques (1953) when he considered the 'phantasy structure and function' of an institution; and it has emerged more latterly as the 'institution in the mind' (Armstrong, 1991), or the 'workplace within' (Hirschhorn, 1995). The culture of a group, organisation or society is reflected in a partially idiosyncratic version, internalised within the individual members. These

---

[58] One strand of Tavistock work that has been less known until recently has persisted within the clinic and does predominantly work with healthcare institutions. The compilation by Obholzer and Roberts (1994) gives a useful window into this work, and it stresses too the importance of intensity and quality of anxiety in relation to working with other human beings. It is, like the Tavistock paradigm in general, work carried out by consultants, those with a particular role to introduce 'external' thinking into the organisation. Such a distancing requirement in the 'external' identity of the consultants may establish a position with regard to their institution that more resembles those consultants in manufacturing industry.

[59] The original draft written in 1950 was never published, and it is not known to me how much redrafting occurred in this version published forty years later.

internal 'cultures' he calls 'psychosocial patterns' which characterise the internal worlds of the participating persons. At the same time, that internal culture is externalised as an influence on the actual culture of an organisation.

Although the work described in this chapter does not necessarily derive directly from Trist's early manifesto, a common thread for several authors is the group or organisational culture and the relation of that culture to the internal states of the individuals.

The inter-group field

In the early work (for instance Jaques, 1951) individuals were seen to interact with each other as members of a group. The psychosocial process links the individual's state of mind with identical or similar states in other people's minds. Jaques found that the middle managers, the workers and the senior managers of an industrial enterprise could all inter-relate *as groups*. Most organisations are made up of a number of groups and are thus multi-group systems, comprising an inter-group field of study.

An elegant research project was conducted by Higgin and Bridger (1964) in this inter-group field. It produced results of fundamental importance. The method involved setting up a conference specifically to study inter-group processes. In this study the conference was invited to form itself into three sub-groups. As it turned out, each sub-group embodied a part, and a part only, of the overall task of study. A number of conference participants reacted to the task with a massive flight reaction, expressed in their abrupt movement to form an instant sub-group; others felt overwhelmed by the task and rejected by others, and in fact enacted that by forming another sub-group, one that displayed dejection and disorganised behaviour; the third group held a kind of guilty reaction to the rejected ones. Thus,

> the three groups took an equal share in the work of the whole conference of which they were all a part and for which the work was being done. There were two tasks to carry out. One was the sophisticated task – the planning task; the other was to contain the intruding basic assumption that was interfering with this. (p. 219)

The emotional (or basic assumptive) task was, as it were, shared out between the groups in a quite unconscious way through 'a pattern of projection and introjection of these emotional forces as a division of labour among the groups' (p. 217). Separate sub-group cultures separated out in a process that split the emotional life of the individuals. The mechanisms of projection and introjection acted as forces that effected a separation of the individuals on the basis of splitting within each. The internal states of the members of the three groups differentiated in three directions. The psychosocial process of the whole conference aroused specific internal states in the individuals during their membership of the conference. This dynamic interplay between the external emotional forces and the internal states in mutual interaction seems an exemplary display of the psychosocial process.

Organisational culture

When individuals identify with separated cultures, it has intense impact on their own intrapsychic states. Miller and Gwynne (1972) conducted a pilot study of residential institutions for the physically handicapped and the young chronic sick. These homes took people who would never get well but might have a substantial amount of time yet to live. Their aim was to examine the quality of life for permanent residents in an institutionalising organisation.

The inmates of the five homes were all severely and permanently handicapped physically, and the task of each home was to create as normal a life as possible for the inmates. Their lives were not short but were afflicted by social attitudes, so 'the disabled generally, no matter what their individual achievements, are non-starters in a world geared to the needs of the able-bodied' (p. 49). The task that these institutions are requested to perform by society in general is 'to cater for the socially dead during the interval between social death and physical death' (p. 80). This task is grisly, since 'the only outputs are dead patients' (p. 85).

> Since it is too painful to acknowledge explicitly what society is implicitly asking these institutions to do, two sets of values are commonly brought in to use as defence mechanisms. These may be labelled the humanitarian or medical values that prolongation of life is a good thing and the liberal or anti-medical value that the handicapped inmates of these institutions are 'really normal'. (p. 82)

Thus the cultural attitudes of the institutions can be distorted by values of a rather extreme kind, in one direction or another.

The humanitarian defence is a defence against the grisly task by reducing the inmates to objects that have to be cared for humanely but who are implicitly incapable of caring for themselves or each other. In effect, as subhuman objects they had lost the essence of their human lives already. The social death implies that life is already over. This set of humanitarian values gave rise in some of the homes to what the researchers called the 'warehousing model' of care for the inmates. This set out simply to prolong life. The inmate is required to accept only the role of incurable dependence on nursing care, and to give up all expectations of using any remaining abilities.

In contrast to the humanitarian values were the liberal ones. They too are a defence against the task, but in the opposite direction. The disabled person is believed to be as acceptable as any healthy person, and potentially as creative and productive if only those resources can be found and brought to work. These values gave rise to a model of care which the researchers termed the 'horticultural model'. In this, rehabilitation is the focus and, unrealistically, the only focus, and aims to convert the deprived and unsatisfied inmate into a fulfilled one again.

Both these models are extremes which cut out important aspects of the choices that inmates need to make. In addressing the period between withdrawal from society into the home and actual death, the researchers claim for the individual his

> right to determine how he would like to spend the intervening period. This
> includes the right to choose dependency or to take advantage of developmental
> opportunities. It then becomes the task of the institution first to help the
> individual to make his decision and second to provide him with the facilities to
> implement it. (p. 90)

The task is somehow to mediate a balance between acceptance of dependence and the struggle against it. However, the pain of recognising real human beings so tragically disabled leads to the defensive cultures that tend to deny either the humanity or else the disablement. So the complexity of the mediating task is distorted and simplified into polarised sets of attitudes.

This study also explored the psychosocial process, in this case one in which the task of the institution reverberates with the internal states of the individuals. The result was to create people who actually hold and embody divergent though linked sets of attitudes.

The large mental hospital

Somewhat similar divergences occur in the much larger and more intricate structure of a mental hospital.

Elisabeth Bott Spillius, originally a social anthropologist and later a psychoanalyst, was concerned in her own early work at the Tavistock Institute (Bott, 1957) with the psychiatric institution's relations with its environment. That work produced the classic study of the social networks of families according to class position. She used the notion of a social defence system as a means to aid understanding of ritual and myth in a third world society (Bott, 1972). However, she also conducted a significant study of a large mental hospital in Britain in the 1950s and, 1960s (Bott, 1976; Bott Spillius, 1990), paying attention once again to the cultural environment of the hospital at that time. Her thesis is that 'the work roles and role relationships inside a mental hospital reduplicate some of the conflicts and untenability that arise between patients and their significant others'. (Bott, 1976, p. 125). The social structure of the hospital was intimately interlinked with individual conflicts. In particular she described an essential conflict between madness and sanity in society at large, which reaches critical proportions amongst the families in whom a psychotic patient lives. Then admission to hospital is a process in which 'mental hospitals inevitably act on behalf of society, not just on behalf of the individual patient' (p. 97). In other words the process of admission is an act within society in which madness, in the form of the patient, is separated from sanity, in the form of the relatives. Admission is an agreement, visibly enacted, on the basis of the assumption

> that madness cannot be contained and accommodated as part of ordinary personal and social life. It is beyond the pale, or it should be beyond the pale. If it is kept inside it will destroy: destroy the individual, the family, the fabric of society. At all costs it must be separated off and sent somewhere else, and the main task of the mental hospital is to be that 'somewhere else'. (p. 121)

The result is that the hospital 'will have divided loyalties to the patient and to society' (p. 138). The separation of mental attributes is concretely enacted by the separation of players who 'represent' them. Or, more precisely, the players and the sub-groups – patients, relatives, staff – separate the emotional reactions just as in the experiential setting of Higgin and Bridger's 1964 study described above. The hospital exists to perform a number of functions: control, care and treatment. That conflict then infuses and complicates all aspects of life in a mental hospital. Each function comes in conflict with others. Different categories of member in the hospital become identified as groups with different functions and on different sides of the conflict. For instance, the doctors are by tradition the authority which they hold 'on behalf of society'. And society looks to them for the job of controlling the mad behaviour. They are required in the first place to discriminate between the mad and the sane, and have to go along with the social process which threw up the patient. At the same time they feel required to prescribe treatment, a function which is, in a mental hospital, therefore closely linked to control, a fact that often makes doctors uncomfortable.

Or for the nurses: 'Madness was safely lodged in the patient . . . the nurse had absorbed all the available willpower and capacity to think . . .

patients lodged much of their capacity to think in the staff' (p. 134). Between the two, a mutual projection system was established with the nurse projecting madness and helplessness into patients, who introject it; and with patients projecting effective willpower and thoughtfulness into the nurses, who introject it. This is the nub of the process of institutionalisation as described by Martin (1955), Barton (1959) and others.

The conflict in society is projected concretely (in the form of the patient) into the hospital, which then deals with the task by separating aspects which are concretely embodied in people. These projection/introjection processes distort the internal states and identities of all parties. It is a complex task involving a major anxiety – about the pollution of sanity with madness – which can be interpreted in at least three separate ways (control, care and treatment amongst four interconnected and anxious groups – relatives, patients, doctors and nurses). The psychosocial process amongst these sub-groups within the institution is clearly mediated by collectively organised mechanisms of projection and introjection in the inter-group field.

A mutual interaction exists between society and the hospital, and between the hospital and its members. It exemplifies Trist's notion of a psychosocial process. There are several steps: the work in the institution creates certain states of mind in the members; and then these states of mind are taken apart and concretely held by different minds. The process embodies splitting, projection and introjection in the minds of the individual members. And finally, the concrete nature of these individual mechanisms ensures that the institution's structure is strictly determined by this.

Psychotherapy and imprisonment

It is common for the primary explicit task of an organisation to be divided up into secondary tasks and different aspects delegated to different people and sub-groups. However, Higgin and Bridger (1964; see above) described how the emotional backdrop to the task may also be split up unconsciously, with different effects on the functioning of the individuals in the varying sub-groups. In Bott's work the primary task of the organisation is conflicted in itself, and often without a recognition of that unconscious division. The unconscious division (splitting) of emotional states leads to the task drifting into two separate directions.

Sub-groups represent those different directions. In another study (Hinshelwood, 1994), in a large mental hospital, the specific anxiety was noted as

the belief that any spark of initiative, and emotional responsiveness between
people, is dangerous and will lead to a serious disruption of one's own mind. It
is an unspoken belief that if something lively starts up, it can only result in a
swift downhill process to a maddened state. If anything stirs a patient on the
ward he will go mad. (p. 286)

This belief seemed to be held by the dominant culture supported by both
patients and psychiatric staff. As a result, an atmosphere of particular
deadness pervades the wards. Techniques to achieve this protective
deadness (Donati, 1989) were very evident and resembled the depersonal-
ising methods described by Menzies (1959) in the nursing service of a
general hospital (also noted by Bott in her study described above).

As a consultant psychotherapist in this organisation, I therefore represented a quite different belief. Psychotherapy is predicated on the
relationships that develop between patient and staff, and thus the 'human
relations which psychotherapists proclaim, pose just that threat of
madness which is the common anxiety' (Hinshelwood, 1994, p. 287).
Psychotherapy therefore represents a counter-culture which is feared and
also denigrated. At times, too, the psychotherapist may be idealised and
turned to for magic – an attitude that the psychotherapist may himself be
tempted to encourage.

There is a deep institutional cleft in the attitudes towards lively
relationships by the different sub-groups: one believes relationships
threaten an outbreak of madness; and the other that they are the epitome
of what is therapeutic (reverse attitudes grow up around drugs).
Psychotherapy represented, unconsciously, something that the dominant
culture had been obliged to abolish – that is, the sense of human life and
liveliness. It appeared therefore to have a particular relevance to the institution at the unconscious level.

An organisational schism appeared to be grounded in, and to promote
psychic splitting at, the individual level. A similar cultural schism was
apparent in the unconscious psychodynamic structure of a prison. There,
psychotherapists occupied a counter-cultural position contrasting with
dominant attitudes (Hinshelwood, 1993). In this case, the prison officers
as well as the prisoners are locked into a complex set of interpenetrating
attitudes. The prisoners have been declared publicly to be guilty to an
unacceptably antisocial degree and incarcerated. They react with a well-
orchestrated system of denials of guilt and of their helplessness. They
engage in counter-accusations, and often they will attempt to trick, cajole
and menace in order to demonstrate prowess and power, which appeared
to them as strength.

Faced with this, the officers respond with a set of attitudes to cope with
the threat of the criminals' antisocial violence. They hold that the

prisoners' dangerousness must be confronted with an iron resistance, all their tricks must be spotted and made useless. Physical control and security is emphasised to support the psychological insecurity. This brings prisoners and officers together in a shared view about the nature of power over others which must be sustained at all costs. In this male prison, a culture of toughness and supremacy over others was dominant.

The prison officers then caricatured the psychotherapists and certain other workers as soft and gullible, a weak point in the system. The prisoners, too, saw these weak people as easy targets to trick and sustain their own prowess. However, at the same time, the psychotherapists and these 'weak' others represent something that the dominant culture has lost – a considerateness and humanity.

However, in the course of these inter-group and psychosocial dynamics, something had happened to ordinary human character traits. In the schism, strength has been distorted into tricky subjugation of others; and considerateness has been distorted as weakness. The institution then fails in its more sensible task of promoting some blend of strength with considerateness. Instead, the hidden terror has caused a divergent drift in the task into two polarised, distorted and self-defeating extremes.

A psychosocial care

The interaction between internal patterns and the external social structure was exploited by two people who devised progressive changes in the therapeutic arrangements for inpatient psychotherapy. Main (1946) inveighed against the traditional mental hospital and the professionalised ritual performance of prescribed behaviour. His notion of the therapeutic community was taken up widely by many others when the large mental hospitals were being abandoned in the 1960s and 1970s, in a number of forms for applying psychotherapy in an inpatient setting (Janssen, 1994; Pestalozzi et al., 1998)

Like Bott, he found a similar cultural divergence in the inter-group relations between nurses and patients:

> [The] helpful will unconsciously *require* others to be helpless while the helpless will *require* others to be helpful. Staff and patients are thus inevitably to some extent creatures of each other. (Main, 1975, p. 61)

But Main wanted to do something about it. His observations were from the institution in which he worked; and which in fact he led. His most important further contribution was to focus on the very rigid, stuck quality of these distorted cultures, and on how the practice in these institutions resembled ritual rather than problem solving. He described how, when a culture drifts, reality-oriented solutions to problems become ritual with a moral force (Main, 1967 [1990]). Things come to be done out of 'ought'. A particular idea that had once been a response to a real problem was hierarchically promoted to a superego requirement. In his psychoanalytic hospital, instead of Freud's dictum, where id was ego shall be, he found that often where ego was, superego had taken over. There is, he claimed, a natural resistance to thinking problems through. For new nurses, their practice was defined and required by their predecessors rather drawing them through a process of rediscovering the problems to which the practices are solutions. Hence there is a preference for a 'freedom from thought'. The internal unthinking states of the individuals became influenced, and in turn influenced by, a ritual manner of performance of the job in the social structure.

Main, as director of the hospital, therefore prescribed a culture of enquiry (Main, 1957, 1967). The idea was to build in a persistent examination of all practices in order to reduce ritual performances in favour of addressing real problems. It is a culture that resembles the descriptive method of psychoanalysis itself. Thus the psychosocial process entails establishing a culture aimed at 'freeing the ego from unconscious enslavement' (p. 62). Main's therapeutic intent was an organisational practice at the level of the organisation itself. The matron of the hospital was Doreen Weddell, who later became an analyst. She was primarily responsible for rethinking the role of the nurse (Weddell, 1968). The work changed 'from working *for* to working *with* the patient' (p. 66). In other words, the nurses worked so 'as to be ordinary human beings, walking alongside and working with their patients' (p. 64). This specific form of psychosocial nursing is not one of psychoanalytic interpretation but an active practice of finding solutions to daily problems (Barnes et al., 1997). Rather than providing care as a one-to-one curative act involving a particular skill or intervention performed by the 'active nurse' upon the 'passive patient' (Main, 1975), nursing is viewed quite differently (Griffiths and Pringle, 1997). If 'a patient is to be viewed as an independent adult [that] means he must also be held responsible for his own actions' (Chapman, 1984, p. 70). The emphasis is on the importance of *real* responsibility, in the community's 'work of the day' as solving practical problems. But responsibility opens a huge intrapsychic domain, gathered around the experience of guilt, regret and defensiveness. The external accompaniment by nurses supports the carrying of responsibility and influences the internalisation of a supporting relationship. The psychosocial process of interaction is, in this practice, harnessed to non-verbal therapeutic ends – albeit a non-interpretative, and often, non-verbal practice.

Conclusion

These studies use a notion of social culture, and specifically the role of culture as a medium to 'bring together the sociological and psychological phenomena'. Each project has tended to stress the two-way trend between individual defences and the social system. To some extent this is a social constructivist point of view in which the individual, determined by the social pressures, adopts certain attitudes, accepts certain behaviours and above all restricts his personality to certain functions and abolishes others. But it is more. It also recognises the pressures individuals bring to bear to steer the organisation's structure and function unconsciously in ways that make it easier for themselves. There is a two-way bargain between the individuals and the organisation. In sociological terms it is structures and roles, but on the other side of the coin it is the introjective and projective processes.

Thus the conception of culture that is in use here is its unconscious aspects. Individuals in roles absorb from the culture certain unconscious sets of values and beliefs. Reciprocally, individuals also tend to push the culture towards sets of values and beliefs, which individually held provide some comfort, and defensiveness against their personal anxieties.

In my view this originating hypothesis set out by Trist remains a strong one. Its benefits are attested by the fact that the studies reported in this chapter continue in some form or other that notion of the unconscious level of the culture, in its individual and social manifestations. Though still a vigorous tradition its specific quality needs distinguishing from the mainstream psychoanalytic social psychology in Britain, and it deserves support as a surviving approach in its own right.

12 CONCLUSIONS
The Baby Grew Up

R.D. HINSHELWOOD

Freud set out to discover the secret of human mental functioning, and then when he found it he wanted to proclaim it not only as the basis of all mental science, but as the fundamental science for the whole of the humanities. At the same time, he was anxious about how those he had proselytised would tinker with his ideas. And tinker they have. And we have down to this day.

There is certainly an uncontrollable progress. Freud in his own view felt he had unleashed a sorcerer's apprentice situation. And he set about establishing a kind of control over the inevitable dilution of psychoanalysis which he feared so much. It was challenging, it was radical, it was revolutionary. Freud knew that, and he believed it would therefore be subverted with easier to digest ideas.

Despite that wish to protect his 'baby', divergences, disagreements and disloyalty have become the history of psychoanalysis. Now there is little that, it seems, can be done about the plethora of psychoanalyses that exist.

Similarly, early on, social scientists became hesitant about his application of psychoanalysis to anthropology there was a strong psychoanalytic reaction to any disagreement. Malinowski for instance is harsh in his first encounter with psychoanalysis. These are his comments on *Totem and Taboo* (Freud, 1913):

> The character of the argumentation and the manner and mannerisms of exposition moreover... contain such glaring surface absurdities and show such lack of anthropological insight (Malinowski, 1923, p. 650).

However, to be fair, this is not his last word, for he continued:

> But with all this, Freud's contribution to anthropology is of the greatest importance and seems to me to strike a rich vein, which must be followed up (p. 650).

Despite a certain degree of balance in Malinowski's appreciation, it was his divergence from Freud's view of the Oedipus complex in society that Jones (1926) responded to. Malinowski had described the Trobriand Islanders' ignorance about procreation and the father's role in conception and pregnancy, and claimed therefore that the Trobriand Islanders had some other complex than the Oedipal one. The Oedipus complex accordingly must be culturally relative, and not the ubiquitous and fundamental building block of human psychology that psychoanalysis claimed. At least some peoples grow up without being confronted with the fertile parental couple, since they denied the link with sexual intercourse, and traced inheritance directly back to the mother only. Jones retorted with evidence that the 'ignorance' was really a repression, a cultural repression, of the knowledge of the true role of sex. It was thus not ignorance at all.[60] In fact the repression of the knowledge only confirmed the power of the Oedipus complex. Jones's response was elegant, logical and devastating – and he demonstrated a considerable mastery of the anthropological data of the time. The early analysts required that psychoanalysis be taken as a complete package.

Jones's was not the last word on the disagreement, since it still rumbles on today (e.g. Gillison, 1993). He did demonstrate just how strongly psychoanalysts insisted at that time that psychoanalysis be accepted wholly and unconditionally – and that it was in effect the Newtonian physics of the mind.

Of course, Freud wrote his tribal fantasy at exactly the time when Einstein was re-casting the whole of Newtonian physics. And we have over the century come to relinquish the notion of a monolithic form of knowledge that stays firm and grows taller – instead, knowledge (of all kinds) has fragmented, demonstrated contradictions, and become infinitely revisable. In fact, taken to an extreme we have a 'post-modern' climate where all these theories (even those of 'hard' science) are simply inspiring narratives, the discourses of special-interest groups.

And the same fate has overtaken psychoanalysis. Its encounter with other disciplines, its spread to other national cultures, and its progress through the currents of history of 100 years have tended to fragment the

---

[60] A distinguished anthropologist, Edmund Leach, supports Jones' attack on Malinowski, though not for quite the same reasons (Leach, 1966). He shows that the supposed ignorance of paternity is a religious belief in which the metaphysical essence of the child is believed to come from an impregnating spirit. This does not mean that the peoples who hold this belief are ignorant of the facts of life – or no more ignorant than a devout Catholic who believes that the Virgin was impregnated by the Holy Spirit.

ideas and the practice. Metapsychology has become almost a supermarket shelf for people to take one or other delicacy of their choosing as it happens to appeal or apply to whatever their intellectual needs require. And in addition there are many other competing psychologies, from which convenient intellectual materials can be quarried.

Today, instead of the question, how can psychoanalysis be applied to certain social phenomena? we must ask another one: which bits of psychoanalytic metapsychology could be tried out in an explanation that might combine bits of other theories too? This relativism of knowledge, and the pragmatic break-up of systematic knowledge, often seem unnerving. There is no chance of restoring psychoanalysis to its pristine state of pure gold. It is irretrievably mixed in an alloy with other ideas. And perhaps the field of psychoanalytic social science is a prime example of that shifting swell of ideas which mixes psychoanalysis together with other brands of ideas. It is therefore of great interest, and we would say importance, to be in a position to know how the particular alloyed mixture has been made up.

Not only that, but the field of psychoanalysis itself, spread globally, and congealed into many institutions, official and otherwise, has itself become a field for social science study and indeed a study that can apply psychoanalytic ideas (Eisold, 1994; Kirsner, 2000). Founded on preserving the ark, i.e. the pure gold of psychoanalysis, but living in a contrasting world of multiple, relativistic knowledge, psychoanalytic institutions everywhere are fascinating examples of the human capacity to tolerate contradiction and to produce fulminating organisational oddities to contain their contradictions.

So, what has happened to Freud's 'baby'? It could be said that it has been dismembered and dispersed. But another way of looking at what has happened is to consider the dispersal as that of a fertiliser that can enrich other disciplines rather than take them over in a psychoanalytic hegemony. Freud might be disappointed, even blanch at the threat to his ideas – but I think he might be intrigued, too, and possibly even proud of the extraordinary variety his own ideas have given rise to in others. And despite his anxiety over rubbing shoulders with those he has not chosen, he could be reassured that psychoanalysis has become such a widespread public property, valued in so many places for its power of explanation and inspiration.

Our ambitions are now slimmed and trimmed. The vision of a psychoanalytic dominance over all branches of human and social science is a lost dream. And instead of Malinowski's aghast exclamation at Freud's extraordinary presumption in a foreign field, there is now a wide respect that psychoanalysis can speak to most other disciplines in the human sciences, whilst according them a respect for their own method and object of study.

References

Adorno, T., Frankel-Brunswick, E., Levinson, D. and Nevitt, S. (1950) *The Authoritarian Personality*. New York: Harper.

Amado, G. (1995) Response to Elliott Jaques. *Human Relations* 48: 351–357.

Amati, S. (1987) Some thoughts on torture. *Free Associations* 8: 94–114.

Anzieu, D. (1975) *Le Groupe et L'Inconscient*. Paris: Bourdas. (English translation 1984 *The Group and the Unconscious*. London: Routledge.)

Anzieu, D. (1983) Progres et problèmes en théorie des groupes. *Bulletin de Psicologie* 27: 363.

Anzieu, D. (1985) *Le Moi-Peau*. Paris: Bourdas. (English translation 1989 *The Skin Ego*. New Haven: Yale University Press.)

Anzieu, D. (1986) *Un Peau pour Penser*. Paris: Clancier-Gluénaud. (English translation 1990 *A Skin for Thought*. London: Karnac.)

Anzieu, D. (1987) (ed.) *Les Enveloppes Psychiques*. Paris: Bourdas. (English translation 1990 *Psychic Envelopes*. London: Karnac.)

Armstrong, D.G. (1991) *The Institution in the Mind: Reflections on the Relation of Psycho-Analysis to Work with Institutions*. London: Grubb Institute.

Armstrong, D.G. (1992) Names, thoughts and lies: the relevance of Bion's later writing for understanding experience in groups. *Free Associations* 26: 261–282.

Armstrong, D.G. (1995) The analytic object in organisational work. Paper at 1995 Symposium of the International Society for the Psychoanalytic Study of Organizations.

Armstrong, D.G. (1996) The recovery of meaning. Paper at 1996 Symposium of the International Society for the Psychoanalytic Study of Organizations.

Asch, S. (1952) *Social Psychology*. Englewood Cliffs, NJ: Prentice-Hall.

Aulagnier, P. (1975) *La Violence de l'Interpretation*. Paris: Presses Universitaire de France.

Babington-Smith, B. and Farrell, B.A. (eds) (1979) *Training in Small Groups: A Study of Five Methods*. Oxford: Pergamon.

Bacciagaluppi, M. (1989) The role of aggressiveness in the work of John Bowlby. *Free Associations* 16: 123–134.

Badcock, C. (1980) *The Psychoanalysis of Culture*. Oxford: Blackwell Science.

Bain, A. (1982) *The Baric Experiment, Occasional Papers*. London: Tavistock Institute.

Bakan, D. (1966) *The Duality of Human Existence: Isolation and Communion in Western Man*. Boston: Beacon Press.

Bakan, D. (1968) *Disease Pain and Sacrifice, Toward a Psychology of Suffering.* Chicago: University of Chicago Press.

Bakan, D. (1979) *And They Took Themselves Wives: The Emergence of Patriarchy in Western Civilization.* New York: Harper and Row.

Bakan, D. (1991) *Maimonedes on Prophecy.* Northvale NJ: Jason Aaronson.

Balint, M., Balint, E., Gosling, R. and Hildebrand, P. (1966) *A Study of Doctors: Mutual Selection and the Evaluation of Results in a Training Programme for Family Doctors.* London: Tavistock.

Baranes, J.-J. (1984a) L'institution thérapeutique comme cadre. *Adolescence* 2: 123–141.

Baranes, J.-J. (1984b) Vers une métapsychologie transgénérationnelle? *Adolescence* 5: 79–93.

Barangers, M. and Barangers, W. (1961) La situacion analitica como campo dinamico. *Revista Uruguya de Psicoanalisis* 26.

Barker, G. (1962) To my Mother. *Penguin Modern Poets* 3 (first series), Harmondsworth: Penguin.

Barnes, B. (1974) *Scientific Knowledge and Sociological Theory.* London: Routledge a id Kegan Paul.

Barnes, E., Griffiths, P., Ord, J. and Wells, D. (1997) *Face to Face with Distress: The Professional Use of Self in Psychosocial Care.* London: Butterworth-Heinemann.

Barton, R. (1959) *Institutional Neurosis.* Bristol: Wright.

Basaglia, F. (1968) *L'Istituzione Negata.* Torino: Einaudi.

Bateson, G. (1972) *Steps to an Ecology of Mind.* London: Chandler.

Beauchesne, H. (1986) *Histoire de la Psychopathologie.* Paris: Presses Universitaires de France.

Bégoin-Guignard, F. (1992) Entre l'arbre et l'écorce. Le psychothérapeute en institution. In Bléandonu, G. (ed.) *Cadres Thérapeutiques et Enveloppes Psychiques.* Lyon: Presses Universitaires de Lyon.

Berenstein, I. (1976) *Familia y Enfermedad Mental.* Buenos Aires: Paidós.

Berger, P. and Luckman, T. (1966) *The Social Construction of Reality.* London: Allen Lane.

Berke, J.H. (1996) The wellsprings of fascism: individual malice, group hatreds, and the emergence of national narcissism. *Free Associations* 39: 334–350.

Bernstein, A.C. (1994) *Flight of the Stork: What Children Think and When of Sex and Family Building.* Indianapolis: Perspectives Press.

Bettelheim, B. (1974) *Home for the Heart.* New York: Alfred Knopf.

Bick, E. (1968) The experience of the skin in early object-relations. *International Journal of Psycho-Analysis* 49: 484–486.

Bion, W.R. (1946) The leaderless group project. *Bulletin of the Menninger Clinic* 10: 77–81.

Bion, W.R. (1948–1951) Experiences in groups, I–VII. *Human Relations* 1–4. Reproduced in Bion, W.R. (1961) *Experiences in Groups.* London: Tavistock.

Bion, W.R. (1952) Group dynamics: a review. *International Journal of Psycho-Analysis* 33: 235–247. Reprinted in Klein, M., Heimann, P. and Money-Kyrle, R. (eds) (1955) *New Directions in Psycho-Analysis.* London: Tavistock, and in Bion, W.R. (1961) *Experiences in Groups.* London: Tavistock.

Bion, W.R. (1961) *Experiences in Groups.* London: Tavistock.

Bion, W.R. (1962) A theory of thinking. Reprinted in *Second Thoughts* pp. 110–119. London: Heinemann (1967).

Bion, W.R. (1965) *Transformations*. London: Heinemann.

Bion, W.R. (1970) *Attention and Interpretation*. London: Tavistock.

Bion, W.R. and Rickman, J. (1943) Intra-group tensions in therapy: their study as the task of the group. *Lancet* 2: 678–681. Reprinted in Bion, W.R. (1961) *Experiences in Groups*. London: Tavistock.

Blackwell, D. (1998) Editorial: Special section on group analysis and organisations. *Group Analysis* 31: 243–244.

Blackwell, R.D. (1994) The psyche and the system. In Brown, D. and Zinkin, L. (eds) *The Psyche and the Social World*. London: Routledge.

Bléandonu G. (1976) *Dictionnaire de Psychiatrie Sociale*. Paris: Payot.

Bléandonu, G. (1984) *W.R. Bion: His Life and Works*, 1897–1979. London: Free Association Books.

Bléandonu G. (ed.) (1987) *Les Groupes Thérapeutiques*. Lyon: Césura.

Bléandonu G. (ed.) (1992) *Cadres Thérapeutiques et Enveloppes Psychiques*. Lyon: Presses Universitaires de Lyon.

Bléandonu G. and Despinoy M. (1974) *Hôpitaux de Jour et Psychiatrie dans la Communauté*. Paris: Payot.

Bleger, J. (1966a) Psicoanalisi del quadro istituzionale. In Genovese, C. (ed.) *Setting e Processo Psicoanalitico*. Milan: Raffaele Cortina.

Bleger J. (1966b) Psychanalyse du cadre psychanalytique. In Kaës, R, and Missenard, A. (eds) (1979) *Crise, Rupture et Dépassement*. Paris.

Bleger, J. (1967) Psycho-analysis of the psycho-analytic frame. *International Journal of Psycho-Analysis* 48: 511.

Bleger, J. (1972) *Sybiosis y Anbiguidad*. Buenos Aires: Paidos.

Bleger, J. (1980) Le groupe comme istitution et le groupe dans le institution. In Kaës, R. (ed.) *L' Institution et les Institutions*. Paris: Dunod.

Bleger, J. (1989a) The group as institution and within institutions. *International Journal of Therapeutic Communities* 10: 109–115.

Bleger, J. (1989b) Administration of groupwork techniques and knowledge. *International Journal of Therapeutic Communities* 10: 117–121.

Bloor, D. (1976) *Knowledge and Social Imagery*. London: Routledge and Kegan Paul.

Bollas, C. (1987) *The Shadow of the Object: Psychoanalysis of the Unthought Known*. London: Free Association Books.

Bollas, C. (1996) *Election Fever*. London: Fabian Society.

Bott, E. (1957) *Family and Social Network*. London: Tavistock.

Bott, E. (1972). Psychoanalysis and ceremony. In La Fontaine, J. (ed.) *The Interpretation of Ritual: Essays in Honour of A.I. Richards*. London: Tavistcck.

Bott, E. (1976) Hospital and society. *British Journal of Medical Psychology* 49: 97–140.

Bott [Spillius], E. (ed.) (1988) *Melanie Klein Today, Vol 2: Mainly Practice*. London: Routledge.

Bott [Spillius], E. (1990) Asylum and society. In Trist, E. and Murray, H. (eds) *The Social Engagement of Social Science*. London: Free Association Books.

Bowlby, J., Figlio, K. and Young, R.M. (1986) An interview with John Bowlby on the origins and reception of his work. *Free Associations* 6: 36–64.

Boxer, P. (1994) Foucault's archaeological method. Working Papers of GOWG (Working Group on Groups and Organisations) (available on www.brl.eom).

Boxer, P. and Palmer, B. (1997) The architecture of quality: the case of the specialist housing consortium. Paper presented at the ISPO Symposium in Philadelphia, June 1997.

Bradford, L.P., Gibb, J.R. and Benne, K.D. (eds) (1964) *T-Group Theory and Laboratory Methods*. New York: Wiley.

Bridger, H. (1946) The Northfield experiment. *Bulletin of the Menninger Clinic* 10: 71–76.

Bridger, H. (1985) Northfield revisited. In Pines, M. (ed.) *Bion and Group Psychotherapy*. London: Routledge.

Bridger, H. (1990a) Courses and working conferences as transitional learning institutions. In Trist, E. and Murray, H. (eds) *The Social Engagement of Social Science, Volume 1, The Socio-Psychological Perspective*. London: Free Association Books.

Bridger, H. (1990b) The discovery of the therapeutic community: the Northfield Experiments. In Trist, E. and Murray, H. (eds.) *The Social Engagement of Social Science, Volume 1, The Socio-Psychological Perspective*. London: Free Association Books.

Brown, N.O. (1959) *Life against Death: The Psychoanalytic Meaning of History*. Middleton, CT: Wesleyan Press.

Burrow, T. (1927) *The Social Basis of Consciousness: A Study in Organic Psychology*. London: Kegan Paul Trench, Trubner.

Cadoret, M. (1984) Les spécificités institutionnelles. *Psychanalystes* 11: 29–43.

Cahn, R. (1978) A propos du processus thérapeutique en institution pour jeunes psychotiques. In Lebovici, S. and Kestemberg, E. *Le Devenir de la Psychose chez l'Enfant*. Paris: Presses Universitaires de France.

Castoriadis-Aulagnier, P. (1975) *La Violence de l'Interprétation: Le Pictogramme et l'Énoncé*. Paris: Presses Universitaires de France.

Chapman, G. (1984) A therapeutic community, psychosocial nursing and the nursing process. *International Journal of Therapeutic Communities* 5: 68–76.

Colman, A.D. and Geller, M.H. (1985) *Group Relations Reader* 2. Washington DC: A.K. Rice Institute.

Cooper, A. and Treacher, A. (1995) Free associations, truth, morality and engagement. *Free Associations* 33: 1–9.

Cooper, D. (1967) *Anti-Psychiatry*. London: Tavistock.

Correale, A. (1991) *Il Campo Istituzionale*. Rome: Borla.

Correale, A. (1992) Campo (modello di). *Interazioni* 0: 124–126.

Correale, A. and Celli, A.M. (1998) The model-scene in group psychotherapy with chronic psychotic patients. *International Journal of Group Psychotherapy* 48(1): 55–68.

Craib, I. (1986) Freud and philosophy. *Free Associations* 4: 64–79.

Craib, I. (1989) *Psychoanalysis and Social Theory*. Hemel Hempstead: Harvester.

Cremerius, J. (1986). Spurensicherung. Die psychoanalytische Bewegung und das Elend der psychoanalytischen Institution. *Psyche* 12:1063–1091.

Curle, A. (1947) Transitional communities and social reconnection, Parts 1 and 2. *Human Relations* 1: 42–68; 240–288.

Dalal, F. (1997) The colour question in psychoanalysis. *Journal of Social Work Practice* 11: 103–114.

Dalal, F. (1998) *Taking the Group Seriously*. London: Jessica Kingsley.

Davids, F. (1996) Franz Fanon: the struggle for inner freedom. *Free Associations* 38: 205–234.

de Board, R. (1978) *Psychoanalysis of Organisations*. London: Tavistock.

de Maré, P. (1983) Michael Foulkes and the Northfield Experiment. In Pines, M. (ed.) *The Evolution of Group Analysis*. London: Routledge.

de Maré, P. and Kreeger, L. (1974) *Introduction to Group Treatments in Psychiatry*. London: Butterworth.

de Maré, P., Piper, R. and Thompson, S. (1991) *Koinonia: From Hate through Dialogue to Culture*. London: Karnac.

de Mause, L. (1991) *The History of Children*. London: Bellew.

Devereux, G. (1967) *From Anxiety to Method in the Behavioral Sciences*. The Hague: Mouton.

Dickinson, E. (1929) Tell all the truth but tell it slant. In *Emily Dickinson: Poems*. London: Everyman.

Diet, E. (1996) Le thanatophore: travail de la mort et destructivité dans les institutions. In Kaës, R., Pinel, J.-P. and Kernberg, O. (eds) *Souffrance et Psychopathologie des Liens Institutionnels*. Paris: Dunod.

Donati, F. (1989) A psychodynamic observer in a chronic psychiatric ward. *British Journal of Psychotherapy* 5: 317–329. (Reprinted in Hinshelwood, R.D and Skogstad, W. (eds) *Observing Organisations*. London: Routledge, 2000.)

Dreyfus, H.L. and Rabinow, P. (1982) *Michel Foucault: Beyond Structure and Hermeneutics*. New York: Harvester.

Duchêne, H. (1959) Raport. Presented at Congrès de Neuropsychiatrie de Langue français, Tours.

Duez, B. (1996) Souffrance et psychopathologie des liens institutionnels. In Kaës, R., Pinel, J.-P. and Kernberg, O. (eds) *Souffrance et Psychopathologie des Liens Institutionnels*. Paris: Dunod.

Durkin, J. (ed.) (1981) *Living Groups: Group Psychotherapy and General System Theory*. New York: Brunner/Mazel.

Elias, N. (1970) *What is Sociology?* New York: Columbia University Press.

Ellwood, J. and Oke, M. (1987) Analytic group work in a boys' comprehensive school. *Free Associations* 8: 34–57.

Emery, F.E. (1976) Professional responsibility of social scientists. In Clark, A.W. (ed.) *Experimenting with Organisational Life*. New York: Plenum.

Emery, F.E. and Trist, E. (1965) The casual texture of organizational environments. *Human Relations* 18: 21–32.

Emery, F.E. and Trist, E. (1975) *Towards a Social Ecology*. New York: Plenum.

Enriquez, E. (1983) *De la Horde à l'Etat*. Paris: Gallimard.

Enriquez, E. (1988) Le travail de la mort dans les institutions. In Kaës, R., Bleger, J., Enriquez, E., Fornari, F., Foustier, P., Rousillon, R. and Vidal, J.-P. (eds) *L'institution et les Institutions. Études Psychanalytiques*. Paris: Dunod.

Evans, D. (1996) *An Introductory Dictionary of Lacanian Psychoanalysis*. London: Routledge.

Ezriel, H. (1950) A psycho-analytic approach to group treatment. *British Journal of Medical Psychology* 23: 59–75.

Fairbairn, W.R.D. (1952) *An Object-Relations Theory of the Personality*. New York: Basic Books.

Figlio, K. (1984) Freud's exegesis of the soul (essay review of *Freud and Man's Soul* by Bruno Bettelheim). *Free Associations*, Pilot Issue, pp. 113–121.

Fisher, S. and Cleveland, S.E. (1958) *Body Image and Personality*. New York: van Nostrand.

Fornari, F. (1966) *Psicoanalisi Della Guerra*. Milan: Feltrinelli.

Fornari, F. (1971) Per una psicoanalisi delle istituzioni. *Tempi Moderni* 8: 59–73.

Fornari, F. (1975) *Psychoanalysis and War*. Bloomington: University of Indiana Press.

Fornari, F. (1976) *Simbolo e Codice. Dal Processo Psicoanalitico all' Analisi Istituzionale*. Milan: Feltrinelli.

Fornari, F., Frontori, L. and Riva-Crugnola, C. (1985) *Psicoanalisi in Ospedale*. Milan: Raffaello Cortina.

Foster, A. and Roberts, V. (1998) *Managing Mental Health in the Community: Chaos and Containment*. London: Routledge.

Foucault, M. (1972) *The Archaeology of Knowledge*. London: Tavistock (original French version 1969).

Foulkes, S.H. (1964) *Therapeutic Group Analysis*. London: Allen and Unwin.

Foulkes, S.H. (1975) *Group Analytic Psychotherapy: Method and Principles*. London: Gordon and Bridge.

Foulkes, S.H. and Anthony, J. (1957) *Group Psychotherapy*. London: Penguin.

Fraser, N. (1996) *Justice Interruptus*. London: Routledge.

Freud, A. (1923) Beating fantasies and daydreams. *International Journal of Psycho-Analysis* 4: 89–102

[All references are to the Standard Edition of Freud's works]

Freud, S. (1895) Project for a scientific psychology. *SE* 1. London: Hogarth Press.

Freud, S. (1905) *Three Essays on Sexuality*, SE 7. London: Hogarth Press.

Freud, S. (1911) Formulations on the two principles of mental functioning. *SE* 12. London: Hogarth Press.

Freud, S. (1913) Totem and taboo. *SE* 13. London: Hogarth Press.

Freud, S. (1917) Transformation of instincts as exemplified in anal erotism. *SE* 17: 127–133. London: Hogarth Press.

Freud, S. (1920) Beyond the pleasure principle. *SE* 18: 7–63. London: Hogarth Press.

Freud, S. (1921) Group psychology and the analysis of the ego. *SE* 18: 65–144. London: Hogarth Press.

Freud, S. (1923) The ego and the id. *SE* 19: 3–66. London: Hogarth Press.

Freud, S. (1926) Inhibitions, symptoms and anxiety beyond the pleasure principle. SE 20: 77–175. London: Hogarth Press.

Freud, S. (1930) Civilization and its discontents. *SE* 21: 59–145. London: Hogarth Press.

Freud, S. (1933) New introductory lectures on psycho-analysis. *SE* 22: 3–182. London: Hogarth Press.

Freud, S. and Bullitt, W. (1967) *Thomas Woodrow Wilson, Twenty-Eighth President of the United States: A Psychological Study*. London: Weidenfeld and Nicholson.

Friedenberg, E. (1964) *The Vanishing Adolescent*, Boston: Beacon Press.

Fromm, E. (1941) *Escape from Freedom*. New York: Farrar and Rhinehart.

Fromm, E. (1942) *The Fear of Freedom*. London: Routledge and Kegan Paul.

Frosh, S. (1991) *Identity Crisis: Modernity, Psychoanalysis and the Self*. Basingstoke: Macmillan.

Fustier, P. (1989) Institution soignante et double prise en charge. *Revue de Psychothérapie Psychanalytique de Groupe*, 13: 59–76.

Gabriel, Y. (1983) *Freud and Society*. London: Routledge and Kegan Paul.

Gay, P. (1989) *Freud: A Life for Our Time*. New York: Anchor Books.

Geahchan, D.-J. (1958) Psychanalyse et organisation hospitalière. *L'information psychiatrique* 44: 21–26.

Giddens, A. (1994) *Beyond Left and Right: The Future of Radical Politics*. Cambridge: Polity Press.

Gillison, G. (1993) *Between Culture and Fantasy: A New Guinea Highlands Mythology*. Chicago: University of Chicago Press.

Glover, E. (1946) *War, Sadism and Pacifism*. London: George Allen and Unwin.

Gordon, P. (1995) Private practice, public life: is a psychoanalytic politics possible? *Free Associations* 35: 275–288.

Gould, L. (1991) Using psychoanalytic frameworks for organizational analysis. In Kets de Vries, M. (ed.) *Organizations on the Couch: Clinical Perspectives on Organizational Behavior and Change*. San Francisco: Jossey-Bass.

Gould, L. (1993) Contemporary perspectives on personal and organisational authority. In Hirschhorn, L. and Barnett, C. (eds) *Psychodynamics of Organizations*. Philadelphia: Temple University Press.

Greene, L. and Johnson, D. (1987) Leadership and structuring of the large group. *International Journal of Therapeutic Communities* 8: 99–108.

Griffiths, P. and Pringle, P. (1997) *Psychosocial Practice within a Residential Setting*. London: Karnac.

Grinberg, I., Langer, M. and Rodrigué, E. (1957) *Psicoterapia de Grupo*. Buenos Aires: Paidós.

Grubb Institute (1984) *Practice and Theory in the Work of the Grubb Institute*. London: Grubb Institute.

Habermas, J. (1987) *The Theory of Communicative Actions:* vol. 2: *Lifeworld and System*. Boston: Beacon Press,.

Hare, P., Borgatta, E. and Bales, R. (1961) *Small Groups. Studies in Social Interaction*. New York: Alfred Knopf.

Harrison, T. (2000) *Rickman, Bion, Foulkes and the Northfield Experiments*. London: Jessica Kingsley.

Hess, R. and Savoye, A. (1981) *L'Analyse Institutionnelle*. Paris: Presses Universitaires de France.

Higgin, G. and Bridger, H. (1964) The psychodynamics of an inter-group experience. *Human Relations* 17: 391–446 (Reprinted in Trist, E. and Murray, H. (eds) *The Social Engagement of Social Science*. London: Free Association Books.)

Hinshelwood, R.D. (1987) *What Happens in Groups*. London: Free Association Books.

Hinshelwood, R.D. (1989) *A Dictionary of Kleinian Thought*. London: Free Association Books.

Hinshelwood, R.D. (1993) Locked in role. *Journal of Forensic Psychiatry* 4: 427–440.

Hinshelwood, R.D. (1994) The relevance of psychotherapy. *Psychoanalytic Psychotherapy* 8: 283–294.

Hinshelwood, R.D. (1999) How Foulkesian was Bion? *Group Analysis* 32: 469–488.

Hinshelwood, R.D. and Skogstad, W. (2000) *Observing Organisations*. London: Routledge.

Hirschhorn, L. (1995) *The Workplace Within: Psychodynamics of Organizational Life*. Cambridge, MA: MIT Press.

Hirschhorn, L. (1997) *Reworking Authority: Leading and Following in the Post-Modern Organization*. Cambridge, MA: MIT Press.

Hirschhorn, L. and Barnett, C. (1993) *The Psychodynamics of Organizations*. Philadelphia: Temple University Press.

Hochmann, J. (1971) *Pour une psychiatrie communitaire*. Paris: Seuil.

Hoggett, P. (1992) *Partisans in an Uncertain World: The Psychoanalysis of Engagement*. London: Free Association Books.

Holmes, J. (1993) *John Bowlby and Attachment Theory*. London: Routledge.

Homans, G.G. (1950) *The Human Group*. New York: Harcourt.

Hopper, E. (1989) Aggregation, massification, fission (fragmentation) and fusion: a fourth basic assumption? Paper for IGAP VIIIth International Conference, Amsterdam.

Horton, R. (1971) African traditional thought and Western science In Young, M. (ed.) *Knowledge and Control*. London: Collier-Macmillan.

Houzel, D. (1987) Cadre et psychothérapie institutionnelle dans un hôpital de jour d'enfants. In Bléandonu, G. (ed.) *Les Groupes Thérapeutiques*. Lyon: Cesura.

Huizinga, J. (1999) *The Waning of the Middle Ages*. London: Dover Publications (originally published in Dutch in 1921).

Hutton, J.M. (1995) Organisation-in-the-mind. Paper presented at Organisational Consulting Master Class, South Bank University, July 1995.

Ingleby, D. (1984) The ambivalence of psychoanalysis. *Free Associations*, Pilot Issue, 39–71.

Jacoby, R. (1983) *The Repression of Psychoanalysis*. New York: Basic Books.

Jacoby, R. (1984) Remembering 'social amnesia'. *Free Associations*, Pilot Issue, 16–22.

Janssen, P. (1994) *Psychoanalytic Therapy in the Hospital Setting*. London: Routledge.

Jaques, E. (1951) *The Changing Culture of a Factory*. London: Tavistock.

Jaques, E. (1953) On the dynamics of social structure. *Human Relations* 6: 10–23.

Jaques, E. (1955a) The social system as a defence against depressive and persecutory anxiety. In Klein, M., Heimann, P. and Money-Kyrle, R. (eds) *New Directions in Psycho-Analysis*, pp. 478–498. London: Tavistock.

Jaques, E. (1989) *Requisite Organization: The CEO's Guide to Creative Structure and Leadership*. Aldershot: Gower.

Jaques, E. (1995b) Why the psychoanalytical approach to understanding organizations is dysfunctional. *Human Relations* 48: 343–349.

Jaques, E. (1995c) Riposte to Gilles Amado. *Human Relations* 48: 359–365.

Jones, E. (1923) *Essays in Applied Psychoanalysis*. London: International Psycho-Analytical Press.

Jones, E. (1926) Mother-right and the sexual ignorance of savages. *International Journal of Psycho-Analysis* 6: 109–130.

Jones, M. (1952) *Social Psychiatry: A Study of Therapeutic Communities*. London: Tavistock.

Kaës, R. (1976) *L'Appareil Psychique Groupal: Constructions du Groupe*. Paris: Dunod.

Kaës, R. (1987) Quelques fondements institutionnels de la vie psychique dans l'équipe soignante. In Bléandonu, G. (ed.) *Les Groupes Thérapeutiques*, pp. 71–80. Lyon: Cesura.

Kaës, R. (1988) Réalité psychique et souffrance dans les institutions. In Kaës, R., Bleger, J., Enriquez, E., Fornari, F., Foustier, P., Rousillon, R. and Vidal, J.-P. (eds) *L'institution et les Institutions. Études Psychanalytiques*. Paris: Dunod.

Kaës, R. (1993) *Le Groupe et le Sujet du Groupe: Éléments pour une Théorie Psychanalytiques des Groupes*. Paris: Dunod.

Kaës, R. (1995) L'exigence de travail imposée à la psyché par la subjectivité de l'objet: contributions de l'approche psychanalytique des groupes à la compréhension des processus et des formations de l'inconscient. *Revue Belge de Psychanalyse* 27: 1–23.

Kaës, R. and Puget, J. (eds) (1986) *Violence d'Etat et Psychoanalyse*. Paris: Dunod.

Kaës, R., Pinel, J.-P. and Kernberg, O. (ed.) (1995) *Souffrance et Psychopathologie des Liens*. Paris: Dunod.

Kanner, L. (1943) Autistic disturbances of affective contact. *Nervous Child* 2: 217–250. Reprinted in Kanner, L. (1973) *Childhood Psychosis*. Chichester: Wiley.

Karterud, S. (1989) On methods and principles of hermeneutics: with reference to psychoanalytic study of small groups. *Free Associations* 18: 73–89.

Katz, D. and Kahn, R.L. (1966) *The Social Psychology of Organizations*. New York: John Wiley.

Keniston, K. (1965) *The Uncommitted*. New York: Harcourt-Brace.

Kennard, D. (1983) *An Introduction to Therapeutic Communities*. London: Routledge.

Kernberg, O. (1979) Regression in organizational leadership. *Psychiatry* 42: 24–39.

Kernberg, O. (1983) Psychoanalytic studies of group process: theory and application. In *Psychiatry 1983: American Psychiatric Association Annual Review*. Washington, DC: American Psychiatric Press.

Kernberg, O. (1998) *Ideology, Conflict and Leadership in Groups and Organizations*. New Haven, CT: Yale University Press.

Kernberg, O. (1998b) Identity, alienation, and ideology in adolescent group processes. In Blum, H., Kramer, Y., Richards, A. and Richards, A. (eds) *Fantasy, Myth and Reality*. Madison: International Universities Press.

Kirsner, D. (2000) *UnFree Associations: Inside Psychoanalytic Institutes*. London: Process Press/Karnac.

Klein, E.B. (1979) Manifestations of transference in small training groups. In Lawrence, W.G. (ed.) *Exploring Individual and Organisational Boundaries*. Chichester: Wiley.

Klein, L. and Eason, K. (1991) *Putting Social Science to Work: The Ground between Theory and Use Explored through Case-Studies in Organisations*. Cambridge: Cambridge University Press.

Klein, M. (1932) The psycho-analysis of children. In *The Writings of Melanie Klein: Volume 2*. London: Hogarth Press (1975).

Klein, M. (1935) A contribution to the psychogenesis of manic-depressive states. In *The Writings of Melanie Klein: Volume 1*. London: Hogarth Press (1975).

Klein, M. (1945) The Oedipus complex in the light of early anxieties. In *The Writings of Melanie Klein: Volume 1*: pp. 370–419. London: Hogarth Press (1975).

Klein, M. (1946) Notes on some schizoid mechanisms. *International Journal of Psycho-Analysis* 27: 99–110. (Reprinted in *The Writings of Melanie Klein Volume 3*. London: Hogarth Press; and Klein, M, Heimann, P., Isaacs, S. and Rivière, J. (eds) *Developments in Psycho-Analysis*, pp. 292–320. London Hogarth Press, 1952)

Klein, M. (1957) Envy and gratitude. In *The Writings of Melanie Klein: Volume 3*. London: Hogarth Press.

Klein, M. (1959) Our adult world and its roots in infancy. In *The Writings of Melanie Klein: Volume 3*, pp. 176–235. London: Hogarth Press

Klein, R. (1981) The patient–staff community meeting: a tea-party with the Mad Hatter. *International Journal of Group Psychotherapy* 31: 205–222.

Kovel, J. (1984) On being a marxist psychoanalyst (and a psychoanalytic marxist). *Free Associations*, Pilot Issue, 149–154.

Kraemer, S. and Roberts, J. (eds) (1996) *The Politics of Attachment: Towards a Secure Society*. London: Free Association Books.

Kris, E. (1952) *Psychoanalytic Explorations in Art*. New York: International University Press.

Kroeber, A.L. (1922) *Totem and Taboo*: An ethnological analysis. *American Anthropologist* 22: 48–55.

Kuhn, T. (1962) *The Structure of Scientific Revolutions* (2nd ed. 1970). Chicago: University of Chicago Press.

Lacan, J. (1966) *Ecrits*. English translation 1977, London: Routledge.

Lacan, J. (1973) *The Four Fundamental Concepts of Psycho-Analysis*. English translation 1979, Harmondsworth: Penguin.

Laing, R.D. (1960) *The Divided Self*. London: Tavistock.

Lakoff, G. (1987) *Women, Fire and Dangerous Things*. Chicago: University of Chicago Press.

Langer, M. (1989) *From Vienna to Managua*. London: Free Association Books.

Laplanche, J. and Pontalis, J.-B. (1973) *The Language of Psychoanalysis*. New York: Norton.

Lasch, C. (1979) *The Culture of Narcissism: American Life in an Age of Diminishing Expectations*. New York: Norton.

Lasch, C. (1995) *The Revolt of the Elites and the Betrayal of Democracy*. New York: W.W. Norton.

Lawrence, W.G. (1979) *Exploring Individual and Organisational Boundaries*. Chichester: Wiley.

Lawrence, W.G., Bain, A. and Gould, L. (1996) The fifth basic assumption. *Free Associations* 6: 28–55.

Leach, E. (1966) Virgin birth. In Laidlaw, J. and Hugh-Jones, S. (eds) (2000) *The Essential Leach*. New Haven, CT: Yale University Press.

LeBon, G. (1895) *Le Psychologie des Foules*. Paris: Seuil.

Levidow, L. and Young, R.M. (eds) (1985) *Science, Technology and the Labour Process: Marxist Studies*. London: CSE Books.

Lewin, K. (1935) *A Dynamic Theory of Personality*. London: McGraw-Hill.

Lewin, K. (1947) Frontiers in group dynamics. *Human Relations* 1: 5–41; 143–153.

Lewin, K. (1951) *Field Theory in Social Science*. New York: Harper and Row.

Lewin, K. (1952) *Field Theory in Social Science: Selected Theoretical Papers*. Cartwright, D. (ed.) London: Tavistock.

Liberman, D. (1956) Conflicto matrimonial e identificación proyectiva. *Revista de 'Psicoanálisis* 13: 1–20.

Liberman, D. (1958) Autismo transferencial, narcisismo, el mito de eco y narciso *Revista de Psicoanálisis* 15: 368–385.

Liberman, D. (1960) *Lingüística, Interacción Comunicativa y Proceso Psicoanalítico*. Buenos Aires, Nueva Visión.

McDougall, W. (1920) *The Group Mind*. Cambridge: Cambridge University Press.

Mahler, M., Pine, F. and Bergman, A. (1975) *The Psychological Birth of the Human Infant*. London: Hutchinson.

Main, T.F. (1946) The hospital as a therapeutic institution. *Bulletin of the Menninger Clinic* 10: 66–70. Reprinted, in Main, T.F. (1989) *The Ailment and Other Psychoanalytic Essays*. London: Free Association Books.

Main, T.F. (1957) The ailment. *British Journal of Medical Psychology* 30: 129–145. Reprinted in Main, T.F. (1989) *The Ailment and Other Psychoanalytic Essays*. London: Free Association Books.

Main, T.F. (1967) Knowledge, learning and freedom from thought. *Australian and New Zealand Journal of Psychiatry* 1: 64–71. Reprinted in *Psychoanalytic Psychotherapy* 15 (1990): 59–74.

Main, T.F. (1975) Some psychodynamics of large groups. In Kreeger, L. (ed.) *The Large Group*. London: Constable. Reprinted in Main, T.F. (1989) *The Ailment and Other Psychoanalytic Essays*. London: Free Association Books.

Main, T.F. (1978) The therapeutic community: variations and vicissitudes (1st Foulkes Memorial Lecture to the Group-Analytic Society, May 1978). *Group Analysis* 10. Reprinted in Main, T.F. (1989) *The Ailment and Other Psychoanalytic Essays*. London: Free Association Books.

Main, T.F. (1983) The concept of the therapeutic community: variations and vicissitudes. In Pines, M. (ed.) *The Evolution of Group Analysis*. London: Routledge and Kegan Paul. Reprinted in Main, T.F. (1989) *The Ailment and Other Psychoanalytic Essays*. London: Free Association Books.

Main, T.F. (1989) *The Ailment and Other Psychoanalytic Essays*. London: Free Association Books.

Malinowski, B. (1922) *Argonauts of the Western Pacific*. London: Routledge.

Malinowski, B. (1923) Psychoanalysis and anthropology. *Nature* 112: 650–651.

Mannheim, K. (1936) *Ideology and Utopia: An Introduction to the Sociology of Knowledge*. London.

Mannoni M. (1975) *Un Lieu où Vivre*. Paris: Seuil.

Marcuse, H. (1955) *Eros and Civilization. A Philosophical Inquiry into Freud*. Boston: Beacon Press. UK edition 1956, London: Routledge.

Marcuse, H. (1964) *One-Dimensional Man: Studies in the Ideology of Advanced Industrial Society*. London: Routledge.

Martin, D. (1955) Institutionalisation. *Lancet* ii: 1188–1190.

Mayo, E. (1933) *The Human Problems of an Industrial Civilisation*. Boston, MA: Harvard University Press.

Mead, G.H. (1934) *Mind, Self and Society*. Chicago: Chicago University Press.

Mellier, D. (1994) De l'emploi du concept de fonction contenante pour l'institution à la notion d'appareil psychique d'équipe, le cas de la crèche. Thesis for doctorate in psychology, Université Lumière, Lyon 2.

Mendel, G. (1968) *La Révolte contre le Père*. Paris: Payot.

Mendel, G. (1996) Itinéraire: sociopsychanalyse, intervention institutionnelle, psychosociologie du travail. In *Les Histoires de la Psychologie du Travail*, pp. 183–201. Paris: Octares.

Mennell, S. (1989) *Norbert Elias: An Introduction*. Dublin: University College Dublin Press.

Menninger, R.W. (1985) A retrospective view of a hospital-wide group relations training program: costs, consequences and conclusions. In Colman and Geller (eds) *Group Relations Reader* 2. Washington DC: Rice Institute.

Menzies, I. (1959) A case study in the functioning of the social system as a defence against anxiety. *Human Relations* 13: 95–121. Reprinted in Menzies (1988) *Containing Anxiety in Institutions*. London: Free Association Books.

Menzies Lyth, I. (1988) A psychoanalytic perspective on social institutions. In Menzies Lyth, I. (1989) *The Dynamics of the Social*. London: Free Association Books. Reprinted in Spillius, E. B. (ed.) (1988) *Melanie Klein Today*. London: Routledge, and reprinted in Trist, E. and Murray, H. (eds) (1990) *The Social Engagement of Social Science*. London: Free Association Books.

Mhlongo, A. (1983) The group analyst as consultant in a social service setting. *Group Analysis* 16: 192–197.

Michaud G. (1977) *Laborde ... un Pari Nécessaire de la Notion d'Institution à la Psychothérapie Institutionnelle*. Paris: Gauthier-Villars.

Milgram, S. (1964) Group pressure and action against a person. *Journal of Abnormal and Social Psychology* 69: 137–143.

Miller, E. (1976) (ed.) *Task and Organization*. Chichester: Wiley.

Miller, E.J. (1990) Experiential learning in groups 1. In Trist, E. and Murray, H. (eds) *The Social Engagement of Social Science*. London: Free Association Books.

Miller, E (1993) *From Dependency to Autonomy: Studies in Organization and Change*. London: Free Association Books.

Miller, E. and Gwynne, G.W. (1972) *A Life Apart*. London: Tavistock.

Miller, E. and Rice, A.K. (1967) *Systems of Organization: Task and Sentient Systems and Their Boundary Control*. London: Tavistock.

Missenard, A. (1986) Refoulement originaire et transmission psychique en petit groupe. In Guyotat, J. and Fédida, P. (eds) *Généalogie et Transmission*, pp. 71–81. Paris: Echo-Centurion.

Mitchell, J. (1975) *Psychoanalysis and Feminism*. Harmondsworth: Penguin.

Modena, E. (1986) A chance for psychoanalysis to change: the Zurich Psychoanalytical Seminar as an example. *Free Associations* 5: 7–22.

Modena, E. (1991) A psychoanalytic glance into microelectronics. *Free Associations* 21: 34–45.

Money Kyrle, R. (1937) The development of war. *British Journal of Medical Psychology* 17: 219–236.

Money-Kyrle, R. (1951) *Psycho-Analysis and Politics*. London: Duckworth.

Moreno, J. (1960) *The Sociometry Reader*. Glencoe, IL: The Free Press.

Moscovici, S. (1996) *The Invention of Society*. London: Polity.

Neri, C. (1993) Genius loci: una funzione del luogo analoga a quella di una divinità tutelare. *Koinos* 14: 161–174.

Neri, C. (1994) The group's emotional biography. *British Journal of Psychotherapy* 10: 383–391.

Neri, C. (1995) *Gruppo*. Roma: Borla. (English translation 1998 *Group*. London: Jessica Kingsley.)

Nitsun, M. (1991) Destructive forces in the group. *Group Analysis* 24: 7–20.

Nitsun, M. (1996) *The Anti-Group*. London: Routledge.

Nitsun, M. (1998) The organizational mirror: a group analytic approach to organizational consultancy, Part 1 – Theory. *Group Analysis* 31: 245–267.

Obholzer, A. and Roberts, V.Z. (1994) *The Unconscious at Work*. London: Routledge.

Oury, J. (1965) Transfer et compréhension en psychothérapie institutionnelle. *Psychothérapie institutionnelle* 1: 179–183.

Palmer, B.W.M. (1996) In which the Tavistock paradigm is considered as a discursive practice. Working Papers of GOWG (available on www.brl.com).

Parin, P. (1985) Freedom and independence: on the psychoanalysis of political commitment. *Free Associations* 3: 65–79.

Parsons, T. (1951) *The Social System*. Glencoe, IL: Free Press.

Perrow, C. (1972) *Organizational Analysis: A Sociological View*. London: Tavistock.

Pestalozzi, J., Frisch, S., Hinshelwood, R.D. and Houzel, D. (1998) *Psychoanalytic Psychotherapy in Institutional Settings*. London: Karnac.

Pichon Rivière, E. (1946) Contribución a la teoría psicoanalítica de la esquizofrenia. *Revista de Psicoanálisis* 4: 1–22.

Pichon Rivière, E. (1965) Grupos operativos y enfermedad unica. In *El Proceso Grupal: Del Psicoanálisis a la Psicología Social*. Buenos Aires: Nueva Visión.

Pichon Rivière, E. (1971) *El Proceso Grupal: Del Psicoanálisis a la Psicología Social*. Buenos Aires: Nueva Vision.

Pichon Rivière, E., Bleger, J., Bauleo, A. and Matraj, M. (1970) Una teoría del abordaje de la prevención en el ámbito del grupo familiar. In: *El proceso Grupal: Del Psicoanálisis a la Psicología Social*. Buenos Aires: Nueva Visión.

Pichon Rivière, E., Bleger, J., Liberman, D. and Rolla, E. (1960) Téchnica de los grupos operativos. *Acta Neuropsychiatrica Argentina* 6. Reprinted in Pichon Rivière, E. (1971) *El Proceso Grupal: Del Psicoanálisis a la Psicología Social*. Buenos Aires: Nueva Vision.

Pietropolli-Charmet, G. (1987) *La Democrazia degli affetti*. Milan: Raffaello Cortina.

Pinel, J.-P. (1989) Les fonctions du cadre dans la prise en charge institutionnelle. *Revue de Psychothérapie Psychanalytique de Groupe* 13.

Pinel, J.-P. (1996) La déliaison pathologique des liens institutionnels. In Kaës, R., Pinel, J.-P. and Kernberg, O. (eds) *Souffrance et Psychopathologie des Liens Institutionnels*. Paris: Dunod.

Pines, M. (1982) Reflections on mirroring. *Group Analysis* 15: Supplement.

Pines, M. (1983) The contributions of S.H. Foulkes to group therapy. In Pines, M. (ed.) *The Evolution of Group Analysis*, pp. 265–285. London: Routledge.

Pontalis, J.-B. (1963) Le petite groupe comme objet. *Les Temps Moderne* 211: 1057–1069.

Prager, J. and Rustin, M. (1993) *Psychoanalytic Sociology, Vols 1 and 2*. Aldershot: Edward Elgar.

Puget, J. (1986) Violencia social y psicanálisis: lo impensable y lo impensado. *Psicanálisis* 8: 307–366. (English translation: Social violence and psycho-analysis in Argentina: the unthinkable and the unthought. *Free Associations* 13 (1988): 84–140).

Puget, J. (1991) The social context: searching for a hypothesis. *Free Associations* 21: 21–33.

Puget, J. (1992) La Elección del debe ser. *Psicoanálisis* 14: 141–145.

Puget, J. and Bernard, M. (1986) Aspectos de curabilidad en grupos terapéuticos. *Revista de Psicología y Psicoterapia de Grupo* 9: 15–28.

Puget, J. and Kaës, R. (1989) *Violencia de Estado y Psicoanálisis*. Buenos Aires: Centro Editor de América Latina.

Puget, J., Bernard M., Games, B.H., Chavez, G. and Romano, E. (1980) *El Grupo y sus Configuraciones: Terapia Psicoanalítica*. Buenos Aires.

Racamier, P.-C. (ed.) (1970) *Le Psychanalyste sans Divan: La Psychanalyse et les Institutions de Soin Psychiatrique*. Paris: Payot.

Rapaport, R. and Rapaport, R. (1990) Dual career families: the evolution of a concept. In Trist, E. and Murray, H. (eds) *The Social Engagement of Social Science*. London: Free Association Books.

Reed, B.D. (1972) *The Dynamics of Religion*. London: Darton, Longman and Todd.

Reed, B.D. (1995) *The Psycho-Dynamics of Life and Worship*. London: Grubb Institute.

Reed, B.D. and Armstrong, D.G. (1988) *Notes on Professional Management*. London: Grubb Institute.

Reed, B.D., Hutton, J.M. and Bazalgette, J.L. (1978) *Freedom to Study: Requirements of Overseas Students in the UK*. London: Overseas Students Trust.

Rees, J.R. (1945) *The Shaping of Psychiatry by War*. London: Chapman & Hall.

Reich, W. (1945) *The Sexual Revolution*. New York: Orgone Institute Press.

Reich, W. (1946) *The Mass Psychology of Fascism*. New York: Orgone Institute Press.

Resnik, S. (1985) The space of madness. In Pines, M. (ed.) *Bion and Group Psychotherapy*. London: Routledge.

Rice, A.K. (1958) *Productivity and Social Organization: The Ahmedabad Experiment*. London: Tavistock.

Rice, A.K. (1963) *The Enterprise and its Environment*. London: Tavistock.

Rice, A.K. (1965) *Learning for Leadership*. London: Tavistock.

Richards, B. (1984a) Civil defence and psychic defence. *Free Associations* Pilot Issue: 85–97.

Richards, B. (ed.) (1984b) *Capitalism and Infancy*. London: Free Association Books.

Richards, B. (1986) Psychological practice and social democracy. *Free Associations* 5: 105–136.

Richards, B. (ed.) (1989) *Crises of the Self*. London: Free Association Books.

Richardson, J.E. (1973) *The Teacher, the School and the Task of Management*. London: Heinemann.

Rickman, J. (1950) The factor of number in individual and group dynamics. *Journal of Mental Science* 96: 770–773.

Rieff, P. (1979) *Freud: The Mind of the Moralist*. Chicago: University of Chicago Press.

Rioch, M. (1979) The A.K. Rice group relations conferences as a reflection of society. In Lawrence, G. (ed.) *Exploring Individual and Organisational Boundaries*. London: Wiley.

Riseman, D. (1961) *The Lonely American*. New Haven: Yale University Press.

Rivière, J. (1955) The unconscious phantasy of an inner world reflected in examples from literature. In Klein, M., Heimann, P. and Money-Kyrle, R.E. (eds) *New Directions in Psychoanalysis*. London: Tavistock.

Roberts, J. (1980) Destructive processes in therapeutic communities. *International Journal of Therapeutic Communities* 1: 159–170.

Róheim, G. (1922) Ethnology and folk-psychology. *International Journal of Psycho-Analysis* 3: 189–192.

Rosenfeld, D. (1982) La noción del esquema corporal psicótico en pacienmtes neuróticos y psicóticos. *Revista de Psycoanálisis* 4: 383–404.

Rosenfeld, D. (1988) *Psychoanalysis and Groups*. London: Karnac.

Rouchy, J.-C. (1978) Un passé sous silence. *Études Freudiennes* 13–14: 175–190.

Roussillon, R. (1988) Espaces et pratiques institutionnelles, le débarras et l'interstice. In Käes, R., Enriquez, E., Fornari, F., Fustier, P., Roussillon, R. and Vidal, J.-P. (eds) *L'Institution et les Institutions*. Paris: Dunod.

Rustin, M. (1991) *The Good Society and the Inner World: Psychoanalysis, Politics and Culture*. London: Verso.

Rustin, M. and Rustin, M. (1987) *Narratives of Love and Loss*. London: Verso.

Sabel, C. (1991) Möbius-strip organisations and open labour markets: some consequences of the reiteration of conception and execution in a volatile economy. In Bourdieu, P. and Coleman, J.S. (eds) *Social Theory for a Changing Society*. Boulder, CO: Westview Press.

Samuels, A. (1993) *The Political Psyche*. London: Routledge.

Sandler, J., Dare, C. and Holder, A. (1973) *The Patient and the Analyst*. London: Allen and Unwin.

Sapir, M. (ed.) (1992) *Formation et Institutions Soignantes*. Grenoble, La Pensée Sauvage.

Sartre, J.-P. (1960) *Critique de la Raison Dialectique*. Paris: Gallimard.

Schilder, P. (1938) *Psychotherapy*. New York: Norton.

Schwartz, H. (1990) *Narcissistic Process and Corporate Decay: The Theory of the Organization Ideal*. New York: New York University Press.

Schwartz, H. (1995) Masculinity and the meaning of work: a response to Manichean feminism. *Administration and Society* 27: 249–274.

Schwartz, H. (1996) The sin of the father: reflections on the roles of the corporation man, the suburban housewife, their son and their daughter in the deconstruction of the patriarch. *Human Relations*, 49: 1013–1040.

Segal, H. (1957) Notes on symbol formation. *International Journal of Psycho-Analysis* 38: 391–397.

Selvini-Palazzoli, M., Anolli, P. and Di Blasio, P. (1987) *The Hidden Games of Organizations*. New York: Pantheon.

Semrad, E. and Day, M. (1966) Group psychotherapy. *Journal of the American Psychoanalytical Association*, 14: 591–618.

Sennett, R. (1992) *The Fall of Public Man*. New York: W.W. Norton.

Shapiro, E. and Carr, W. (1991) *Lost in Familiar Places*. New Haven: Yale University Press.

Shapiro, R. (1991) Psychoanalytic theory of groups and organizations. *Journal of the American Psychoanalytic Association*, 39: 759–781.

Sherif, M. (1936) *The Psychology of Social Norms*. New York: Harper.

Simon, H. (1929) *Une therapeutique plus active des malades mentales*. Paris: W. de Gruyter.

Slavson, S.R. (ed.) (1947) *The Practice of Group Psychotherapy*. New York: International Universities Press.

Sofer, C. (1972) *Organizations in Theory and Practice*. London: Heinemann.

Spiro, M. (1993) *Oedipus in the Trobriands*. New Brunswick: Transaction Publishers.

Stanton, A. and Schwartz, M. (1954) *The Mental Hospital*. New York: Basic Books.

Stapley, L.F. (1996) *The Personality of the Organisation: A Psycho-Dynamic Explanation of Culture and Change*. London: Free Association Books.

Stokes, J. (1994a) The unconscious at work in groups and teams: contributions from the work of W.R. Bion. In Obholzer, A. and Roberts, V. (eds) *The Unconscious at Work*. London: Routledge.

Stokes, J. (1994b) Institutional chaos and personal stress. In Obholzer, A. and Roberts, V.Z. (eds) *The Unconscious at Work*. London: Routledge.

Strachey, A. (1957) *The Unconscious Motives of War*. London: George Allen and Unwin.

Sturgeon, T. (1954) *More than Human*. London: Gollancz.

Sulloway, F. (1979) *Freud: Biologist of the Mind: Beyond the Psychoanalytic Legend*. London: Burnett Books.

Tagliacozzo, R. (1986) Il servizio di un DSM visto da un punto di vista dello psicoanalista. *G.F.A.* 8.

Temperley, J. (1984) Our own worst enemies: unconscious factors in female disadvantage. *Free Associations* Pilot Issue: 23–38.

Thompson, E.P. (1978) *The Poverty of Theory and Other Essays*. London: Merlin.

Tosquelles, F. (1966) Histoire critique du mouvement de psychothérapie institutionnelle dans les hôpitaux psychiatriques français. *Psychothérapie institutionnelle* 2–3: 21–64.

Trist, E. (1985) Working with Bion in the 1940s: the group decade. In Pines, M. (ed.) *Bion and Group Psychotherapy*. London: Routledge and Kegan Paul.

Trist, E. (1990) [1950] Culture as a psychosocial process. In Trist, E. and Murray, H. (eds) *The Social Engagement of Social Science*. London: Free Association Books.

Trist, E. and Bamforth, K.W. (1951) Some social and psychological consequences of the longwall method of coal getting. *Human Relations* 4: 3–38.

Trist, E. and Murray, H. (1990a) *The Social Engagement of Social Science, Volume 1*. London: Free Association Books.

Trist, E. and Murray, H. (1990b) Historical overview of the foundation and development of the Tavistock Institute. In Trist, E. and Murray, H. (eds) *The Social Engagement of Social Science, Volume 1. The Socio-Psychological Perspective*. London: Free Association Books.

Trist, E. and Murray, H. (eds) (1993) *The Social Engagement of Social Science, Volume II*. London: Free Association Books.

Trist, E.L., Higgin, G.W., Murray, H. and Pollock, A.B. (1963) *Organizational Choice: Capabilities of Groups at the Coal Face under Changing Technologies*. London: Tavistock.

Trist, E.L., Higgin, G.W., Murray, H. and Pollock, A.B. (1990) The assumption of ordinariness as a denial mechanism. In Trist, E. and Murray, H., *The Social Engagement of Social Science, Volume 1*. London: Free Association Books.

Trotter, W. (1916) *Instincts of the Herd in Peace and War*. London: T. F. Unwin.

Tubert-Oclander J, (1990) *El grupo operativo de aprendizaje*. Guadalajara: University of Guadalajara and the Jalisco Psychoanalytic Association.

Turkle, S. (1978) *Psychoanalytic Politics: Jacques Lacan and Freud's French Revolution* (Critical Perspectives). New York: Basic Books.

Turkle, S. (1984) *The Second Self: Computers and the Human Spirit*. New York: Simon and Schuster.

Turkle, S. (1995) *Life on the Screen: Identity in the Age of the Internet*. New York: Touchstone.

Turquet, P.M. (1974) Leadership: the individual and the group. In Colman, A.D. and Geller, M.H. (eds) *Group Relations Reader 2*, pp. 71–87. Washington, DC: Rice Institute.

Turquet, P. (1975) Threats to identity in the large group. In Kreeger, L.C. (ed.) *The Large Group: Dynamics and Therapy*. London: Constable.

Usandivaras R. (1957) La regresión en el grupo terapéutico. *Primer Congreso Latinoamericano de Psicoterapia de Grupo*. Buenos Aires, September 1957. Facultad de Ciencias Médicas de la Ciudad de Buenos Aires.

Usandivaras, R. (1970) *Test de las Bolitas*. Buenos Aires: Paidós.

Vinar, M. (1989) Pedro or the demolition: a psychoanalytic look at torture. *British Journal of Psychotherapy* 5: 353–362.

Vinden, F.H. (1977) The introduction of War Office Selection Boards in the British Army: a personal reflection. In Bond, B. and Roy, I. (eds) *War and Society* 2. London: Croom Helm.

von Bertalanffy, L. (1950) An outline of general systems. *British Journal of the Philosophy of Theory, Science* 3.

von Bertalanffy, L. (1968) *General Systems Theory: Foundation, Development, Application*. New York: George Braziller.

Vygotsky, L.S. (1978) [1934] *Mind in Society*. Boston, MA: Harvard University Press.

Waddell, M., Richards, B., McNeill, M. and Levidow, L. (1978) Psychoanalysis, marxism and feminism. *Radical Science Journal* 6/7: 107–117.

Watzlawick, P., Beavin, J.H. and Jackson, D.D. (1967) *Pragmatics of Human Communication*. New York: Norton.

Weddell, D. (1968) Change of approach. In Barnes, E. (ed.) *Psychosocial Nursing*. London: Tavistock.

Weiner, N. (1949) *Cybernetics*. New York: Technology Press.

Whitaker, D.S. (1992) Transposing learnings from group psychotherapy to work groups. *Group Analysis* 25: 131–149.

Whiting, C. D'A. (1958) La psicoterapia de grupo como complemento del psicoanálisis. First Latin-American Congress of Group Psychotherapy, Buenos Aires, September 1957. Facultad de Ciencias Médicas de la Ciudad de Buenos Aires, p. 85,.

Wilden, A. (1972) *System and Structure*. London: Tavistock.

Williams, R. (1958) *Culture and Society*. London: Hogarth Press.

Williams, R. (1989) *Resources of Hope: Culture, Democracy, Socialism*. London: Verso.

Winnicott, D.W. (1958) *Collected Papers: Through Paediatrics to Psycho-Analysis*. London: Tavistock.

Winnicott, D.W. (1965) *The Maturational Process and the Facilitating Environment*. London: Hogarth Press.

Winnicott, D.W. (1967) The location of cultural experience. Reprinted 1971 in *Playing and Reality*. London: Tavistock.

Winnicott, D.W. (1971) *Playing and Reality*. London: Tavistock.

Wolf, A. and Schwartz, E.K. (1962) *Psychoanalysis in Groups*. New York: Grune and Stratton.

Wolfenstein, E.V. (1990) Group phantasies and 'the individual'. *Free Associations* 20: 150–180.

Young, R.M. (1989) Transitional phenomena: production and consumption. In Richards, B. (ed.) *Crises of the Self*, pp. 57–72. London: Free Association Books.

Young, R.M. (1994) *Mental Space*. London: Process Press.

Zaleznik, A. (1989) *The Managerial Mystique: Restoring Leadership in Business*. New York: Harper and Row.

Zaretsky, E. (1999) 'One large secure, solid background': Melanie Klein and the origins of the British welfare state. *Psychoanalysis and Welfare* 1: 136–154.

Zimmermann, D. (1958) Aplicación de la psicoterapia de grupo a la enseñanza de la Psiquiatría Dinámica. *Primer Congreso Latinoamericano de Psicoterapia de Grupo*. Buenos Aires, September 1957. Facultad de Ciencias Médicas de la Ciudad de Buenos Aires.

Zimmermann, D.E., Osorio L.C. et al. (1997) *Como Trabalhamos com Grupos*. Porto Alegre: Artes Médicas.

Zinkin, L. (1983) Malignant mirroring. *Group Analysis* 16: 113–126.

Index

237

child
  guidance 47
  primary narcissism of 18
  psychiatry 98
  sacrifice 56–8, 59, 60
childhood
  play 44
  unconscious trauma 3
children 46–7
  autistic 122
  groups 128
Chile 125, 129, 139, 141
Christ, Jesus 6, 57, 58, 59
Christianity/Christians 6, 59, 65, 68
chronicisation 101, 108
church 149
  see also Christianity/Christians
circumcision 57
Civil Resettlement Units 145
civilisation 4, 6
Civilization and Its Discontents (Freud)
    ix, 6
class
conflict 52
  dynamics 185
claustrophobia 141
Cleveland, S.E. 17
clinical counselling service 82
clinical psychologists 82
cloth-mother 17
coal mine, innovation and conflict in a
    171–6
coal mining 205–6
code
  analyst 83
  interpretations 83–4
co-evolution 168
co-forgetting 19
cognitive behaviour 9
cognitive distance 114
collective consciousness 17
collective human unconsciousness 5
collective psychotherapy 100–1
Colombia 128, 129
colonisation of the life world 37
commensal interaction between mystic
    and establishment 68
communication
  structured 101

theory 9
community
  care 152
  treatment in 103
compassion 45
competence 46
complementary objects, search for 113
composite working 172
compromised nature of psychoanalysis
    from a Marxist perspective 196
compulsory behaviours 88
computers 39, 49, 52
  living with 50
  and sexuality 51
concentration camps 98
conception 57
Coney Island amusement park, NY 36
Conference of Socialist Economists 189,
    190
confidentiality, patient 40
conflict
  and innovation in a coal mine 171–6
  resolution in groups 70–1
  in society projected into mental
      hospital 211
conformism/conformity 52, 62
co-inherence 115
Congrès de Neuropsychiatrie de Langue
    française, Tours 102
conscious behaviour 9
consistency 122
consultation 103
container 23, 115, 160
  for client anxieties 164
  institution as 80, 86, 90, 91
  of emotions and bodily experiences
      95, 96
container–contained 121, 160
container–function 111, 121, 187
  setting, institutional envelopes and
      figurability 121–3
containment 122
continuous reversal 115
Cooper, A. 200
Cooper, D. 78, 107
co-participation 21
co-remembering 19
core practice 163–5
Correale, A. xvii, 22, 77–96

Printed in Great Britain
by Amazon